Britain's Revival in the Gulf

Britain's relationship with the Gulf region remains one of the few unexplored episodes in the study of British decolonization. The decision, announced in 1968, to leave the Gulf within three years represented an explicit recognition by Britain that its 'East of Suez' role was at an end. In this book, Simon C. Smith analyses the decision-making processes which underpinned this reversal and which are clearly central to achieving an understanding of Britain's repositioning in the post-war world. Additionally, this book presents an examination of the interaction between British decision-making on the one hand, and local responses and initiatives on the other, in shaping the modern Gulf. Using sources previously unavailable to scholars, *Britain's Revival and Fall in the Gulf* is a valuable addition to the studies on the modern Gulf and will be of interest to both academic and general readers.

Simon C. Smith is Senior Lecturer in International History at the University of Hull. He has published widely on British imperial history and his books include *Kuwait, 1950–65: Britain, the al-Sabah, and Oil* (1999).

RoutledgeCurzon Studies in the Modern History of the Middle East

1 **Britain's Revival and Fall in the Gulf**
Kuwait, Bahrain, Qatar, and the Trucial States, 1950–71
Simon C. Smith

Britain's Revival and Fall in the Gulf

Kuwait, Bahrain, Qatar, and the Trucial States, 1950–71

Simon C. Smith

Routledge
Taylor & Francis Group
LONDON AND NEW YORK

First published 2004 by Routledge Curzon

This edition published 2013 by Routledge

Routledge
Taylor & Francis Group
711 Third Avenue
New York, NY 10017

Routledge
Taylor & Francis Group
2 Park Square, Milton Park
Abingdon, Oxon OX14 4RN

First issued in paperback 2013

Routledge is an imprint of the Taylor & Francis Group, an informa business

Typeset in Times by
Florence Production Ltd, Stoodleigh, Devon

British Library Cataloguing in Publication Data
A catalogue record for this book is available from the British Library

Library of Congress Cataloging in Publication Data
A catalog record for this book has been requested

ISBN13: 978-0-415-33192-0 (hbk)
ISBN13: 978-0-415-64621-5 (pbk)

Contents

Preface and acknowledgements

Despite the fact that the smaller states of the Persian Gulf have often been reduced to the periphery in the study of British imperialism and decolonization, they are worthy of attention, not least because of their economic value to Britain. Referring to Kuwait in the turbulent month of July 1958, Prime Minister Harold Macmillan described it as 'the key to the economic life of Britain – and of Europe'.[1] With the discovery of oil in commercial quantities in the Lower Gulf as well, the importance of the British-protected states became more important than ever in the post-war period. Oil produced by Britain's Persian Gulf clients was prized for the favourable terms under which it was purchased. As sources of oil independent from other major Middle Eastern producers, the British-protected states also appeared to stand in the way of Britain, and the Western world in general, being held to ransom. Moreover, the apparent inconceivability of separate independence for the smaller states of the Lower Gulf, not least on account of the deep-seated rivalries between them, militated against their swift movement towards independence in the post-war era.

As the first two chapters of this study attempt to show, far from stemming from an unquestioning imperial mind-set, British policy derived from an assessment of the national interest in which different shades of opinion within Britain's decision-making establishment were heard and debated. This tendency was particularly pronounced in the post-Suez era when the Persian Gulf States, in keeping with other British dependencies, were subjected to a cost-benefit analysis. Consistent with the tendency in areas as diverse as Central Africa, South-East Asia, and South Arabia, Britain also sought to foster closer association among the small Gulf States, a subject which is addressed in Chapters 3 and 4. Learning the painful lessons of failed 'Whitehall' federations elsewhere in the empire, however, British policy-makers were decidedly less conspicuous in moves for unity in the Gulf, preferring instead to rely on local actors to provide the stimulus. In formulating its approach to the multifarious issues affecting the Gulf States, Britain also had to take account of actors on the international stage, not least the United States. Chapters 5 and 6 examine Anglo-American relations in the Gulf context, seeking to demonstrate that any transfer of power from Britain to America was partial, and neither sought nor welcomed by either power. Only with Britain's impending departure from the Gulf following the 1968 decision to withdraw by the end of 1971, did both countries seek actively to encourage regional proxies to fill the vacuum.

For funding a research trip to the US National Archives, College Park, I should like to thank the British Academy. I should also like to record my gratitude to the University of Hull for funding a research trip to the JFK Library, Boston. Thanks are also due the staff at the JFK Library, as well as the National Archives in both the UK and the US.

Simon C. Smith
History Department,
University of Hull
August 2003

Abbreviations

ADDF	Abu Dhabi Defence Force
AIOC	Anglo-Iranian Oil Company
ARAMCO	Arabian American Oil Company
BAPCO	Bahrain Petroleum Company
COMIDEASTFOR	Commander, Middle East Force
FCO	Foreign and Commonwealth Office
FO	Foreign Office
FRUS	Foreign Relations of the United States
GOK	Government of Kuwait
HMG	His/Her Majesty's Government
IRG	Interdepartmental Regional Group
MoD	Ministry of Defence
OPEC	Organization of Petroleum Exporting Countries
TSDO	Trucial States Development Office
UAE	United Arab Emirates/Union of Arab Emirates
UAR	United Arab Republic

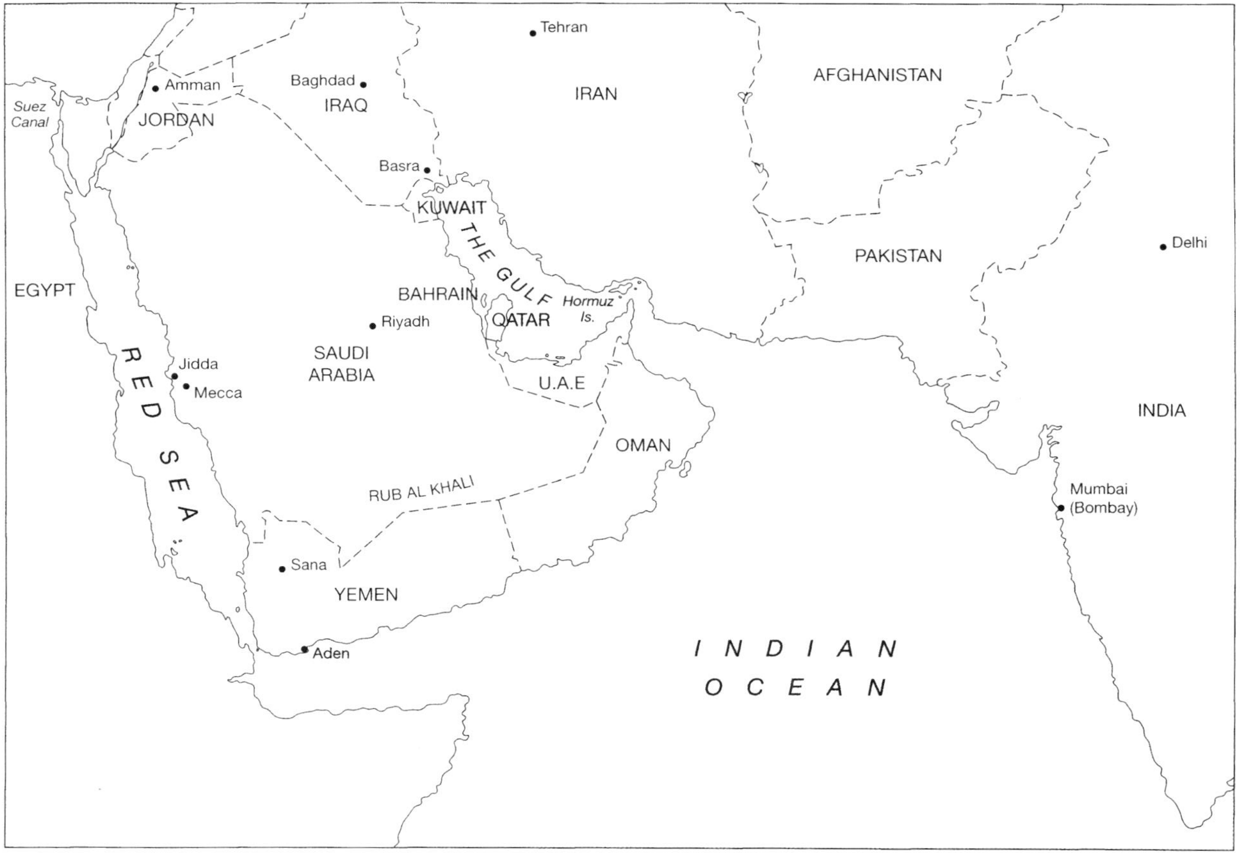

The modern Gulf in its regional context.

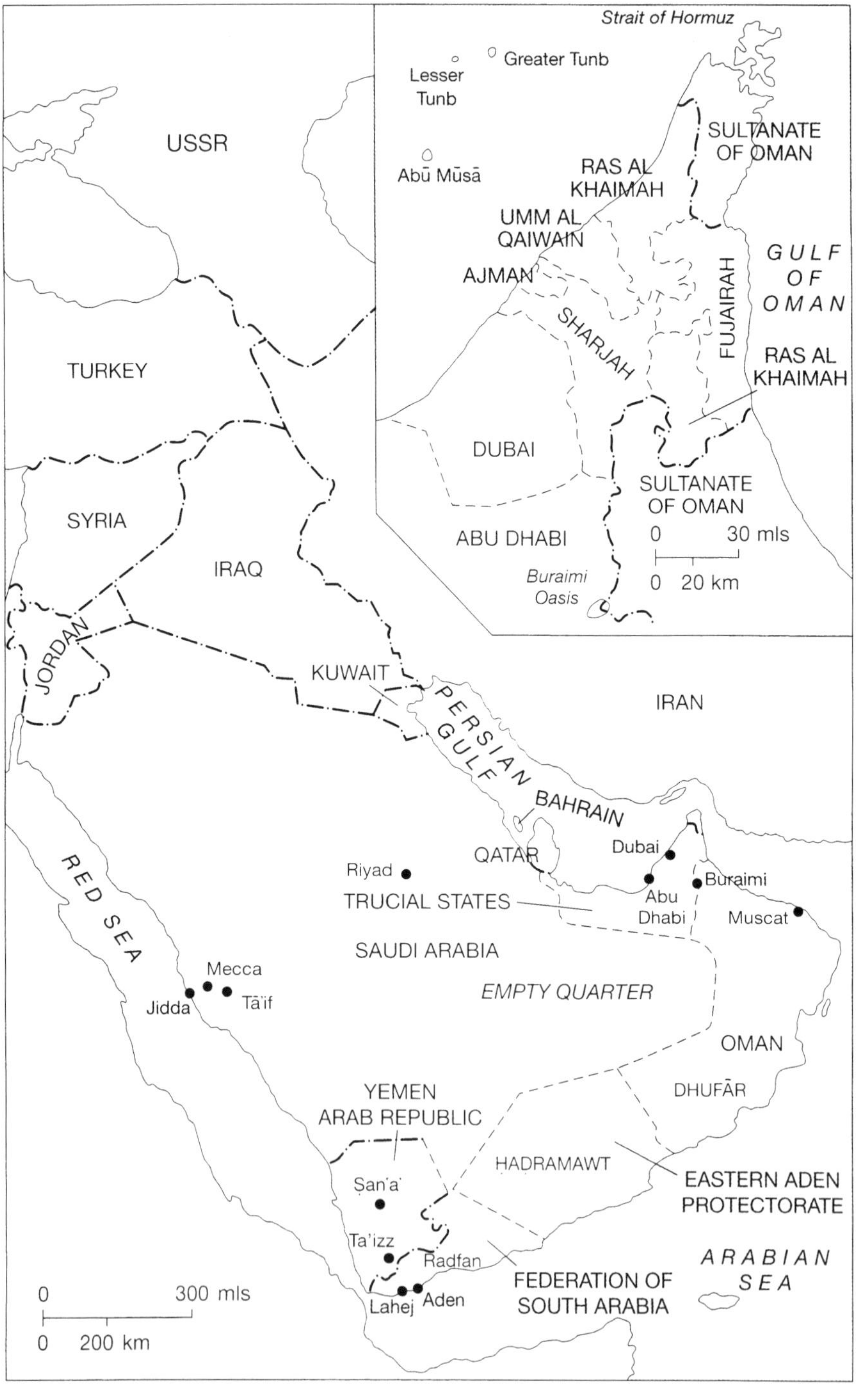

The Gulf States, *c.* 1963.

Introduction

Until recently, the smaller Gulf States have been overlooked in the study of British decolonization. Indeed, they often appear as mere footnotes to Britain's departure from larger, and ostensibly more important, territories. Yet in many ways, the British egress from the Gulf was at least as significant in Britain's re-positioning in the post-war world than its departure from other dependent territories. The transfer of power in India in 1947 was accompanied by a strengthening of Britain's commitment not merely to what remained of its Asian empire (especially Malaya), but also to the African colonies. Equally, the quickening of the pace of decolonization in Africa in the late 1950s and early 1960s did not foreshadow a repudiation of Britain's global role. Nevertheless, the decision, announced in January 1968, to leave the Gulf and South-East Asia within three years represented an explicit recognition by Britain that its 'East of Suez' role was at an end. Reflecting upon this reversal, the Labour grandee Patrick Gordon Walker described it as 'the most momentous shift in our foreign policy for a century and a half'.[1] Even allowing for some hyperbole, this depiction does reflect the import of a series of decisions which saw the renunciation of the world role which had been so much a part of British external policy and identity since the early nineteenth century, if not before. The demise of the commitment to the role outside Europe, of which the politico-military presence in the Gulf was a vital part, is perhaps all the more noteworthy since not only was there strong local support for a continuation of Britain's traditional role, but also British interests in the region, which had grown markedly since the early 1950s, still remained strong.

The economic importance of the small oil-bearing Gulf States to Britain in terms not merely of the supply of large quantities of oil under favourable terms, but also of the investment of surplus revenues in the sterling area, had witnessed a post-war revival of British interest in the Gulf States. A corollary of this was a move towards greater interference in their internal affairs at a time when preparations for transferring power were advancing apace in other dependent territories across the empire. As the Political Resident in the Persian Gulf, Sir William Luce, presciently noted towards the end of 1961,

> it is no exaggeration to say that Britain at this moment stands more deeply committed in the Persian Gulf, both politically and militarily, than at any time since the last war, a situation which stands in marked contrast with the great contraction of our political and military commitments elsewhere in the world over the past fifteen years.[2]

Referring to Britain's total defence bill of £1500m, an official of the Foreign Office contemporaneously remarked that the tiny Amirate of Kuwait was 'perhaps the only place where it can be shown to yield a positive dividend, if only by helping us to preserve a state of affairs which is still very favourable to us financially'.[3] By the mid-1960s the economic potential of the Lower Gulf was becoming increasingly apparent as well.

In the mid-1960s, it was predicted that this area would be producing 100m tons of oil per annum within ten years. Describing the Lower Gulf as 'an increasingly valuable asset to Britain and the sterling area', the report of a conference of British Political Agents held in 1965 concluded that the 'importance of stability in the area would therefore grow rather than diminish'.[4] Kuwait itself was already producing 123m tons of oil, or 27 per cent of Persian Gulf production, while British companies accounted for 40 per cent of total output from the area.[5] The willingness of Persian Gulf Rulers to invest their surplus revenues in sterling was also prized by the British. Summarizing British economic interests in the region in May 1967, the Cabinet's Official Defence and Oversea Policy Committee recorded that 'we are concerned to maintain and develop our oil investments and supplies; to avoid shocks to sterling from the movement of Kuwaiti and other deposits; and to promote our export trade'.[6] Three years earlier, the Treasury, Foreign Office, and Ministry of Power had produced a joint memorandum in which they stressed that Britain's interest in the region was based both on 'the need for the continued flow of oil to the West and on the financial and economic benefits to the United Kingdom of the arrangements under which British companies operate'.[7] The value of an 'independent and friendly' Kuwait in ensuring that Britain and the West continued to receive oil supplies from the Middle East 'on acceptable terms' was specially highlighted.[8] This apparent unanimity, however, concealed an ongoing and controversial debate about the costs and benefits of the British presence in the Gulf.

Britain's position in the region rested on a series of agreements[9], dating back to the General Treaty of 1820, designed to suppress piracy. By signing the Perpetual Maritime Truce of 1853, the Shaikhdoms of Abu Dhabi, Sharjah, Dubai, Ajman, Ras al Khaimah, and Umm al Qaiwain became known as the Trucial States, a name which they retained until British withdrawal in 1971. In the more competitive international environment of the late nineteenth century, Britain sought to consolidate its standing in the Gulf. Under two agreements, the first signed in 1880, the second twelve years later, the Ruler of Bahrain undertook not merely to desist from entering into negotiations or receiving representatives from any other power, but also to avoid alienating territory without the sanction of the British government. In 1892, the Trucial States entered similar exclusive agreements. Fujairah was not included in these agreements since it was considered part of Sharjah. In 1952, however, the British recognized its separate existence under British protection.

Initially, Kuwait and Qatar remained outside the British system. Anxious to escape the sway of the Ottoman empire, however, the two Shaikhdoms signed treaties with Britain in 1899 and 1916 respectively, under which they pledged neither to alienate land nor receive representatives of a foreign power. British influence was exercised through officials, known as Political Agents, supervised by a Political Resident whose headquarters were transferred from Bushire in southern Persia to the island of Bahrain in 1946. Although the Rulers also bound themselves not to grant oil concessions without the prior approval of HMG, the nature of the agreements concluded with the Rulers necessarily limited Britain's role in the internal affairs of the Shaikhdoms.[10] Before the Second World War, this abstinence was raised to the level of declared policy. 'The policy of the Political Agent has been, and is, to intervene as little as he possibly can with the internal administration of the State', adumbrated Britain's representative in Kuwait in 1931.[11] Referring to the Rulers on the eve of the Second World War, the Political Agent in Bahrain expostulated: 'We certainly do not want to administer their disgusting territories and people.'[12]

The post-war expansion of oil revenues, however, witnessed a more interventionist stance by the British, a policy which was facilitated by the transfer of responsibility for the Gulf States from the former imperial authorities in India to the Foreign Office in April 1948.[13] This shift was underlined by the instructions Bernard Burrows received from the Foreign Office upon taking up the post of Political Resident in 1953:

> The Shaikhdoms of the Gulf have become of first importance to the United Kingdom and to the Sterling Area as a whole. It is essential that Her Majesty's Government should exert sufficient influence in them to ensure that there is no conflict between the policies of the Rulers and those of Her Majesty's Government.[14]

This directive was by no means easy to implement. 'If we seek to interfere directly', observed Burrows' successor, Sir George Middleton, 'we are decried as old-fashioned imperialists. If we appear to acquiesce in the existing state of affairs we are decried as the prop of outmoded reaction.'[15] '[W]e are held responsible for internal mismanagement of the Gulf States' affairs, while we have no legal (or moral) right to intervene in them', lamented a Foreign Office official.[16] Referring specifically to Kuwait, the Political Agent there remarked: 'If the Kuwaitis have always been jealous of their domestic independence, they are hyper-sensitive about it now.'[17]

Indeed, the tradition of internal autonomy in the Gulf States made the invasion of this hallowed realm by the British a challenging and controversial enterprise. Summarizing the British dilemma, Glen Balfour-Paul has remarked that 'the high point in Britain's conviction of the necessity, and therefore the propriety, of intervention in the internal affairs of the states was reached just when it was becoming impracticable'.[18] Despite the renewed importance ascribed to the Shaikhdoms, of which British attempts to intervene in their internal affairs were a function, there were marked differences of opinion in British decision-making circles about the efficacy of maintaining Britain's Gulf presence.

Writing shortly after Britain's withdrawal from the Gulf, Philip Darby depicted Britain's military posture East of Suez as a role which was 'too deeply rooted in Britain's outlook and history to be vulnerable to routine questioning and criticism'.[19] Extending his argument, Darby asserts that 'British policy flowed naturally along established channels guided more by the experience of an imperial past than by any conception of a post-imperial future'.[20] He has also reflected that 'in the sixties, when the sense of purpose was strongest and to some extent Britain's [East of Suez] role was broadened as a result, its economic rationale was weakest'.[21] Equally, John Darwin has contended that the preservation of the presence East of Suez was founded on a conception of British interests which was fundamentally 'emotional and romantic'.[22] Only when such thinking had been replaced by governing principles which were 'coldly rational and cost-effective' was withdrawal possible. In the estimation of William Roger Louis, such clear-sighted logic had to await the advent of the Labour administration of Harold Wilson:

> The British did not plan to leave the Gulf because they wanted to, or for reasons concerning the Gulf itself. They left, in short, because of the decision of Harold Wilson's Labour Government to rescue the British economy by taking severe measures including the evacuation of all troops from South-East Asia as well as those from the Gulf.[23]

In a similar vein, F. Gregory Gause has suggested that 'It was not until the 1960s, especially with the advent of the Labour party in 1964, that Britain's commitments East of Suez in the Middle and Far East were called into serious question'.[24]

Far from supporting the idea that Britain blindly clung to an imperial past until cold economic reality forced a withdrawal decision under Harold Wilson, the documentary record demonstrates that British policy-makers were constantly reviewing the costs and benefits of Britain's deployments in the Gulf, especially following the 1956 Suez War. With respect to South Arabia, Britain's other principle responsibility in the Middle East, Karl Pieragostini suggests that 'there was no careful, analytical appraisal of the need for a military presence'.[25] In the Gulf, by contrast, the advantages and disadvantages of a continuing British commitment to the area were subjected to ongoing scrutiny. The costs of maintaining the British military establishment in the Gulf were continually weighed against the economic benefits which Britain derived from the region. On the one hand, the cost-cutting instincts of the Treasury, coupled with the scepticism of some diplomats, led to a questioning of the need for a military presence. On the other, British officials in the Gulf, along with the Foreign Office itself, tended to stress the dangers to British interests of allowing a power vacuum to develop in the Gulf. By mid-1967, several months before the devaluation of sterling and the subsequent announcement of Britain's departure from the Gulf, the decision had already been taken in principle to withdraw. Devaluation, and the ensuing political shifts within the Labour cabinet, merely accelerated the process of withdrawal upon which the government had already resolved. Despite promising to reverse this decision, the Conservative government of Edward Heath pragmatically concluded that there was insufficient local support for the preservation of Britain's special position, and that to remain increased the risk of instability which had traditionally been Britain's mission to guard against. Similar pragmatism underpinned British attempts to weld the states of the Lower Gulf together in advance of withdrawal.

Pieragostini insists that 'attempts to form a workable Federation of South Arabia seem based, to a large degree, on programmed decision making'.[26] In particular, he argues that the federal doctrine which had been employed in other parts of the empire, such as Central Africa and the West Indies, was uncritically applied to South Arabia. While this might have been the case for South Arabia, British policy-makers' approach to the Gulf was much more subtle. Learning from failed efforts at nation-building elsewhere in the empire, they scrupulously abstained from any attempt at imposing a British solution to the problem of closer association, thus permitting a greater degree of organic growth. As the former Political Agent in Bahrain, Anthony Parsons, recalled: 'Britain had gained experience of unsuccessful attempts to persuade small regional states into political unions which they had not themselves conceived. The fate of the West Indies Federation and the Federation of South Arabia was fresh in our minds.'[27] Although Britain had encouraged moves towards closer association and warmly welcomed the creation of the United Arab Emirates, this structure derived essentially from the initiative of the Rulers themselves, most notably those of Abu Dhabi and Dubai. The fact that the UAE has endured, while other efforts to bring former dependencies together failed ignominiously, owes much to the means of its inception.

The United States, while also favouring convergence between the small states of the Lower Gulf, remained decidedly inconspicuous in the affairs of the region. In contrast with more conventional accounts which stress the assumption of Western leadership by the United States in the Middle East following the Suez crisis, an exploration of Anglo-American relations in the Gulf context reveals that the Americans, far from wishing to supplant the British, continued to rely upon them to preserve regional stability. Even after the announcement of Britain's intention to withdraw by the end of 1971, the Americans initially hoped that Britain would retain influence and that the Rulers would continue to see Britain as their main source of external advice. While recognizing the importance of securing American co-operation, Britain, for its part, stoutly defended its regional paramountcy and neither anticipated, nor hankered after, a transfer of responsibility to the United States. Indeed, an examination of the Gulf in this period casts doubt on John Darwin's contention that the Suez crisis 'led to the abandonment of all British claims to manage Western interests in the Middle East'.[28] The growth of Britain's interests and involvement in the Gulf, which will be the subject of the first chapter, precluded any such luxury.

1 Responsibility without power

British policy towards the Gulf, 1950–67

As Britain's economic stake in the Gulf increased from the early 1950s, the laissez-faire approach which had characterized British policy before the war gave way to greater pro-activity. This manifested itself in attempts at greater intervention in the internal affairs of the states of the Lower Gulf. At the end of the decade, the problems entailed in this policy shift were highlighted by the Political Resident, Sir George Middleton. 'Our difficulties', he averred, 'derive from our having special responsibilities without enjoying the exercise of executive powers. We can persuade, advise or cajole, but we cannot command.'[1] Moreover, in the aftermath of the 1956 Suez war, the British position in the Gulf was seriously challenged for the first time not only by progressive forces in the region, but also by growing scepticism among British policy-makers themselves about the long-term viability of Britain's special position there. Indeed, from the end of 1956 an ongoing debate started which culminated in the 1967 decision that Britain should aim to leave the Gulf by the mid-1970s. This decision was all the more momentous in the context of the post-war expansion of Britain's interests in the region, especially following Iran's nationalization of the British-owned Anglo-Iranian Oil Company in 1951 (see Chapter 5).[2]

The increased importance of Persian Gulf oil in view of the nationalization of Anglo-Iranian, coupled with the prospect of immense and growing wealth pouring into the primitive Gulf Shaikhdoms, argued the Permanent Under-Secretary at the Foreign Office, Sir William Strang, necessitated a comprehensive review of the situation in the Persian Gulf.[3] Sir Roger Makins was selected for the task, visiting the Gulf between 12 February and 12 March 1953. In the resulting report,[4] Makins haughtily asserted that 'the efficiency of the administration in an Arab country is proportionate to the amount of British administration and advice which they have received in the past'. In calling for more wide-ranging British advice to be dispensed, Makins did recognize that 'Her Majesty's Government are responsible only for the external affairs of the States and have no direct responsibility for their internal administration'. Nevertheless, he insisted that these responsibilities could not 'remain in watertight compartments', and that the 'administrative efficiency and economic stability of the States must be a matter of concern to Her Majesty's Government'. 'The provision of British advisers', insisted Makins, 'is essential in order to preserve the administrations from collapse and to protect the great interest of Her Majesty's Government arising from the prospective accumulation of sterling balances in the hands of Kuwait and Qatar'. Acknowledging that there was a 'latent dislike and suspicion of foreign advisers derived from the pride and the national feeling of the Arab', Makins stressed that they 'must be as high in quality and as few in number as possible'. While the latter condition was met, the former rarely was.

In return for recognition by Britain, the new Ruler of Qatar, Shaikh Ali, who had come to power in a palace coup in November 1949, requested a British adviser. The man selected for the post, Group Captain Phillip Plant, proved unequal to the challenges confronting him. As early as June 1950, the Political Resident, Sir Rupert Hay, reported that 'Plant is floundering a good deal in Qatar largely on account of his inexperience.'[5] Plant's deficiencies also came to the attention of the US Consul in Dhahran, M. R. Rutherford, who noted that the adviser gave the impression of feeling 'harassed and impatient'.[6] 'I feel certain', continued Rutherford, 'that he does not treat his responsibilities with any amount of amusement or imagination'. Although the Foreign Office considered attempting to replace Plant, the embarrassment of engineering his removal so soon after his appointment was recognized.[7] Plant's inadequacies, moreover, actually strengthened his position locally since he was susceptible to pressure from Shaikh Ali for an uneven distribution of state revenues in favour of the ruling family and its retainers. A Foreign Office official lamented that 'It would therefore be useless for us to suggest to the Shaikh that he should get rid of Plant, who, if there has to be a British Adviser, admirably suits the Shaikh's book'.[8] Despite grumbling about Plant's lack of drive and administrative experience, Hay came to the conclusion that 'we should make the best of him'.[9] The modest benefits of securing a British adviser for Qatar were replicated in Kuwait.

At the end of 1950, the new Ruler of Kuwait, Shaikh Abdullah, consented to the appointment of a financial adviser.[10] The position of financial expert went to Colonel G. C. L. Crichton, a former secretary to the government of India in the Foreign Department. The position, however, carried no formal powers and was made not by the FO, but by the Ruler's London representative, H. T. Kemp. Crichton, moreover, soon proved unequal to the challenges confronting him. '[P]artly no doubt through his lack of Arabic', mused a Foreign Office official, 'Col. Crichton is not in a position to influence affairs in Kuwait to the extent which is desirable'.[11] The Treasury also expressed disquiet about Crichton's appointment, arguing that he possessed 'neither the personality nor the knowledge to be able to advise the right courses of action and to put them across to the Ruler'.[12] There was also concern that, far from being consulted over the revision of the Kuwait Oil Company concession in 1951, Crichton was denied even a sight of the new oil agreement.[13] The development expert, W. F. Hasted, fared little better. Early in 1953, the president of the department of public works, Shaikh Fahad, engaged a Syrian engineer, Majadin Sabri, to head the department.[14] At the end of March, Hasted was obliged to place his staff under Jabri's control and confine himself to giving technical advice.[15] A year later, he was forced to resign. Even during his time in post, Hasted acted in a manner which caused alarm and consternation in official British circles.

Towards the end of 1950, the Political Agent, H. G. Jakins, observed: 'Experts engaged by local government tend to show a sturdy independence of His Majesty's Government and we must, I think, expect that they should consider their first loyalty is to the local government.'[16] Hasted, who was described by Jakin's successor, C. J. Pelly, as regarding development work with 'an almost fanatical enthusiasm',[17] certainly conformed with this stereotype. Despite British reservations, he encouraged the government of Kuwait to commit itself to an ambitious development plan for the period 1952–7 involving capital expenditure of over £90m, dismissing any suggestions that state revenues should be put aside for investment purposes as 'typical Treasury fussing'.[18] C. E. Loombe of the Bank of England went so far as to comment: 'I get the impression that Hasted has built up a small kingdom for himself and there is a danger that he will be carried away by his enthusiasm and the desire to see the results of his work in a short period.'[19] Attempts by the British government to foist a 'senior adviser' on Abdullah, which included direct pressure from Prime Minister Churchill,[20] were stubbornly resisted. A few months earlier, D. A. Greenhill of the FO's Eastern Department had presciently warned that 'if we attempt to press our advice against the Rulers' will or to drive them faster than they are ready to go we are likely to achieve nothing permanent but resentment'.[21] Alienating the populations of the Shaikhdoms by asserting overweening advice was another potential danger, especially in the more sophisticated political environment provided by Bahrain.

In 1954, elements within Bahrain, alienated by the autocratic rule of the al-Khalifah family, coalesced to form the Gulf's first political party, the Higher Executive Committee.[22] Influenced by Arab nationalism and committed to a more participatory form of government, the Committee agitated for the removal of Sir Charles Belgrave who, since his appointment in 1926, had acted as adviser to successive Rulers. The incumbent, Shaikh Salman's, refusal to part with Belgrave fuelled discontent culminating at the beginning of March 1956 in the stoning of the Foreign Secretary, Selwyn Lloyd's, car shortly after his arrival in Bahrain for a brief visit. Although the precise origins of the disturbances were obscure, anti-Belgrave, as well as anti-colonial, slogans indicated the mood of the demonstrators.[23] Coming hard on the heels of King Hussein of Jordan's dismissal of Sir John Glubb, the British commander of the Arab Legion, the agitation against Belgrave was taken extremely seriously at the highest levels in Britain.

On 5 March, Prime Minister Eden called a meeting at 10 Downing Street to discuss the situation. In his diary, Evelyn Shuckburgh (Assistant Under-Secretary of State, Foreign Office) recorded that 'Ministers – led by the PM – were mad keen to land British troops anywhere, to show that we are still alive and kicking; and thought Bahrain a good place because of the recent stoning of Selwyn Lloyd'.[24] Subsequently, Eden expressed his fear that 'the situation in the Persian Gulf may become highly dangerous at any moment', adding: 'We have the resources. We must take the necessary measures to make them available.'[25] As regards Belgrave, Eden was insistent that

> we cannot accept the removal of another high ranking British adviser to an Arab ruler in the foreseeable future.
>
> The Glubb business did us quite enough harm and the result of any such event internationally could be disastrous for our whole position in the Middle East.[26]

The Prime Minister's insistence on Belgrave's retention contradicted the evolving view among British officers in the Gulf, and within the Foreign Office itself, that the British adviser was becoming a liability and should be eased out of his position. The Political Resident, Bernard Burrows, reported that the Political Agent in Bahrain had informally told members of the Higher Executive Committee that, while nothing would be done imminently, Belgrave's appointment would be brought to an end in the not too distant future.[27] In his diary entry for 15 March 1956, Shuckburgh wrote: 'The PM has seen Bahrain telegrams and is in a state of excitement, which he has communicated to Nutting.[28] He seems to want to march troops in and arrest the "Higher Executive Committee" with which Bernard [Burrows] is now negotiating.'[29] In a prescient remark which foreshadowed Eden's approach during the Suez crisis, Shuckburgh wrote: 'The PM has never understood that it is far more courageous to accept a humiliation than to do a damn silly "bold" act.'[30] '[E]verybody knows that Belgrave ought to go and soon', he added.

Eden's penchant for military intervention in Bahrain was also questioned by FO officials, most notably the head of the Eastern Department, D. H. M. Riches. '[I]f we intervened with troops', he remarked,

> we should in fact be committing ourselves, (and would be so regarded both by the Ruler and the opposition) to taking Bahrain over. We therefore could not allow the Ruler to go his own autocratic way with the aid of British soldiers and we should find ourselves imposing a constitutional pattern and in fact assuming an overtly "colonial" role. This would be an entirely new departure and one which would run completely against the stream of asiatic thought of contemporary ideas on the advance of backward states towards self-government.[31]

In a similar vein, an FO colleague of Riches warned against ignoring the reformist movement on the grounds that it was well-organized and could rely on widespread public support.[32] No doubt with such considerations in mind, Burrows favoured Belgrave's departure in 1956 rather than waiting until the following year.[33] On a practical level, the Political Resident had already criticized Belgrave's tendency to allow government work to fall into arrears, while the Political Agent in Bahrain described the adviser as an 'anachronism' whose continued presence was likely to build up popular feeling against Britain.[34] While recognizing the temptation to side with the Ruler against the reform movement, Selwyn Lloyd counselled against this course of action.

> It would be likely [he wrote] to lead to a popular rising in favour of reform and before long British troops would be shooting down people whose claims are in accord with our own proclaimed beliefs and practices. We could maintain control only by taking over Bahrain, which is legally independent, as a colony and holding it down by force. The effect on our friends, particularly the Americans, would be deplorable, and the operation would be a propaganda gift to the Egyptians and our other enemies.[35]

During the cabinet discussion on his memorandum,[36] Lloyd expressed concern that local distrust of Belgrave might develop into 'general opposition to British influence and interests in Bahrain'. With this in mind, Lloyd recommended the taking of appropriate steps to secure Belgrave's retirement. The Foreign Secretary's colleagues, however, were worried lest the abrupt departure of Belgrave, following so closely on the dismissal of Glubb, would represent a 'blow to British prestige in the Middle East'. Consequently, it was decided that the impression would have to be given that Belgrave was retiring of his own volition to make way for a younger man. Eden, however, remained sceptical. Commenting on a report that Shaikh Salman was losing confidence in Britain, the Prime Minister averred: 'I feel sure that we are heading for something worse than a Glubb situation if we lose both the Ruler and Belgrave.'[37] In response, Lloyd pointed out that 'Belgrave has become the epitome of the present system of rule in Bahrain and the focus of all the discontent it has engendered.'[38] The alternative to easing Belgrave out of office, Lloyd cautioned, would be to risk another crisis in which the Bahrain adviser would be the central figure. 'Then', he proceeded to tell the Prime Minister, 'either he will have to go abruptly in the Glubb manner or we shall have to use British troops to impose his retention and the continuation of an entirely autocratic regime.' Such a situation, predicted Lloyd, would result in the types of protest – strikes, boycotts, and sabotage of the oil industry – which would not only have serious effects on Britain's prestige in the Persian Gulf, but also undermine confidence in its ability to maintain the British presence there. Lloyd's attempts to manoeuvre Belgrave out of office were frustrated by the adviser's unwillingness to go.[39]

In July 1956, Lloyd was obliged to tell his cabinet colleagues that Belgrave's obduracy placed in jeopardy the plan to appoint a new financial adviser to the Ruler.[40] In a confirmation of Lloyd's prediction, the Committee of National Union (the renamed Higher Executive Committee) demanded Belgrave's dismissal under threat of widespread strike action.[41] In a perverse twist of logic, the Ruler used the possibility of disorder to justify the retention of Belgrave's services 'until things were more settled'.[42] Clearly searching for a scapegoat, Shaikh Salman scolded the Foreign Secretary for the lack of support he had received in his conflict with the Committee of National Union, and threatened to look elsewhere for support if Britain turned against him.[43] Pressure for change, both internal and external, proved irresistible, however. In August, Belgrave's retirement was announced, his departure date set for sometime in the first half of the following year. Before this could happen the Gulf was subjected to the shock waves produced by the Suez crisis.

In early 1952, a Foreign Official noted that although the Rulers and peoples of the Gulf Shaikhdoms were traditionally pro-British, it was natural for them to 'sympathise with the attitude and the aspirations of the other Arab States of the Middle East'.[44] On the eve of the Suez crisis, Burrows warned that 'These Shaikhdoms can act in the knowledge of British protection and at the same time can think as Arab nationalists adhering to the Cairo–Riyadh political philosophy. There is no difficulty for an Arab in the divorce of thought and action.'[45] Foreign Secretary Lloyd was somewhat more circumspect, remarking that the

> principal threat to the British position in the Gulf seems to come, immediately, not from the Rulers who recognize the value to themselves of our relationship with them but from the dissident and reformist elements over whom Egypt exercises the greatest influence.[46]

Lloyd's analysis was soon to be tested.

The deterioration in Anglo-Egyptian relations, which culminated in the nationalization of the Suez Canal on 26 July 1956, set the British government on a collision course with the Egyptian president, Gamal Abdul Nasser. In protest at the calling of the Conference of Maritime Nations in London, Nasser exhorted his fellow Arabs to hold a series of strikes in mid-August. On the sixteenth, a crowd threw stones at the British Agency in the Qatari capital, Doha, breaking all the front windows. Two platoons from the Royal Navy had to be landed to restore order.[47] In Kuwait, around 4000 people gathered to hear pro-Nasser speeches. Although the crowd dispersed quietly, a hard core of 200 demonstrators clashed with the Kuwaiti security services. By 16 August, while most government offices functioned normally, 90 per cent of shops remained closed. It was the

Anglo-French attack on Egypt, which began on the night of 31 October/ 1 November, that provided the real test for British relations with the Gulf Shaikhdoms.

Increasingly frustrated by Nasser's defiance, and determined to remove the Egyptian president from power, Eden searched for a pretext to employ military force. This was provided by the French who, convinced that Nasser was fuelling the Algerian uprising against them, had their own reasons for wishing to see Nasser's demise. During a meeting at Chequers on 14 October, the Deputy Chief of the French Air Force, Maurice Challe, presented a plan which involved clandestinely encouraging the Israelis to attack Egypt, thereby providing a justification for despatching an Anglo-French force to Suez ostensibly to separate the combatants. The collusive plan was firmed up at a meeting of representatives of the British, French, and Israeli government at Sevres, just outside Paris on 22 October. The flimsy façade the British had created to conceal their real motives was quickly seen through. Referring to first reactions from Bahrain, Burrows noted 'wide acceptance of view that we and the French instigated the Israeli attack in order to have an excuse to reoccupy the Canal'.[48] From his vantage point in Doha, Political Agent Carden reported:

> The Ruler and every Arab that I have heard has condemned our attack on Egypt. At worst they suspect us of collusion with the Israelis, whom they loathe; at best they suspect us of wishing to unseat Nasser and regain control of the Canal.[49]

Minor demonstrations and a strike among workers of the Qatar Petroleum Company ensued. In Bahrain and Kuwait rather more serious disturbances broke out.

In the absence of legal political parties, reform-minded individuals in Kuwait came together under the auspices of social clubs. Some degree of co-operation among these various bodies was provided by the establishment of the Committee of Clubs. It was this organization which coordinated the protest at the attacks on Egypt. Strikes and a mass meeting were called for 3 November which resulted in a two-hour running battle between demonstrators and police in the centre of Kuwait town. On the same day disorder broke out in Manama, the capital of Bahrain. Whereas the al-Sabah proved able to deal with the situation without outside intervention, the government of Bahrain, fearing a loss of control, called on British troops to clear the streets of Manama.[50] Turning the unrest to his own advantage, the Ruler arrested leading members of the Committee of National Union. Convicted of attempting to assassinate Belgrave and Shaikh Salman himself, two were sentenced to ten years in a Bahraini jail, the other three to fourteen-year terms to be served outside Bahrain.[51] With the Committee of National Union temporarily emasculated, both adviser and Ruler attempted to delay Belgrave's departure, Shaikh Salman even floating the idea of retaining him as his personal adviser.[52] Apart from jeopardizing the Foreign Office's painstaking efforts to effect Belgrave's removal, any postponement of the adviser's retirement would, as Riches noted, 'lend colour to the suspicions of the moderate reformists who believe that the Ruler has used the trial of the Committee of National Union leaders as an excuse to relapse into his former obstinate refusal to make changes'.[53] However, ill-health and an enforced return to Britain for medical treatment foiled any hopes that Shaikh Salman had of keeping his adviser. In final grudging recognition that after over thirty years of service Belgrave would not be returning, the Ruler appointed G. W. R. Smith to the new post of Secretary to the government of Bahrain in June 1957.

The reaction to the Suez war on the Trucial coast was considerably less extreme than in the more politically sophisticated Shaikhdoms of Kuwait, Qatar, and Bahrain. With the exception of the Union Jack being stolen from the car of the Political Agent in Dubai, the Trucial States remained relatively peaceful. The Ruler of Dubai promised his unequivocal support, while the Abu Dhabi ruling family expressed satisfaction with British actions, the Ruler's brother, Shaikh Zaid, reportedly punctuating BBC news bulletins with cries of 'come on Israel'.[54] Zaid also told the British political officer in his state that Britain should have 'done to Cairo what the Russians did to Budapest'.[55] Although the Ruler of Sharjah was more circumspect, he did promise to do his utmost to restrain Egyptian and Jordanian teachers and other possible agitators from condemning Britain.[56] Burrows had already recognized that Britain was having to 'draw very deeply on accumulated fund of goodwill of the Persian Gulf Rulers'.[57] With respect to Kuwait, the Political Agent, G. W. Bell, recognized that Britain had been forced to move closer to 'reactionary elements of the Ruling family' at the precise moment that it had hoped to achieve 'closer co-operation with younger and more liberally minded members'.[58] The American Consul in Kuwait, William D. Brewer, agreed with this analysis. 'While the basic British position remains,' he mused, 'reliance for its preservation must increasingly be placed, at least temporarily, on a few senior shaykhs and on force'.[59] The changed atmosphere in the Gulf led some to doubt the long-term prospects and viability of the British presence there.

Sir Roger Stevens and Sir Michael Wright, British Ambassadors in Tehran and Baghdad respectively, were the principal sceptics. Wright warned that the British role in the Gulf was perceived in the Arab world as '"imperialistic" and anachronistic',[60] while Stevens questioned its whole basis.[61] 'With the liquidation of our Indian Empire,' he maintained, 'the traditional reason for our presence in the Persian Gulf ceased to exist; and our positions there became stations on a road leading nowhere.'

> It is not clear to me [he continued] that our political position in Kuwait and Qatar is essential to the maintenance of our commercial interests,

> nor am I sure how effective it is in the long run for ensuring that the Ruler of Kuwait does not try to spend his vast resources outside the sterling area. At any rate, recent events seem to have shown that our token military presence in the Gulf does not ensure the flow of oil any more than a military occupation foothold in the Plate would guarantee our supply of beef.

'It is surely better to devise a constructive way out of this dead-end even at the loss of a little prestige,' he concluded, 'rather than wait to be overwhelmed by events and thrust onto the inevitably disastrous defensive.'

The Political Resident rebuffed such ideas.[62] Underpinning his approach was the notion that existing relations with the Persian Gulf States should 'continue to be regarded as a major British interest'. 'It is surely a principle borrowed from America and alien to our own system of political thought', he condescended, 'that anything which has existed for a hundred years, such as our relations with the Gulf States, must necessarily be wrong or must change.' Not surprisingly, Burrows saw any alteration in the relationship between Britain and the Gulf Shaikhdoms as unjustified. Summing up the debate, Selwyn Lloyd recommended that the policy of the British government had to lie somewhere between the two extremes. While recognizing a rapidly changing world situation would not permit stagnation in the Gulf, he did shy away from drastic or fundamental changes. '[B]y taking too sudden or far-reaching initiatives we may well not forestall trouble but precipitate it', he cautioned.[63] Implicitly rejecting without necessarily addressing the points raised by Stevens, Lloyd adhered to the traditional argument that the British presence facilitated the supply of oil, 50 per cent of Britain's needs by 1957 being satisfied by Kuwait alone. The expulsion in 1955 of Saudi forces from the disputed Buraimi oasis territory on the border with Abu Dhabi, coupled with the deployment of British forces in Bahrain the following year, symbolized for Lloyd Britain's determination to fulfil its responsibilities in the region. 'Even the future decline in our conventional military strength need not be locally reflected in the Gulf', he confidently predicted.[64] The Foreign Secretary's willingness to embrace change where appropriate, however, is demonstrated most clearly with respect to Kuwait.

In September 1958, the government of Kuwait requested British recognition of its right both to conduct relations with other Arab countries and to join international organizations such as the International Telecommunications Union.[65] The following year Kuwait began to press for an abandonment of Britain's extra-territorial jurisdiction,[66] and at the beginning of 1961 the Ruler insisted on the replacement of the 1899 agreement which he felt had fallen into desuetude.[67] At each of these stages, Britain was prepared to facilitate Kuwait's requests. Kuwait was granted the right to conduct relations with her Arab neighbours in October 1958,[68] and the Cabinet decided to support the Shaikhdom's application to join international organizations in November.[69] The first transfer of jurisdiction from Britain to Kuwait took place in February 1960,[70] while the 1899 agreement was terminated on 19 June 1961.[71] Britain acquiesced so readily to Kuwait's requests for a number of reasons. First, Kuwait was willing to maintain economic and military links with Britain. Not only did Kuwait repeatedly express a preference for continuing to invest her oil revenues in London,[72] but was also prepared to remain within the sterling area,[73] and administer exchange controls on the same broad principles as the Bank of England.[74] Moreover, paragraph d) of the letter which terminated the 1899 agreement contained the following clause: 'Nothing in these conditions shall affect the readiness of Her Majesty's Government to assist the government of Kuwait if the latter request such assistance.'[75] The recognition of Kuwait's independent status also came to be seen as the best means of protecting British interests.

Referring to Kuwait's growing independent status in October 1959, the head of the Eastern Department at the FO, R. A. Beaumont, argued that 'it may well be advantageous to encourage this process, provided that existing friendly relations between HMG and Kuwait and our unimpaired access to oil on beneficial terms remain'.[76] The British, furthermore, increasingly recognized the inexorable pressures for Kuwaiti independence. 'The essential consideration must be,' observed the Political Agent in August 1959,

> . . . that in the course of nature Kuwait, because of her cohesive political identity, backed by great wealth, must some day achieve independence. . . . I submit that we must accept this necessity and be prepared to meet it before it becomes too urgent and a cause for dissension between us.[77]

Writing earlier in the year, moreover, Foreign Secretary Lloyd, had emphasized that:

> The irreducible interest of the United Kingdom in Kuwait is that Kuwait shall remain an independent state having an oil policy conducted by a Government independent of other Middle Eastern producers . . . and also having a policy independent of Communist or satellite influence.[78]

Indeed, it was felt that the maintenance of an independent oil policy by Kuwait, which was still supplying Britain with about 40 per cent of its oil needs, would prevent other oil-producing states from holding Britain, and the rest of Western Europe, to ransom.[79]

By fostering international recognition of Kuwait, it was also hoped that potential aggressors in the Middle East would be deterred from seeking to absorb the oil-rich Shaikhdom,[80] a calculation belied by Iraq's continuing territorial ambitions. The British were even prepared to acquiesce in the distribution of part of Kuwait's accumulated reserves to other Arab countries. In 1961, the Economic Counsellor to the Political Resident, W. P. Cranston, argued:

> It may well be that the promise of substantial Kuwaiti financial contributions to future Arab economic development may be part of the price which Kuwait will have to pay in order to secure her future independence and to remove the current feeling of resentment, not wholly justified, that Kuwait is retaining her wealth and not sharing it with her neighbours.[81]

Kuwait had already made some gestures with respect to contributing towards economic development in the Lower Gulf. Such assistance became less significant following the discovery of oil in commercial quantities in Abu Dhabi.

An oil strike at Das Island by Abu Dhabi Marine Areas Limited,[82] coupled with discoveries by Petroleum Development Trucial Coast,[83] promised to turn Abu Dhabi into a major oil producer. Indeed, the Political Resident, Sir George Middleton, prophesied that by the end of 1961 Abu Dhabi would be 'in the "big money"'.[84] Oil wealth among the Gulf Shaikhdoms, however, aroused the envy of the poorer states of the Arab world. Referring to Jordan's lack of sympathy for Kuwait following the renewal of the Iraqi claim to the Amirate in mid-1961, the British Ambassador in Amman, John Henniker-Major, noted: 'Of moral indignation at the threat to a small and independent country, there was hardly a trace'.[85] Henniker-Major also pointed out that the British presence presented a target for Arab nationalists, as well as providing a potential source of friction with the Arab world. 'As far as the Middle East and the world in general is concerned', chimed an FO official, 'there is also the drawback of being saddled with what looks like being one of our last major colonial responsibilities'.[86] Another official expressed concern that in the United Nations, the Afro-Asian and Soviet blocs would soon 'run out of straight "colonial" targets and almost certainly turn the searchlight on to the Persian Gulf'.[87] 'We cannot afford in the twentieth century to risk giving the (false) impression that HMG look upon the Gulf with the blinkered eyes of a nineteenth-century Pro-Consul', he continued. Middleton's successor, Sir William Luce, however, was a firm believer in the efficacy of the continued British presence in the Gulf.

In early 1963, Luce revisited a question first posed in the aftermath of the Suez crisis, namely the extent to which the West in general, and Britain in particular, could afford to rely solely on normal commercial processes for the uninterrupted supply of oil.[88] To answer this question in the affirmative, Luce argued, it would be necessary to foresee the time when the Arab world had moved from instability to stability and when Cold War tensions had eased sufficiently for the West to trust the Soviet Union not to expand into the Gulf region. In Luce's opinion, neither prospect was realistic. Equally, Luce dismissed the argument that because the Arabs could not drink their oil it would always find its way to overseas markets. 'They are quite capable of damaging themselves economically for political reasons,' he observed, 'and, in any case, if they were under Communist influence they would not have the final say.' In warning of the dangers of a power vacuum in the Gulf, Luce asserted that 'we should not allow ourselves to become obsessed with the inevitability of early and total withdrawal from our special position in the Persian Gulf or to suffer from any quite unnecessary guilt complex about the respectability of that position'. He concluded:

> Our position here is not a tottering one nor is it in danger of rapid erosion by any internal influences. It remains acceptable to most of the people of the area and particularly to those in power, and provided we play our cards skilfully, I see no reason why it should not remain so for many years.

Luce's views were not allowed to pass unchallenged in the FO. R. S. Crawford of the Arabian Department questioned whether Middle East oil producers would subordinate economic considerations to political ones. Casting his mind back to the decimation of the Iranian economy following the nationalization of Anglo-Iranian Oil in 1951, he noted that 'Arabs as well as Iranians do seem to have learned the lesson of Abadan'.[89] Focusing on another aspect of Luce's thesis, Britain's Ambassador in Amman, Roderick Parkes, cast doubt on the long-term viability of preserving Britain's commercial interests in the Gulf by means of a military presence. While accepting that there was no immediate pressure to liquidate the military position, Parkes stressed: 'we should now be thinking in terms of an orderly withdrawal, and the avoidance of a series of last-ditch retreats that might win us weeks of breathing space, at the cost of years of diplomacy undoing the damage done'.[90] As if to underline his point, the Ambassador mused:

> I simply cannot see, in 1963, a tight community of friendly, contented Arabs going about their business in the Peninsula under Western protection and casting no sidelong glances at the fomenting Arab world outside. Nationalism and Nasserism both have a long start and I doubt whether, for example, the students who stoned Mr Selwyn Lloyd's car in 1956 have either materially outgrown their youthful enthusiasm or will readily be diverted from a compulsive interest in Arab politics.

Parkes' counterpart in Kuwait, Sir John Richmond, was equally sceptical about Luce's analysis: 'An island of British paramountcy, evolving very slowly towards limited political autonomy, protected by constitutional monarchies, seems to me a last-ditch defence of the nineteenth century which cannot possibly succeed in the second half of the twentieth century.'[91] Instead, Richmond urged that the object of policy should not be to retain Britain's military and political position indefinitely, but to 'transform it into a mutually profitable and equal relationship'. In the future, argued Richmond, Britain would have to rely 'solely on normal commercial procedures backed by increasing international inter-dependence, for the uninterrupted supply of oil'. Taking a calculated swipe at Luce, Richmond concluded with this peroration: 'I do not believe, as he appears to do, that in the second half of the twentieth century you can dig oil with bayonets'. The Treasury was also sceptical about the effectiveness of Britain's military structure in preserving oil supplies from the Gulf.

Drawing conclusions from the failure to prevent violent change in either Iraq or Yemen, R. L. Sharp (Assistant Secretary, Treasury) cast doubt on whether the British military presence could protect either Iran or Saudi Arabia in the future.[92] Sharp's Treasury colleague, J. E. Lucas (Principal), added that it was 'doubtful in the extreme whether any conceivable British military presence in the Middle East could have any value against a major Russian attack'.[93] As regards security of supplies, Sharp argued that, since the Middle East producers were dependent on their oil revenues to fund not only ordinary expenditure, but also growing development programmes, it was unlikely that they could afford any protracted stoppage of oil production.[94] Summing up, Sharp suggested that 'oil companies' profits are more likely to be affected by other factors, such as pressure from producing countries, and increasing competition, than they are by anything that our military presence in the Gulf area will protect them from'.

Using figures from a 1961 inter-departmental report on Britain's economic and financial interests in the Gulf, the Treasury also tried to undermine the case for a continued military presence. The report estimated that if British companies were excluded from the Middle East, there would be an additional cost to the balance of payments of at least £200m.[95] Nevertheless, in the likelier scenario that British companies were able to continue operating in the Middle East, but with a substantially reduced share of profits, the report concluded that the extra burden on the balance of payments would be closer to £100m. Since the cost of Britain's Gulf effort was put at £120 to £125m, rising to between £150 and £160m over the next ten years, the Treasury questioned the economic sense of maintaining it. 'The premium is too high in relation to the sort of risks which it is designed to ensure against',[96] emphasized Sharp, while Lucas urged that 'from the financial and economic standpoint, there is no need for a UK military presence in the Persian Gulf after 1970'.[97] The Treasury also pointed out that British forces 'could not prevent a peaceful change which might adversely affect the bargaining power of the oil companies *vis-à-vis* the producing countries'.[98] Undeterred by such arguments, the Political Resident continued to make the case for a continuing military role in the Gulf.[99]

Luce ascribed the relative stability of the Gulf by comparison with the rest of the Middle East to the British presence. Returning to earlier arguments, he identified a power vacuum in the Gulf which Britain, over the previous century-and-a-half, had filled. With the discovery of oil, he continued, 'power pressures on the vacuum have increased and we correspondingly have had to fill it more strongly'. Luce characterized the argument of those who stated that the stationing of British forces in the Gulf was not the best way to ensure the flow of oil as 'dangerously facile and naïve'. Only by filling the power vacuum with the exercise of power, argued Luce, could the necessary political and economic stability be provided to ensure the flow of oil on reasonable terms and in ever-increasing quantities. 'Our political position here', he insisted, '. . . would collapse under external pressures were it not supported, and seen to be supported, by military power.' FO mandarins were impressed by the force of Luce's arguments. J. A. Snellgrove found Luce's theory of vacuums 'persuasive', adding that 'It is one thing to modernise and streamline ouur relationship with the Rulers . . . but quite another to abandon our special position of friend and protector'.[100] D. J. McCarthy of the Arabian Department agreed with this analysis, as he put it, 'not because I like our anachronistic posture (largely responsibility without power) but because in a region of instability full of feckless people in a world in upheaval it is hard to think of an alternative that works'.[101]

A Foreign Office memorandum for the Cabinet Defence and Oversea Policy Committee's long-term study group revealed the influence of Luce's ideas. On the one hand, the FO argued that the presence of British forces created the conditions of order necessary for oil production, transportation, and exploration to continue. On the other, the FO contended that the stability which the military presence brought to the region provided the oil companies with 'the best chance they can have of ensuring that oil is available to their Western and other markets in growing quantities and on reasonable terms'.[102] The Treasury, however, countered that 'the peaceful combination of producing countries in OPEC is already extracting a larger share of the profits from the oil companies, and may continue the process, in which military force is entirely irrelevant'.[103] With the election of a Labour government in October 1964, the British role in the Persian Gulf came under renewed scrutiny.

As early as November, the new Foreign Secretary, Patrick Gordon Walker, expressed his wish to 'work towards a situation in the protected Gulf States which would be broadly analogous with Kuwait, where we had a Defence treaty but no more'.[104] When Luce presented his desire to remove the recalcitrant Ruler of Abu Dhabi, Shaikh Shakhbut, Gordon Walker expostulated: 'I will need a lot of persuading that this James Bond scheme is a good one. This would not fit in with my idea for a change of posture in the Gulf.'[105] Sensing that change was in the wind,[106] Luce urged the Foreign Secretary that federation should be seen as the road to modernizing Britain's relationship with the Gulf and advised against the shedding of British functions to the individual Shaikhdoms until the achievement of the federal goal. Despite his antipathy towards Shakhbut, the Political Resident also mounted a strong defence of shaikhly institutions. Noting that the ruling families of the Gulf were 'deeply rooted' and commanded the respect of the majority of their people, he stressed his belief that the 'only alternative at present to the continuation of shaikhly rule is violent revolution, either by the local security forces or by some group within the population'. Accepting that there were some bad Shaikhs in the Gulf, he insisted that it should be Britain's aim to 'improve the performance of the curable, rather than to sweep away the whole system'. He concluded that any change in Britain's relationship with the Gulf should 'not involve such sudden or drastic change as would shake the confidence of the Rulers in our intention to continue to support the integrity of their States, and so drive them into reinsuring elsewhere'.

Although Gordon Walker accepted the case for maintaining the British military presence on strategic grounds, he questioned its necessity with respect to preserving oil supplies.[107] Equally, he was distinctly unhappy about the nature of Britain's relationship with the Rulers which, having stemmed from the former Indian imperial government, was in need of modernization. Explaining what the modernization of relations with the Shaikhdoms would involve to Phillips Talbot (Assistant Secretary for Near East Affairs at the State Department), Crawford identified the confinement of British activities to defence and foreign affairs and the relinquishment of British jurisdiction of non-Muslim foreigners once a suitable legal system for the Gulf States had been established.[108] Relaying the new emphasis to British diplomats, the FO pointed out that 'Our policy is to modernize our relationship with the States while retaining our military presence in the Gulf'.[109] No doubt bearing the imprint of Gordon Walker's views, the FO also focused on the role of the military presence in maintaining stability and preventing the emergence of a political vacuum, rather than preserving oil supplies. Luce's views were by no means rejected *in toto*, however. Gordon Walker's successor, Michael Stewart, accepted the need to persist with the shaikhly system in the Gulf on grounds of British self-interest and the lack of any viable alternative.[110] Furthermore, the Political Resident's gradualist agenda found favour. While Stewart recognized the need to dispense with those aspects of Britain's special position which detracted from the Gulf States' internal autonomy, he acknowledged that this should be done 'in such a manner as neither to alarm our friends nor to weaken our ability to maintain our position and defend the integrity of the Gulf States'.[111] Referring to the Gulf in a memorandum to the Cabinet, Stewart explained that

> In our absence there would be a security vacuum which would be likely to do grave harm to political stability throughout the area and

to the production and transportation of oil, as well as encourage a renewal of Soviet southward pressure.[112]

Stewart's more cautious approach than his predecessor's can, at least in part, be accounted for with reference to events in Bahrain in the early months of 1965.

In the first half of March, disturbances broke out in Bahrain. Initially demonstrators focused their anger on the Bahrain Petroleum Company's redundancy scheme, but later extended their activities to agitation in favour of the formation of unions. From the FO's perspective, however, the demonstrations were designed 'more as a trial of strength with authority than to achieve any particular objective'.[113] Luce traced the origins of the troubles to the influence of the UAR-directed Arab Nationalist Movement operating through Kuwait.[114] In these circumstances, he sought authority to commit British forces should the Bahrain Ruler request assistance in maintaining order. In December 1964, Britain had renewed an undertaking, first given in 1958, that HMG would 'as in the past, and on the basis of existing treaties and engagements, support Bahrain, should the need for help arise, and maintain Bahrain's independence'. Having taken legal advice, the FO accepted that this commitment extended to a need for assistance against internal as well as external attack.[115] On a more self-interested note, an FO official remarked that 'it is very much in our own interest to avoid prolonged disturbances which might jeopardize British lives and would certainly attract hostile publicity'.[116] As a result of such calculations, Luce was authorized on 13 March to commit British forces to the maintenance of internal security if so requested by the Ruler. A day later, having received such a request, the Political Resident ordered the use of naval helicopters to assist local police in identifying demonstrators and, where necessary, to drop tear gas to disperse them.[117] By 18 March order had been restored sufficiently to permit the withdrawal of the helicopters. The suppression of the Bahrain disturbances did not signal the end of challenges to British interests in the Lower Gulf, however.

Having been seduced by offers of economic aid, Shaikh Saqr of Sharjah declared his intention in mid-May 1965 to permit an Arab League presence in his territory. For good measure he told the Minister of State at the Foreign Office (George Thomson), who was visiting the area, that he had 'little or nothing to thank the British government for over the years', adding that the Trucial Oman Scouts were of no value to him and were intended only to protect British interests.[118] The Political Agent in Dubai, H. G. Balfour-Paul, was concerned not merely by the style of Saqr's declaration, which he described as remarkable for its 'unabashed effrontery', but also by the 'serious implications of his action in flaunting his Treaty obligations and deliberately opening the gates to this most obvious instance of a Trojan horse'.[119] While Britain was not in principle opposed to Arab League aid to the Trucial States, there was a determination to prevent it being used as a pretext for political penetration into the region. In order to provide some measure of control over the purposes to which Arab League assistance was put, Britain was insistent that aid was channelled through the Trucial States Development Office and Fund which the British had been instrumental in establishing. Since to insist upon this the Rulers risked losing League offers of help, the FO recognized that alternative sources of funding would have to be found.[120] Foreign Secretary Stewart told his colleagues on the Cabinet Defence and Oversea Policy Committee that 'If we wish to maintain our position we must compete with the Arab League and contain its activities.'[121] To this end, Stewart proposed that Britain provide up to £1m in economic aid to the Trucial States. In support of his case, Stewart warned that 'if we withdraw we should leave a power vacuum which would result in the embroilment in conflict of the neighbouring countries with consequent serious risk to our oil supplies.'[122] He added that a withdrawal imposed by the Arab League would not merely involve a breach in Britain's treaty obligations, but also jeopardize the pro-Western stance of Iran. Despite opposition from the Minister of Overseas Development, Barbara Castle, who argued that Britain was in danger of diverting to the Trucial States funds which were urgently needed for development elsewhere in the Arab world,[123] Stewart won backing for his proposal.[124] Despite this victory, the situation in the Trucial States deteriorated rapidly.

Even with the £1m grant, Britain's position was weak especially in the absence of aid from other friendly sources. Although Shaikh Shakhbut reluctantly agreed to provide £100,000 by the end of the year, this did little materially to improve the situation.[125] Shakhbut also dragged his feet on the question of a fixed percentage contribution from his revenues for development in the Trucial States.[126] Emboldened by the brazen self-confidence of Shaikh Saqr, first his kinsman and namesake, Shaikh Saqr of Ras al Khaimah, and subsequently the Rulers of Ajman and Umm al Gawain, joined his confrontational stance.[127] The legal opinion that the treaties contained no provision for sanctions against recalcitrance and could be denounced at will by the Rulers merely underlined the fragility of Britain's position. No doubt playing devil's advocate, Luce recommended that Britain permit an Arab League presence on the Trucial Coast, rather than risk the denunciation of its treaties.[128] Although this was considered by the Cabinet Defence and Oversea Policy Committee, it was felt that if the two Saqrs were allowed to flaunt Britain's advice with impunity, its standing in the area would be undermined.[129] Luce reported that there was an air of expectancy in the Gulf in the face of the overt challenge which had been thrown down to Britain. Belying his earlier defeatist attitude, the Political Resident stressed: 'It is inconceivable to me that Her Majesty's Government could abandon their peace-keeping role in this economically vital area at the first flick of the whip by Nasser and a couple of insignificant, self-serving Sheikhs.'[130] The deposition of Shaikh Saqr by members of the ruling family of Sharjah at the end of June precipitated a capitulation by the other dissident Rulers who informed the Secretary-General of the Arab League that aid must be channelled through the Trucial States Development Fund.[131] Predictably, the League refused to acquiesce. Perhaps more troubling from the British perspective, King Feisal equivocated over contributing to the Fund, justifying his stance with the comment that Saudi Arabia, as a member of the Arab League, had a 'most difficult path to steer'.[132] The Kuwaiti representative on the Arab League Gulf Committee had already declared that 'Kuwait would never contribute to the "British Fund"'.[133] By October, the Rulers were beginning not only to question the prudence of turning down Arab League aid, but also to lose confidence in Development Fund itself.[134] Feisal's reticence was particularly troubling in view of a growing mood among British policy-makers that Saudi Arabia was a possible successor to Britain's special position in the Gulf.

As early as September 1960, the Political Resident, Sir George Middleton, had urged that British policy should be 'political rather than military and be designed as a holding operation and a period of preparation for the time when the old Saudi Arabia emerges as a more modern Arab state to take our place in the Gulf'.[135] Despite accepting that the scale of British interests precluded withdrawal from the Gulf in the immediate future, the Cabinet Official Committee on Defence and Oversea Policy anticipated that it would become necessary sometime after 1970.[136] In these circumstances, the Committee recommended that 'we should be preparing our present clients for the choice they will have then to make between associating with each other or achieving some dependent relationship with Saudi Arabia'. Taking a pragmatic line, the Committee observed that 'Geography is the basic reason for thinking of Saudi Arabia as, in a sense, our eventual heir in the Persian Gulf some time after 1970.'[137] 'Surely the only answer to all these absurd little states is for them to be absorbed by Saudi Arabia as rapidly and decently as possible', snapped the Head of the FO's United Nations (Political) Department, Sam Falle.[138] 'Absorption by Saudi Arabia', admitted the Arabian Department's Head, T. F. Brenchley, 'is the best medium-term answer'.[139] Aware of the unhappy precedent set by British attempts to foster federations among other dependent territories, Brenchley's colleague, E. M. Rose, was prepared to countenance a federation of Gulf Shaikhdoms on the understanding that it was 'only a stage on the road to ultimate Saudi domination of the Gulf'.[140] Even Luce accepted that Saudi Arabia had to be the 'keystone of any solidarity between the Gulf States and the Arabian Peninsula'.[141]

From his vantage point in Jedda, Britain's Ambassador to Saudi Arabia, Morgan Man, reported that Feisal had gained the 'distinct impression' that Her Majesty's Government recognized the 'predominant position and influence of Saudi Arabia in the Gulf area'.[142] Commenting on the possibility of the extension of the Saudi riyal to the Gulf States, a Treasury official remarked: 'I have long felt that these States ought to move into the Saudi orbit and this currency move would be in the right direction'.[143] The Foreign Office, however, was more circumspect over the currency question. On the one hand, it was felt that the adoption of the riyal so soon after Britain's announcement to withdraw from Aden by 1968 would confirm local fears that Britain was preparing to abandon its position in the Gulf as well.[144] On the other, the acceptance of the Saudi currency would have an 'adverse effect' on the development of closer co-operation between the Gulf States.[145] Certainly there was little chance of Abu Dhabi accepting the riyal in view of the long-running and bitter territorial dispute with Saudi Arabia over the Buraimi oasis (see Chapter 5). The idea of a transfer of power to Saudi Arabia resurfaced in the wake of the British decision to leave South Arabia.

Aden, which had joined the British-sponsored federation of South Arabian states in January 1963, formed a key link in Britain's military structure in the Middle East. Indeed, the resources of the British base in Aden had been an important component in the 1961 operation to deter Iraqi adventurism in Kuwait.[146] The South Arabian Federation proved an unhappy constitutional experiment, however. As the Governor of Aden, Sir Charles Johnston, had been forced to concede: 'the entry of Aden into the Federation is not an easy matter to provide for. It is a bringing together not only of urban and rural, but of different centuries as well: modern Glasgow, say, and the eighteenth-century highlands'.[147] The speed with which the merger was completed prompted the American Consul in Aden to liken it to a 'Midnight marriage by Justice of the Peace rather than [a] Church affair with trimmings'.[148] To make matters worse the overthrow in September 1962 of the imamate in neighbouring Yemen brought revolutionary Arab nationalism, backed by Nasser's United Arab Republic, to the very doors of the fledgling federation. The internal contradictions, coupled with the external pressures, provided a recipe for instability. By mid-1965, the Secretary of State for Defence, Denis Healey, told his colleagues on the Defence and Oversea Policy Committee that five battalions in Aden were engaged in preserving internal security in the federation and the military base itself, making them unavailable for use elsewhere in the region.[149] In other words, far from providing a secure base from which British power could be projected in the Gulf, South Arabia was in fact absorbing military resources. At the beginning of September, the speaker of Aden's legislative assembly, Sir Arthur Clarke, was assassinated. The refusal of the Chief Minister, Abdul Mackawi, to condemn such acts of terrorism led to the dissolution of the Aden government and the imposition of direct rule.

Independence for the federation had already been set for 1968 (subsequently brought forward to 1967). It remained to be decided whether Britain would maintain a military presence in, or commitment to, South Arabia after that date. Bearing in mind the costly, and seemingly intractable,

'Confrontation' with Indonesia in which Britain had become embroiled after the creation of Malaysia in 1963, the Cabinet Official Committee on Defence and Oversea Policy advised against undertaking the defence of any part of South Arabia after independence.[150] On 24 November 1965, the committee's ministerial counterpart agreed that Britain should not maintain any obligations to, or defence facilities in, Aden or the South Arabian Federation after independence.[151] Despite the decision not merely to depart from South Arabia, but also to cut all defence ties, no similar egress from the Gulf States was envisaged. 'In the Gulf our major interests preclude our political or military withdrawal in the present decade', asserted the Official Committee on Defence and Oversea Policy.[152] To compensate for the loss of Aden, plans were set in train to expand British forces stationed in the Gulf. This had the advantage of reassuring not merely nervous Gulf Shaikhs, but also the principal pro-Western leaders of the region, the Shah of Iran and King Feisal of Saudi Arabia.[153]

The pro-Western alignment of Iran was described by the Cabinet Official Defence and Oversea Policy Committee as a 'major British asset'.[154] Besides being valued as a non-Arab source of oil in the Middle East, Iran was seen as a moderating influence on other oil producers. The Committee also pointed out that an unfriendly government in control of the northern shore of the Gulf would require Britain to station considerably larger and more costly military forces to protect British interests. Subjected to nationalist criticism and Soviet overtures, the Shah's pro-Western stance was seen as 'brittle', however. Although it was recognized that he would never voluntarily join the Soviet camp, it was feared that if he became disenchanted he would 'revert to the traditional Iranian policy of neutralism and of playing off East and West'. 'For these reasons,' stressed the Committee, 'the Shah needs constant reassurance of Western support, if he is to remain convinced that his present game is worth the candle.' The decision to redeploy to the Gulf following the departure from Aden can clearly be seen in this context. Indeed, the Committee speculated that the Shah regarded the British presence in the Gulf as his 'main security against enemies in the area'. There was also recognition that Saudi Arabia had a legitimate and profound interest in the future of the Gulf States. Nevertheless, the drawbacks of a Saudi take-over of these states were soon realized.

The Defence Review Working Party for the Cabinet Official Defence and Oversea Policy Committee[155] pointed out that, under the treaties with the Gulf States, Britain could not appoint Saudi Arabia to succeed it without their consent. Although envisaging a situation in which the Gulf States might seek Saudi protection if it became clear that Britain was about to depart, the Working Party feared that the Saudis would be 'almost bound to insist first on Buraimi as their pound of flesh. Abu Dhabi would certainly reject Saudi protection on such terms, and the attitude of at least some of the other Rulers might harden in sympathy.' There was also some doubt about whether the sparsely populated desert kingdom had the resources to provide the Gulf States with meaningful diplomatic and military protection. The Working Party also warned that

> There is always the danger of a change of regime in all or part of Saudi Arabia, and if we had gone too far in promoting the Saudis as our successors we might not be able to draw back if a government hostile to our interests came to power in Riyadh.

Nevertheless, the importance of securing 'Saudi co-operation and at least Iranian acquiescence' was recognized. Although the two monarchies were described as 'near the ideal as we are ever likely to get', it was recognized that each regime was 'dangerously dependent on the life of one man'.

Despite the perceived fragility of Iran and Saudi Arabia, and the inherent problems in grooming them as successor states, the Working Party anticipated the ending of Britain's special role in the Gulf:

> After our decision to withdraw militarily as well as politically from Aden by 1968, no one really believes that we shall be able (or even wish) to stay indefinitely in the Gulf. By the mid-1970s we must expect a world where almost all colonial and quasi-colonial traces have disappeared and the overseas deployment of British power has contracted further than at present. If we have not gone from the Gulf, the pressures on us to go are likely to be very severe indeed.

Fearing that a continued British presence would represent a 'tempting target for the rising forces of Arab nationalism', the Working Party urged that 'we should clearly be wise to go before the consequences of staying become more dangerous to local stability than the consequences of departure.' In spite of the recognition that after Britain's withdrawal oil supplies would become concentrated in the hands of fewer local governments, the conclusion was still reached that it was not in Britain's interests to remain in the Gulf beyond the mid-1970s. The Working Party consoled itself with the thought that 'unity has managed over the last twenty years to elude the best efforts of the Arab world, and centralized control of Arab "oil power" seems unlikely to follow an orderly British departure from the Gulf'.

In spite of the Defence and Oversea Policy Committee's attempts to draw comfort from such predictions, the significance of its recommendation was inescapable. In the ongoing discussions which had been started by Sir Michael Wright and Sir Roger Stevens following the Suez war, the advantages and disadvantages of the retention of Britain's special position in the Gulf had been endlessly debated. Although British officials in the Gulf, especially Burrows and Luce, had extolled the virtues of a continued presence, other voices, not least from the cost-conscious Treasury, questioned the need for maintaining Britain's military commitments, preferring instead to rely on normal commercial processes for the preservation of Britain's economic stake in the region. What appears to have swung the argument in favour of those who backed relinquishment was the related decision to withdraw from Aden. Although initially the commitment to the Gulf was restated, the loss of military resources in Aden struck a severe blow to the long-term viability of Britain's presence in the Gulf. Not content with a determination to leave by the mid-1970s, some members of the Labour government pushed for an even earlier departure. Events not directly connected to the Gulf, in particular the Six Day War and the devaluation of the pound, served to facilitate this objective.

2 Defence reviews, devaluation, and Britain's departure from the Gulf

Despite being on the left of the Labour Party, Prime Minister Harold Wilson had the reputation of being a firm proponent of Britain's presence East of Suez. In 1965, he had even optimistically declared that Britain's frontiers were 'on the Himalayas'.[1] Referring to Wilson's dealings with Lyndon Johnson, Chris Wrigley suggests that he gave the US President 'commitments in line with the policies he intended pursuing anyway – resisting devaluation and maintaining a role East of Suez'.[2] By the end of 1967, however, domestic and international events had conspired against both objectives. The impact of the devaluation of sterling on the subsequent decision to withdraw from East of Suez, including Britain's Persian Gulf commitments, has produced differing interpretations. While Jeffrey Pickering places importance on shifts in the balance of power in the Labour Cabinet following devaluation in facilitating withdrawal, others, most notably Saki Dockrill and Matthew Jones, stress the incremental erosion of the commitment to a defence posture East of Suez stretching back over a number of years. Certainly senior figures within the Labour government were highly sceptical of Britain's role outside Europe.

For the impatient mind of the Lord President of the Council, Richard Crossman, a withdrawal from the Gulf in the mid-1970s envisaged by the Defence and Oversea Policy Committee was far too leisurely a timescale.[3] Referring to the fact that the Labour government was in the midst of its second major defence review in just three years, he argued that it was 'surely unwise to try to allay our allies' anxieties about our intentions by committing ourselves to revised plans that will shortly require yet another revision'. As regards the Gulf, Crossman favoured the cancelling of Britain's treaty obligations, justifying his comments with the remark that 'In the Arab world a British military presence is an embarrassment to our friends and provocation to our enemies and does not seem to strengthen our own hands in negotiations.' During Cabinet discussions on defence expenditure,[4] Crossman reiterated his case for early withdrawal from Britain's overseas commitments:

> it would not be credible either in this country or abroad to announce a plan to withdraw slowly from the Middle East and Far East over a

> period of eight to ten years, during which time our military strength would steadily and obviously diminish. Events would overtake us and we should be forced to withdraw more quickly; it would therefore be better to decide now on a plan for as rapid a withdrawal as possible.

Although there was sympathy for Crossman's position, early scaling down of Britain's commitments was rejected. Since Malaysia and Singapore were concerned at Britain's proposal for a final pull-out by 1975–6, and vehemently opposed to the announcement of a specific date, the Cabinet conceded that 'we could not now contemplate going back to our Allies with proposals for an earlier final withdrawal'. Since so many in Singapore were dependent on the British military infrastructure there for employment, it was felt that a precipitate withdrawal could trigger 'social and economic chaos' leading to the collapse of the government of Lee Kuan Yew. As regards the Middle East, there was general agreement that no date for withdrawal should be given since departure 'did not involve serious logistic problems for the forces, nor lengthy planning preparation such as were involved in the Far East'. In consequence, the Cabinet agreed that there was 'no requirement to take a decision on withdrawal until events made it in accord with our interests to do so'. If anything, the British were keen to reassure Gulf Rulers of their fealty, especially in view of the fighting retreat from Aden and the South Arabian Federation which began in the summer of 1967.

The Head of the Arabian Department, M. S. Weir, underlined the importance of not allowing the impression to develop that HMG may be reconsidering their Gulf policy in the light of events in South Arabia on the grounds that to do so would 'destroy confidence, promote instability, and make it harder for us to disengage'.[5] In talks with Dr Rashad Pharaon, Counsellor to King Feisal, W. P. Cranston of the British Embassy in Jedda told his Saudi host that it was 'our intention to remain firmly where we were in the Gulf for as long as required in order to ensure some stable system and to avoid a repetition of what happened in South Arabia'.[6] The Political Resident, Sir Stewart Crawford, pointed to the need for HMG to 'carry conviction in their assurances to the Rulers of their intention to stay in the Gulf for a long time yet, to back the Rulers and to go on helping them with developing their states'.[7] 'If we ourselves show that we have made up our minds to ensure stability in this area and we are not contemplating an early walk-out,' he concluded, 'then we have a good chance to succeed'. Just such an assurance was given to the Rulers during the visit to the Gulf of the Foreign Office Minister, Goronwy Roberts, in early November 1967. Indeed, among his objectives was a determination to convince the Rulers that the British presence would continue as long as it was necessary to maintain peace and stability in the area (see Chapter 3). Following a series of sterling crises which had scarred the Labour government's period in power, the currency was finally devalued on 18 November

1967. The significance of devaluation for the British decision to accelerate the timescale for withdraw from the Persian Gulf is a much debated issue.

Saki Dockrill attempts to downplay the significance of devaluation in the reformulation of Britain's world role. In justifying this stance, she focuses on the Defence Expenditure Studies Report of July 1967 which determined that Britain would depart from East of Suez by the mid-1970s.[8] Although the Persian Gulf was not specifically mentioned, there was an understanding among ministers that the withdrawal decision would include this region.[9] Dockrill stresses that 'the July decision was a definitive one',[10] and that consequently Britain had already 'crossed the rubicon' before devaluation.[11] Taking her interpretation still further, she contends that the July 1967 Report was 'the logical outcome of a series of reviews which Whitehall had conducted over a number of years'.[12] Within months of coming to office, Labour had placed a ceiling on defence expenditure of £2000m at 1964 prices until the end of the decade. 'Ministers and officials were *not unconscious* of the implications of defence cuts for the eventual decline of Britain's East of Suez role', argues Dockrill.[13] '[I]f we are to maintain any aspirations to a world role in the 1970s on a defence budget restricted to £2000m,' observed Defence Secretary Healey, 'we cannot at the same time maintain the full range of military capabilities which we might otherwise plan to have'.[14] As a result of such logic, major defence projects with East of Suez applications, not least the development of the Tactical Strike and Reconnaissance aircraft (TVR-2) and the construction of a new aircraft carrier (the CVA01), were scrapped. Referring to the Cabinet's resolution at the beginning of 1968 to accelerate withdrawal, Dockrill concludes: 'In terms of the nature and scope of Britain's withdrawal East of Suez, the January decision made little difference to that which had been taken in July.'[15]

Jeffrey Pickering, by contrast, places more emphasis on devaluation, focusing on its political, rather than economic, consequences. 'The nucleus of the Wilson Cabinet', he argues, 'consisted of men from the old Labour right who fervently supported the overseas military role.'[16] Labelling these men 'Bevinites' due to their adherence to principles established by the post-war Labour Foreign Secretary, Ernest Bevin, Pickering emphasizes their commitment to maintaining Britain's world role. Among this group were the Chancellor, James Callaghan, the Defence Secretary, Denis Healey, and successive Foreign Secretaries, Patrick Gordon Walker, Michael Stewart, and George Brown. Despite being seen as a standard bearer for the left of the Labour Party, the Prime Minister was also wedded to the notion of Britain's East of Suez role. Pickering contends that 'the political transformations set in motion by devaluation had a greater impact on the East of Suez role than economic concerns, either immediate or long-term'.[17] He justifies this interpretation with reference to internal changes within the Labour Cabinet which 'punctured the Bevinite consensus at the heart of the Cabinet'.[18] The most significant element in these developments was the resignation of Callaghan as Chancellor and his replacement by Roy Jenkins who was not merely fervently pro-European, but also a long-standing critic of Britain's East of Suez posture. 'The long-standing wall of senior ministerial support for Britain's east of Suez commitments now had a gaping hole in it,' observes Pickering, 'and soon it began to crumble.'[19] The first significant waverer was the Prime Minister himself who, politically wounded by the traumas of devaluation, 'was content to agree with his Chancellor that, at this stage in his government, only one policy calculation was truly important: what was good for the balance of payments was good for Labour and, by extension, Britain as a whole'.[20] Equally important was Healey's defection to the side of the reformers.[21] The American Embassy in London explained Healey's refusal to resign over defence cuts with the comment that 'he is relatively young, politically ambitious, and has no place else to go'.[22] Changes within the British decision-making establishment, argues Pickering, also contributed to the victory of those in favour of retrenchment. In 1964, the three service departments had been merged into a unified Ministry of Defence. This loss of autonomy by the services resulted in a dwindling of influence on the part of the Chiefs of Staff. As a result, 'one of the most visible barriers to retrenchment was eliminated' since from the mid-1960s 'the military could not stand in the way of a decision to abandon the world role'.[23]

Pickering's arguments have much explanatory power. Indeed, it is difficult to account for the Cabinet's decision to sanction a rapid run-down East of Suez without reference to the influence of Roy Jenkins and the sagging of Wilson's commitment to Britain's world role in the wake of the devaluation of sterling. Nevertheless, his ideas have by no means survived unscathed. Focusing on South-East Asia, Matthew Jones challenges the notion that the Wilson Cabinet contained a 'Bevinite' caucus wedded to preserving Britain's military establishments overseas. '[S]enior ministers, including the so-called Bevinite core of 1968,' he suggests, 'held a far more realistic grasp of Britain's position than some accounts have allowed for'.[24] According to Jones, leading figures, such as Brown and Healey, were openly sceptical about Britain's world role. In July 1966, for instance, Brown told a Cabinet colleague 'We've got to turn down their [America's] money and pull out the troops: all of them. I don't mean Germany. I want them out of East of Suez.'[25] A month earlier, Healey and Callaghan were reported as disagreeing with the Prime Minister's line on upholding the notion of world power and an East of Suez role, while Brown was characterized as 'unenthusiastic'.[26] Pickering's interpretation, therefore, fails to take account of shades of opinion within the 'Bevinite' core. Pickering is also guilty of exaggerating the significance of the decisions taken in the wake of devaluation which, as Dockrill has ably demonstrated, had been anticipated by previous reviews of Britain's defence and overseas commitments, not least the seminal Defence Expenditure Studies Report of July 1967. The fracturing of support for a continued role East of Suez, however, was due not so much to a weakening commitment, but to a determination to ensure that overseas responsibilities did not over-stretch Britain's military capabilities.

In a joint memorandum to the Cabinet, George Brown and the Secretary of State for Commonwealth Affairs, George Thomson, confessed that

> We accept . . . that the stage has been reached where there can be no further cuts in defence expenditure unless the overseas commitments on which much of it is based are themselves reduced. We agree with the Secretary for Defence that to attempt to cut defence expenditure further without reducing our overseas commitments would be to endanger the morale of the armed forces.[27]

Following discussions between Healey and US Embassy staff, Ambassador Bruce reported that 'By making common cause with Brown and Thomson and Callaghan . . . he had succeeded in getting firm Cabinet agreement that if more cuts were to be made they had to be preceded by and related to cuts in commitments'.[28] In his memoirs, Healey admitted that 'My problem was to extricate our forces from their commitments East of Suez with the least possible damage to Britain's influence in the world, and to the stability of the areas where they were present'.[29] Such concerns, underlined by strong representations from Singaporean premier Lee Kuan Yew, persuaded the Cabinet to push back Britain's military withdrawal from the original date of 31 March 1971 to the end of that year.[30] The Treasury, however, was mindful to ensure that this was indeed a terminal date with respect to British commitments towards the Gulf. This was especially so in the context of the Gulf Rulers' offer to contribute towards the costs of a continuing British military presence. '[T]he idea has the makings of a useful red herring to defer a decision on withdrawal from the Gulf', commented one official.[31] '[O]nce we got into discussion with the Rulers', remarked another, 'we would gradually get towards the slippery slope of maintaining our military commitments for some indefinite period'.[32] In a similar vein, yet another official dismissed the idea of 'turning British troops into Sheikhs mercenaries' on the grounds that it would promote an 'indefinite, escalating and unhappy presence in the Gulf'.[33] The Treasury even pressed for a withdrawal in advance of the 31 December 1971 deadline.[34] Demonstrating how far opinion had evolved, an official remarked that 'we do not accept that a military presence is necessary or desirable to protect British commercial interests and investments (the Japanese, Germans, Swedes, Swiss and many other countries manage very well without such burdens)'.[35] With the election of a Conservative government in Britain in June 1970, nevertheless, the possibility of extending the British presence beyond the end of 1971 was raised.

Towards the end of 1968, the former Governor of Aden, Sir Kennedy Trevaskis, toured the Gulf, ostensibly on business but in fact using his visit to gather information for the Conservatives. 'Heaven knows what report Trevaskis will turn in to the Conservative Party on his return to London', expostulated Bahrain's Political Agent, A. D. Parsons, 'but I think it will probably be anti-UAE, pro a pattern of mini-states and . . . encouraging as regards a reversal of the decision to withdraw if the Conservatives win the next general election.'[36] Whatever Trevaskis told his masters on his return, the Conservative leader, Edward Heath, soon began making the case for the retention of British forces in the Gulf. In an article for the *Sunday Times*, Heath, who had himself recently returned from a trip to the area, pledged: 'if when the time comes, our friends in the area want us to continue a presence in some form, then after my visit I am even more convinced than before that it would be in our interests to do so'.[37] While admitting that a number of Rulers would privately welcome a reversal of the withdrawal decision, the Foreign and Commonwealth Office pointed out that 'probably only the Rulers of Dubai and Sharjah (plus of course the Sultan) among those who count, and no radical elements, would be willing to have such views attributed to them publicly'.[38] The FCO view was that 'talk of a change of policy can take the Rulers' eyes off the ball and do damage'.[39] No doubt influenced by party political rivalry, the Minister of State, Goronwy Roberts, added: 'if we reversed our decision, even "partially", we would run very grave risks of sparking off revolutionary propaganda and activity, perhaps creating an Aden-type situation and certainly tempting the Shah and Feisal to "take action"'.[40] With Heath ensconced in Number 10 the debate about the merits and demerits of reversal was reignited.

During Heath's visit to the Gulf in 1969, British officials identified two principal objections to a major volte-face in the policy of withdrawal: the likely removal of the Rulers' incentive to pursue unity and the provocation of hostile forces both within and without the Gulf to drive out British forces and topple the existing regimes. A year on, the Deputy Political Resident, M. S. Weir,[41] admitted that the first objection had waned since the Union was 'still languishing'. The second, by contrast, had 'gained weight with the sharpening of tension between outside powers with an interest in the Southern Gulf, principally Iran, Iraq and Saudi Arabia, and their attempts to promote their rival interests through political pressure and subversion'. Weir also drew attention to the claims of subversive groups within the Shaikhdoms themselves that British withdrawal policy was a 'sham' and that imperialism would 'endeavour to maintain its stranglehold by some other means'. Any indication confirming this, he warned, risked provoking the intensification of propaganda, demonstrations, and even acts of terrorism directed against both the Rulers and the British presence.

The new Foreign Secretary, Alec Douglas-Home, quickly called for a period of consultation to assist in determining future British policy for the Gulf. He also defined the two main aims of British policy as 'the earliest possible settlement of issues in dispute through negotiation and the building up of stability in particular through settling on a practical basis the political future of the Trucial States, Qatar and Bahrain'.[42] The Political Resident, Sir Stewart Crawford, argued strongly that reversing the withdrawal decision would not contribute to these objectives, justifying his position with the comment that 'it would reduce such incentive as the Rulers have to make compromises and encourage them to relax'.[43] Looking at the issue more broadly, the British Ambassador in Kuwait, Sam Falle, cautioned that a prolongation of the British presence would 'provoke Arab nationalists to try and drive us out of the Gulf and give them the excuse for violent action that they at present lack'.[44] He even foresaw an 'Aden situation arising in Bahrain' if withdrawal were delayed. From a UN perspective, Britain's Deputy Permanent Representative, F. A. Warner, forecast that 'the communists, the Iranians, and those Afro-Asians committed to the eradication of foreign military bases, would use any prolongation as an additional stick with which to beat us'.[45] Britain's Ambassador in Tehran, Sir Denis Wright, confirmed that 'in the Shah's view there is no place for continued British military presence in the Gulf and that withdrawal should be completed as planned'.[46] Shaikh Sabah, the Kuwaiti Minister of Foreign Affairs, was equally sceptical about procrastination on the grounds that all the time the Rulers of the Lower Gulf thought a change of policy was likely, 'they would do nothing further towards Federation'.[47]

Counsellor at the British Embassy in Cairo, D. L. Stewart, alerted the FCO to the danger of assuming that, following talks with Heath in 1969, President Nasser would acquiesce in the maintenance of Britain's military presence in the Gulf. 'It seemed to me', recalled Stewart, 'a classic instance of the kind of semi-assurance which Nasser has so often given in private conversation to Western statesmen which proved to be entirely valueless when the time came to deliver.'[48] As regards opinion in Washington, the British Embassy there identified two distinct schools of thought, the first hoping for a delay in Britain's military pull-out, the second arguing that a continued presence beyond 1971 might 'exacerbate the situation, rather than contribute to the stability of the area'.[49] Only King Feisal and his advisers, who believed that Britain had left insufficient time to bequeath stability and feared 'another South Yemen on their door', were thought to favour a reversal of British policy.[50] Despite the Saudi position, the Arabian Department's Head, A. A. Acland, admitted that 'There seems little doubt that a change in British policy would lay HMG open to a good deal of criticism and to the accusation of trying to perpetuate the colonialist and paternalistic relationship in the Gulf'.[51] Certainly in discussions with Douglas-Home, the Shah made it clear that he would 'oppose a reversal of the present policy on the grounds, at any rate publicly, that this would represent the perpetuation of a colonialist arrangement'.[52] A few days later, the Kuwaiti Prime Minister, Shaikh Jabir, declared in the National Assembly that 'we, in Kuwait, neither welcome nor accept any foreign presence in our region, be it British or otherwise'.[53]

In discussions with Ambassador Falle, the Kuwaiti Foreign Secretary, Shaikh Sabah, reiterated Kuwait's opposition to the maintenance of the British presence, pointing out that it was 'not clear against whom residual British forces would be expected to defend the Gulf States'.[54] Taking a pragmatic line he also argued that the prolongation of the 'imperialist presence' would provide a pretext for those who wished to make trouble in the Gulf.[55] Even Shaikh Zaid of Abu Dhabi was reported to be against a reversal of the withdrawal decision on the grounds that it was 'the only incentive the Rulers had to federate'.[56] Similarly, Crawford, in his final despatch as Political Resident, remarked that 'A postponement of withdrawal would remove any pressure the Rulers now feel under to unite . . . and in this situation Bahrain can hardly be expected to wait much longer before seeking to go ahead on its own into full independence'.[57] With an eye to Britain's long-term reputation, Crawford concluded that 'The presence of British forces in the Gulf has always in the past been a steadying element and has never attracted local hostility. It would be preferable for them to leave while this is the case, rather than risk overstaying their welcome.'[58] The Foreign Secretary's newly-appointed personal representative in the Gulf, Sir William Luce, was of the same mind. '[A]t the time of the termination of the Exclusive Agreements', he argued, 'there is very unlikely to be any identifiable threat of external aggression (including support by a contiguous territory of internal revolt) against which it could be in HMG's interest to undertake a defence commitment to the Union'.[59] The corollary of this was that 'there would be no valid military reasons for retaining any British forces permanently stationed in the Gulf or its near vicinity'.[60] In the report of his recommendations submitted towards the end of 1970, Luce was even more definite on this point.

Luce had already reached the conclusion from his consultations that all the large countries surrounding the Gulf, as well as the UAR, were of the opinion that the withdrawal of British forces should take place as planned and that failure to do so would create 'dangers for the stability of the area'.[61] Noting in his report[62] that the real threat to stability in the Gulf came from 'subversion and revolution by Arab nationalist and left-wing elements', he indicated that 'the presence of a British battalion will not deter the threat, indeed it could encourage it'. Consequently, he concluded that any new agreement reached with the Gulf States should include no specific defence commitment and the withdrawal of British units stationed in the Gulf be completed by the end of 1971 as planned. Luce also recommended that the existing exclusive agreements with the Gulf States be terminated by the same date, justifying this stance with the observation that the British announcement in January 1968 had 'generated a firm expectation, and indeed a determination in and around the Gulf, that the nine States will become fully responsible for the conduct of all their affairs in the course of 1971'. Even in the event of a viable union failing to materialize, Luce still argued against extending British protection and responsibility for the external affairs of the Trucial States. On the one hand, he insisted that it would be a 'fallacy to think that the prolongation would provide further opportunity to bring about a viable Union'. On the other, he calculated that 'HMG would be entering into a hazardous commitment with no positive advantages to be gained.' Coming from a man who during his tenure as Political Resident had been such a passionate advocate of the British presence in the Gulf, Luce's views carried considerable weight.

Summing up the Cabinet Defence and Oversea Policy Committee's discussion of Luce's recommendations, the Prime Minister observed that, while pressure should continue to be brought to bear on the Rulers to unite, 'We should make it clear to them that we could not remain in the Gulf on the present footing'.[63] At a subsequent meeting of the same Committee, it was agreed that an early statement to the House of Commons should be made to this effect.[64] When discussed by the full Cabinet, ministers consoled themselves with the thought that 'By offering training facilities, and other support to the local forces we were making it clear that we did not intend to abandon our friends'.[65] During the Commons debate on the Persian Gulf on 1 March 1970, Douglas-Home informed MPs that HMG were prepared to offer a Treaty of Friendship to the Gulf States, to hand over the Trucial Oman Scouts to form the nucleus of a Union army, to provide training teams for the Union security forces, to participate in training exercises involving the British army and air force units, and finally, to pledge regular visits to the area by Royal Navy ships.[66] Summing up, the Foreign Secretary maintained that 'arrangements of this kind will form a sound basis for a continuing and effective British contribution to the stability of the area, and a new and up to date relationship between Britain and the States concerned'.[67] Although Denis Healey mocked the government for its apparent volte-face on the permanent stationing of British forces in the Gulf, Douglas-Home retorted by pointing out that on the Gulf the previous Labour government had 'vacillated, then acted precipitately, with no thought to the future'.[68] The announcement of Britain's military withdrawal from the Gulf had been prefigured by the Kuwaiti decision to terminate its defence agreement with Britain.

At the beginning of 1961, Shaikh Abdullah indicated his belief that the provisions of the 1899 Anglo-Kuwaiti agreement were outmoded and his wish for its replacement with a new understanding more in line with Kuwait's evolving status. Reviewing the whole issue, a Treasury official questioned the rationale behind a commitment to continue to protect the Shaikhdom from external attack.[69] '[E]ven if the worst came to the worst and a hostile Iraqi regime were to entrench itself in Kuwait,' he contended, 'the consequences might not necessarily be so tragic as is generally thought', justifying his analysis with the observation that the oil industry had 'astonishing powers of recuperation and improvisation, and reacts very quickly and effectively to any emergency'. Provided that Iranian oil was still available and accessible to Britain, he concluded, 'it is possible that the consequences both on the supply side and the balance of payments side might not be catastrophic'. Assessing the merits and demerits of the Kuwait commitment, another Treasury mandarin pointed out that any indication of a reluctance to support the Shaikhdom would 'shock the Ruler'.[70] In his opinion, this risked oil interests at a time when Britain was having to 'nurse Kuwait in continued good practices as a large holder of sterling in her new state of independence, and when, with the establishment of the Organization of Petroleum Exporting Countries to advance their financial interests, it is important to maintain the good will which the British oil companies enjoy in Kuwait'. On the other hand, he described the defence commitment to Kuwait as 'expensive and uncomfortable': expensive because of the cost of troops on the ground and the backing which they required; uncomfortable because of doubts over Britain's security of tenure over the Aden and Kenya bases which were necessary to support the commitment. However, in the discussions on the reformulation of Anglo-Kuwaiti relations following Shaikh Abdullah's request for the revision of the 1899 Agreement, ministers affirmed their determination to continue defending Kuwait.

'Access to Kuwait's oil resources on the best financial terms possible', stressed the Lord Privy Seal, Edward Heath, 'remain vital interests for the United Kingdom and these would be endangered should Kuwait lose her independence. It therefore remains in the interest of Her Majesty's Government to continue to afford assistance to Kuwait in maintaining its independence.'[71] Echoing these sentiments, Foreign Secretary Home observed that:

> Access to the oil of Kuwait on present terms strengthens the position of British oil companies and of the British economy in their relations with other oil-producing countries and prevents the latter from holding Britain and indeed the rest of Western Europe to ransom.[72]

Prime Minister Macmillan was convinced that 'Any new agreement must recognize our right to intervene if Kuwait's independence were threatened and this would . . . equally involve recognizing our obligation to do so'.[73] The FO, however, was sceptical about this line of reasoning, one official remarking: 'I very much doubt whether the Ruler would be prepared to sign any agreement which gave us the right to intervene in Kuwait otherwise than with the agreement of the Government of Kuwait.'[74] This analysis was born out by events, the Ruler making clear that he would not accept the right of uninvited intervention.[75] In view of Iraqi dictator Abdul Karim Qassem's declaration of 25 June 1961 that Kuwait was an 'integral part' of Iraq, Shaikh Abdullah invoked paragraph d) of the letter terminating the 1899 agreement (see Chapter 1). Recalling the Kuwaiti Ruler's reaction to news of the impending arrival of British troops, Luce mused:

'I have seldom seen a man more relieved or grateful than was the Amir'.[76] Even before the departure of the last British troops on 10 October to be replaced by an Arab League force, policy-makers began analysing the efficacy of the defence guarantee to Kuwait.

Towards the end of September 1961, a Foreign Office and Ministry of Defence paper[77] concluded that 'Our economic stake in Kuwait itself, and the central position of Kuwait to our oil operations in this whole area, are such that we should take all reasonable measures that we can to protect Kuwait.' Kuwaiti independence was especially valued since it was seen as blocking 'a consolidation of control of Middle East oil by one or more of the remaining major Middle East producers', thus ensuring that oil would continue to flow from the Middle East 'in adequate quantities and on reasonable terms'. Kuwait's membership of the sterling area and willingness not merely to accept payment for oil in sterling, but also to hold substantial reserves in sterling, were also highlighted. Looking at the impact of Britain's approach to Kuwait, the FO and MoD hypothesized that 'if we fail to ensure the security of Kuwait, we might expect a crumbling of our position in the remainder of the Gulf'. This was particularly troubling in view of oil discoveries in Abu Dhabi and the possibility of oil strikes in Oman. Anticipating the loss of military facilities in Kenya as that country progressed towards full independence, the paper called for a redeployment of forces to the Gulf. Justifying the costs involved in this re-organization, the FO and MoD argued that 'compared with the size of the economic benefits which we derive from the maintenance of the independence of Kuwait under the present regime, the expenditure is well worth while'. Recognizing that no Arab ruler wished to be beholden to foreign, especially non-Arab, armed forces, the two departments posited that 'the Amir and the ruling family, though anxious to have a British force in readiness to intervene again, will be reluctant to invite our armed forces to return to Kuwait once they have left'. As regards the political options open to the Amir to reduce the threats to his regime, the FO and MoD recommended a policy of increasing Kuwait's regional standing through a programme of investment in Arab countries 'even if it should mean that there was a risk that Kuwaiti investments in London would in time be somewhat run down'.

Towards the end of 1961, Luce threw his ideas into the debate about the future of Anglo-Kuwaiti relations. Not surprisingly, he was a strong advocate of the military guarantee to Kuwait:

> I am . . . forced to the conclusion that so long as Qasim controls Iraq, Kuwait must rely on external military aid to secure her independence, that only Her Majesty's Government can effectively provide that aid and that the present Amir will expect them to do so. Equally, so long as Kuwait oil retains its present importance to us, it is in our interests to continue to bear this responsibility.[78]

The British Ambassador in Kuwait, J. C. B. Richmond, however, challenged the basis of Luce's reasoning.[79] On the one hand, he pointed out that the maintenance of existing policy towards Kuwait would become 'more difficult and more expensive as Kenya reaches independence'. On the other, he argued that preserving Kuwaiti oil on favourable terms would become 'less important as these terms are progressively eroded by the greater effectiveness of OPEC and the pressure of the producing countries on their oil companies'. In conclusion, he urged that Britain should be looking for ways to extricate itself from the military obligations to the Ruler of Kuwait.

The Treasury also cast doubt on the viability of the defence commitment. One official questioned whether British forces could successfully stop Qassem and preserve the status quo if he were determined to take Kuwait 'whatever the cost'.[80] 'It is inconceivable', he continued, 'that we could move our forces in and out of Kuwait every time Qasim might move his troops towards the border, only to withdraw them'. While recognizing the potential costs of replacing oil from Kuwait, another official recorded that 'we have to face the fact that, even if Kuwait maintains an independent existence, she will follow the example of all the oil producing countries in trying to extract better terms for herself and thereby limit our present oil profits'.[81] From this reasoning he deduced that 'in 10 years' time we are likely to lose less from an Iraqi take-over than we do now since our assets will not be giving us so high a return'. In a similar vein, yet another Treasury mandarin remarked that 'the peaceful combination of the producing countries in OPEC is already extracting a larger share of the profits from the oil companies, and may continue the process, in which military force is entirely irrelevant'.[82] Scepticism even infected the Foreign Office.

The overthrow of Qassem in February 1963, coupled with growing doubts about whether Kuwait would ever call on British assistance again,[83] prompted an FO official to conclude that 'we are paying a premium of 100 per cent for indifferent cover against an improbable risk'.[84] Even more galling was Kuwait's continued reliance on British military protection, while at the same time sheltering radical groups who threatened to undermine the British structures in the Gulf on which the Kuwaitis depended. Referring to this paradox, the British Ambassador in Kuwait, G. N. Jackson, bemoaned the ruling family's tendency to 'pay protection money to the housebreakers while publicly criticizing the police'.[85] Following the disturbances in Bahrain in March 1965, for instance, the Kuwait National Assembly had condemned the 'ferocious acts' committed by 'imperialist British forces'.[86] In conversation with the Kuwaiti Crown Prince, Shaikh Sabah al-Salim, Jackson 'labelled as duplicity the extremist public statements later followed by contrary private assurances'.[87] Despite his evident frustration, Jackson did not support a fundamental revision of relations with Kuwait: 'Any other regime that we should be likely to get could be much worse, and, quite apart from considerations of oil, could cause wide political repercussions all over the Persian Gulf and beyond.'[88] The Cabinet Official Committee on Defence and Oversea Policy also supported the maintenance of existing Anglo-Kuwaiti relations. Examining the issue from an economic point of view, the Committee emphasized that

> Kuwait has special importance because of its immense oil resources in which B.P. has a fifty per cent share, and because of its position as an independent producing country. So long as these retain their value, as they seem certain to do into the seventies, the basis for Her Majesty's Government's support of Kuwait will remain.[89]

Taking a slightly different line, Foreign Secretary Stewart argued against a denunciation of the 1961 defence guarantee on the grounds that 'To do so would not only risk Kuwait's future but would certainly undermine our position in the rest of the Gulf and the confidence of Iran'.[90]

D. J. McCarthy (Political Advisor, Middle East Command), however, continued to question the viability of the Kuwait commitment.[91] On the one hand, he reported the British Ambassador in Kuwait's view that 'any Kuwaiti Government would rather let a coup succeed than depend for its suppression on the actual use of British force in the streets'. On the other, he doubted the effectiveness of British intervention in answer to a coup backed by Iraq: 'The difficulty here . . . is that by the time it had become clear that outside fomenting was involved and that the Iraqis were moving, we should probably be left with too little response time'. Clearly disillusioned with the Kuwaitis, whom he described as keeping Britain 'on the military hook without accepting any serious inconvenience to help us', McCarthy suggested that the Kuwait commitment be revisited. Even Political Resident Luce began producing powerful arguments against maintaining the Kuwait commitment.[92]

For Luce, the prospective loss of British facilities in Aden undermined the political viability of the guarantee to Kuwait. Recalling growing Kuwaiti sensitivity towards the British defence connection, Luce predicted that a relocation of military forces from Aden to the Gulf would cause leading Kuwaitis 'acute embarrassment and . . . lead to their public denial that they needed the presence of these British forces and very probably to an irresistible demand for the abrogation of the 1961 Agreement'. Developing his theme, the Political Resident indicated that once Britain had left Aden, the Gulf would become the final target for Nasser in his plan to expunge the last remnants of the British presence in the Middle East. 'If he saw us moving substantial forces out of Aden and into the Gulf', maintained Luce, 'he would regard this as a last-ditch challenge, and he would react with redoubled vigour, particularly in the mobilization of subversive and terrorists elements.' In such a situation, insisted Luce, 'we should be sealing the fate of the Shaikhly regimes in the Gulf and destroying whatever hope there is of peaceful evolution in this area'. '[I]t would be in our interest', he concluded, 'to get off the hook of the Kuwait commitment before, or simultaneously with, the loss of our military facilities in Aden'. Adding his voice to the debate, Ambassador Jackson pointed out that the most likely threat to Kuwait, an internal coup, was one which the British would find difficult to combat, not least because the Kuwaitis would not wish them to perform such a task.[93] '[I]n maintaining internal security in Kuwait', expatiated Jackson, 'we should inevitably be cast in the role of propping up an unpopular regime, which could hardly further either our case or theirs'.

The death of Shaikh Abdullah on 24 November 1965, and the shifts in the balance of power within the al-Sabah ruling family which resulted, put a further question mark over the defence guarantee. Although Shaikh Sabah, Abdullah's brother and a firm proponent of the British connection, ascended the throne, the change of ruler had the effect of strengthening the hand of Shaikh Jabir al-Ahmad, who became Prime Minister. Jabir came from a rival branch of the al-Sabah family which tended to place more emphasis on relations with the Arab world, and correspondingly less on those with Britain.[94] An opportunity to reassess the defence commitment to Kuwait arose in the wake of the publication of the Defence White Paper of February 1966.

Referring to the White Paper, Karl Hack observes that a 'psychological barrier, a pain threshold in decline, had been breached'.[95] Under these conditions, military assistance to Kuwait soon came under scrutiny. Although the defence commitment itself was retained, the terms under which it would operate were decisively altered. Henceforth, military assistance to Kuwait was to be restricted to air cover, with ground troops being made available only if the Amir provided sufficient notice to enable them to be brought in from Britain or the Far East.[96] Even this reduced obligation was queried by the Defence Secretary, Denis Healey: if Britain continued to offer help in the form of ground forces, he argued, it could find itself 'landed with a commitment almost as onerous as the present one – in financial as well as military terms'.[97] In consequence, Healey favoured the restriction of British assistance to air support alone. The FO, however, resisted this pressure.

The Head of the Arabian Department, T. F. Brenchley, pointed out that the Amir would only call on British forces 'in the last extremity' due to concern over the likely reaction of Arab nationalist regimes.[98] Equally, the improbability of Shaikh Sabah being able to provide Britain with sufficient notice of an impending coup to allow the introduction of British troops was a 'strong argument' against putting Britain's 'extremely valuable relationship with Kuwait at risk in order to avoid such a contingency'.[99] Foreign Secretary Brown was also decidedly uneasy about limiting British assistance still further. 'If we speak to the Amir as you suggest', he told Healey, 'we are likely to give him the impression that HMG are taking a unilateral step away from their former close relationship with Kuwait.'[100]

Healey accepted Brown's arguments about 'treating the Ruler gently'.[101] In consequence, Shaikh Sabah was simply informed that, as from 1 January 1967, Britain would not be able to make special provision for ground forces to assist Kuwait. Since it would take some time to assemble such forces from elsewhere, he was also told that Britain would need considerable warning.[102] The FO admitted to Ambassador Jackson that more time than the two to three weeks originally envisaged would be necessary to assemble ground forces from outside the Gulf if intervention were contemplated. Nevertheless, the FO impressed upon him the importance of not spelling this out to the Amir for fear that he would take this as a sign that Britain's military position in the Gulf was weakening.[103] With the knowledge not only that he could call on the Arab League and the United Nations to defend Kuwait, but also that Kuwait was widely recognized and respected, he declared himself satisfied with the revised defence plans.[104]

The defence commitment continued to cause problems, however. A comment by the Chancellor of the Duchy of Lancaster (George Thomson) that a slight increase in British force levels in the Gulf was designed to carry out Britain's commitment to Kuwait and the other Gulf States[105] alarmed the Kuwaiti Minister of Defence, Shaikh Sa'ad.[106] As he explained to the British Ambassador, 'it was [a] difficult thing for any Arab Government to acknowledge dependence on western forces', adding 'the less said about the link between our forces in Bahrain and Sharjah and the commitment to Kuwait, the better'. Ambassador Jackson described this attitude on the part of Sa'ad, who was seen as one of Britain's best friends in Kuwait, as 'disheartening, but not surprising'. The reluctance of the Kuwait government to take a stouter public line over the British commitment presented Britain with a dilemma. 'On the one hand', observed Jackson,

> Kuwait wishes the part that British forces in the Gulf play to be concealed. On the other . . . in Bahrain and in the other states of the Lower Gulf it is a positive help in gaining acceptance of the presence of our forces that they should be thought to be there for Kuwait's benefit.

By describing the role of Britain's forces in the Gulf as the fulfilment of its obligations to the states in the area without specifying Kuwait separately, Jackson hoped to reconcile these contradictory presentational needs.

The practical problems of maintaining the Kuwait commitment were equally acute.[107] Imminent military withdrawal from Aden would leave only two squadrons of ageing Hunter aircraft available for defending Kuwait. To make matters worse, not only would the Hunters be operating at maximum range, but also they would be heavily out-numbered by the Iraqis who would be using airfields much closer to the battlefield. The MoD proposed to replace the Hunters with two squadrons, one consisting of eight Phantoms, the other of eight or nine Harriers. Four Phantoms would be needed for air defence of the base at Bahrain, leaving the remaining over-stretched force to cover the roles of fighter reconnaissance, the air defence of Kuwait, ground attack against Iraqi tanks and vehicles, the protection of Kuwaiti troops, and the interception of Iraqi aircraft in the battle area. The Harriers presented their own particular difficulties: since their functions were limited to ground attack only, they would have to be purchased specifically for the Kuwait operation. The problems of maintaining the guarantee to Kuwait were considered by the Cabinet Official Committee for Defence and Oversea Policy.[108]

The Committee identified oil and sterling balances as Britain's twin interests in Kuwait. As regards the former, it was estimated that Britain's stake in the oil industry benefited its balance of payments to the tune of £40–£50m a year. The Committee was also keen to stress that there was a wider British, and Western, interest in guaranteeing that Kuwait remained an independent source of oil: 'Diversity of independent sources of oil ensures a greater security of supply'. As regards sterling balances, it was pointed out that there was a strong British interest in averting 'any major change in the present state of the Kuwaiti sterling balances', not least because Kuwait was the largest external holder of sterling. A change of regime in Kuwait leading to domination by, or absorption in, another Arab power, it was feared, would have serious consequences. On the one hand, if Kuwait's balances were at the disposal of a more populous, poorer country, the likelihood was that they would be run-down over a number of years. On the other, 'the new authorities might seek to diversify the balances or part of them into another currency'.[109]

If Britain had an economic interest in maintaining Kuwait's independence, it had a political one as well. 'If she were absorbed by Iraq, or if her present regime were replaced by one more subject to Iraqi or UAR influence, our own position in the Southern Gulf . . . would be seriously weakened', the Committee concluded. More generally, drastic change in Kuwait would upset the stability of the Gulf region as a whole. Not merely would Iran and Saudi Arabia find their position *vis-à-vis* the revolutionary Arab states much weakened, but also the two monarchies 'would be tempted to make counter moves to redress what they considered the balance of power in the Gulf'. Since the Shah set much store by continuing Kuwaiti independence, it was feared that he would treat any change in the Amirate's status as 'of the kind described as a Western betrayal'. While recognizing that one section of the al-Sabah, led by Prime Minister and Heir-Apparent Jabir al-Ahmad, found the build-up of British forces in the Gulf 'embarrassing', the ruling family as a whole was described as 'united in favour of our commitment'. Equally, the Committee did not consider that pressure from the Arab world would be sufficiently strong to persuade Kuwait to renounce dependence on British assistance against its own better judgement. The foregoing convinced the Committee that there was 'no reason why either Her Majesty's Government or the Kuwait government should wish to change the Anglo-Kuwaiti agreement, in the period up to 1970–71'. This recommendation was soon to come under pressure as a result of Kuwait's response to Arab defeat in the Six Day War.

The devastating speed and decisiveness with which Israel secured victory stimulated Arab claims that it had received outside assistance. Kuwait immediately came under pressure to impose an oil embargo on Britain and the United States. Shaikh Sabah al-Ahmad confirmed the stoppage of oil during an interview with the British Ambassador, G. G. Arthur, on 6 June.[110] The Kuwaiti Foreign Minister, however, confidently predicted that it would be temporary, adding that 'Kuwait relied on Her Majesty's Government for protection and wanted to retain her friendship with Great Britain.' He also assured Arthur that his government would take 'all measures necessary to protect British lives and property'. Arthur described the encounter as the 'turning point in the crisis of Anglo-Kuwaiti relations', since by this date it had become clear not merely that the Arabs were beaten, but also that 'Kuwait's survival in an uncertain future might well come to depend once again on the support of her oldest friend'.[111] Shaikh Jabir al-Ali, Kuwait Minister of Guidance and Information, confidently predicted that the oil embargo would not be effective since the other Arabs, especially the Egyptians, wanted economic assistance which Kuwait could only provide if it exported the maximum amount of oil.[112] Although the Minister's prediction proved accurate, the Arab powers agreeing to lift the oil embargo at the Khartoum Conference in August, Kuwait's susceptibility to Arab pressure raised doubts in Britain about the long-term viability of the defence agreement. Drawing conclusions from the events of mid-1967, Political Resident Stewart observed:

> the way in which the embargo on oil exports to Britain and America has been imposed on unwilling Rulers by the consensus of the main Arab oil-producing countries and by members of their labour forces, teaches us that in the future we must expect the political aspects of oil policy in these States, other than the Sultanate [of Oman], to tend to follow fairly closely those of the other main Arab producing countries.[113]

The Six Day War and its immediate aftermath precipitated a mini-defence review in which the efficacy of maintaining the defence agreement with Kuwait was once more debated. Foreign Secretary Brown and Defence Secretary Healey were of the opinion that the Middle East crisis presented an opportunity for Britain to extricate itself from the 1961 exchange of letters.[114] FCO officials marshalled counter-arguments. Putting the additional defence costs attributable solely to the Kuwait commitment at a mere £650,000, the head of the Arabian Department, M. S. Weir, concluded that 'it would not be worth risking our very substantial interests in Kuwait in order to save this modest insurance premium'.[115] Assistant Under-Secretary of State, T. F. Brenchley, added that the exchange of letters 'had a restraining influence on the Kuwait Government'.[116] George Brown, however, remained unconvinced and asked for further consideration to be given to the question. Weir recapitulated the arguments presented by the Defence and Oversea Policy Committee, focusing in particular on the British interest in preserving Kuwait's independence.[117] Brenchley was in full agreement, stressing what a good return Britain received for 'a very small investment of defence support'.[118] Brown was still sceptical and asked specifically what Britain was gaining from the Kuwait commitment. 'The short answer', responded Brenchley, 'is confidence – on the part of the Shah, King Faisal and especially the Rulers of the protected shaikhdoms – and thus co-operation in our policies'.[119] In the absence of confidence, he predicted, orderly disengagement from the Gulf region in the future would be compromised. As regards the necessity of a continuing British role in Kuwait's defence, Brenchley presciently remarked that 'Iraq would one day attempt to assert her claim to Kuwait by force'.[120] The Permanent Under-Secretary added his voice to the debate arguing that Britain's military presence in the Gulf had helped it to weather the recent crisis in the Middle East.[121] '[A]t the present difficult moment', he summed up, 'we enjoy some, possibly temporary, advantage from a military commitment we have tended to regard as purely a liability'.

Support for the maintenance of the Defence Agreement also came from British officials in the Gulf. In the heightened atmosphere following the Six Day War, suspicion of Iraqi intentions increased. In these circumstances, Arthur reported that 'the Kuwait Government, as well as many private Kuwaitis of the older generation, set great store by what they regard as our commitment to defend them'.[122] [I]f we wish to exploit current Kuwaiti fears of Iraq and their attachment to a defence link with us,' he continued, 'we must clearly not whittle down the defence agreement any further'. Crawford warned that 'the ending of the commitment by us at a time when the Kuwaitis wish to retain it, could hardly fail to be followed by action by them against our material interests'.[123] He also urged that 'the ending of the Kuwait commitment, when it happens, should not result from a United Kingdom initiative which led to Kuwaiti recriminations'.

Under the weight of official opinion, Brown accepted that there was more to gain than lose by retaining Britain's pledge to assist in Kuwait's defence. Nonetheless, he was reported to be 'not happy about the present situation in which the Kuwaitis feel free to discriminate against British interests while we remain committed to their defence'.[124] He also declared himself willing to 'look at the question again if it appeared that the Kuwait Government were contemplating substantial further moves to damage British interests for political reasons'. Although the MoD agreed that the balance of advantage remained with retaining the defence guarantee, it also expressed dissatisfaction at the way in which the Kuwaitis were able to damage British interests with impunity.[125] An opportunity to bring what was becoming for Britain an increasingly inconvenient arrangement to an end was provided by the decision taken in early 1968 to withdraw from the region altogether.

The FCO favoured a formal amendment to the 1961 exchange of letters in which paragraph d) would not be interpreted as implying an obligation to provide military assistance.[126] Ambassador Arthur perceptively predicted that 'As "good Arabs" some Kuwaitis might prefer to terminate their formal connection with us when it no longer offers them the advantage of military protection'.[127] To circumvent this problem, Arthur suggested that the existing agreement should simply be re-interpreted in such a way as to exclude the defence commitment. Although the Amir was attracted by this idea, he was eventually persuaded by the Prime Minister, Shaikh Jabir al-Ahmad, to terminate the 1961 agreement. Explaining Kuwait motives, Arthur noted: '[The] Kuwait Government clearly want to extract maximum "Arab" propaganda advantage out of what they regard as a disagreeable necessity'.[128] On 13 May 1968, Shaikh Jabir informed Arthur that 'since Kuwait has achieved success in her international relationships, the obligations arising from the Agreement of the nineteenth June, 1961, were no longer appropriate'.[129] Although the Kuwait government attempted to salvage as much face as possible from the termination, Arthur reported that 'no native Kuwaiti . . . , young or old, conservative or nationalist, seriously wished to be rid of the 1961 Agreement; and everybody will know that it was we who in fact, if not in form, gave the notice of its termination'.[130] Explaining the attraction which the 1961 agreement had held, Arthur recorded that 'it sat lightly on the Kuwaitis, who enjoyed protection without foreign troops or any visible sign of the "Imperialist" presence'.[131] Although the Ruler of Kuwait, Shaikh Sabah, had been 'dismayed' by the British decision to withdraw and remained 'all for its reversal', the rest of the Kuwait government was reported to be 'reconciled to the new circumstances'.[132] In response to a question from British Embassy staff about whether he would be prepared publicly to say that the Amirate wanted British forces to stay in the Gulf, the Minister of Defence simply laughed and said 'never'.[133]

Arthur's successor, Sam Falle, described Anglo-Kuwaiti relations in the aftermath of the termination of Britain's special position as being on a 'modern, realistic and business-like basis'.[134] He went on to state that he perceived 'neither bitterness nor sentimentality about the past'. Although Arthur had predicted that the end of the 1961 agreement would mean 'a decline, which may be quite swift and sharp, in our influence and ability to protect our interests in Kuwait', Falle was able to report these fears had not been realized. Kuwait self-interest played an important part in this. Referring to oil, Falle remarked: 'there is no reason to suppose that a new government here would adopt policies which would cut off its only major source of revenue'.[135] Nevertheless, change of a 'revolutionary, socialist character', prophesied Falle, would lead to a running down of

Kuwait's sterling balances.[136] The Libyan revolution of 1 September 1969, which witnessed the overthrow of King Idris, gave added relevance to Falle's warning.

A. C. Goodison (Counsellor, British Embassy, Kuwait), nevertheless, was quick to point out the differences between Libya and Kuwait:

> Libya is a huge empty country and the King was isolated at the top. Kuwait is a compact little state with a Royal family so numerous that they and their protégés can occupy all the nodal points of power including those in the army: indeed the Sabah form almost a political party on their own. They marry widely among the leading merchant families and are part of the social fabric, not a superimposed clique. Idriss was old and distant and the first Arab to unite the country; the Sabah have been here for 200 years and many of them are young and accessible. Egypt, Algeria, and the Soviet Fleet were more uncomfortable neighbours for Libya than Iraq, Saudi Arabia, and Iran are at present for Kuwait. It was generally thought that a Republic would follow the death of King Idriss; none is talked of here. Libya has foreign bases: Kuwait is rather more successful at preserving a non-aligned, anti-Israeli posture which does not make Arab enthusiasts ashamed.[137]

Goodison also pointed out that since the Kuwaiti armed forces were among the most highly paid in the world, they were unlikely to suffer from material grievances. Falle himself conceded that the al-Sabah maintained their grip on power by filling the main offices of state and by rigidly controlling the intelligence and security apparatus.[138] The latter tactic ensured that noone was able to oppose their will without the ruling family's knowledge. The termination of Britain's defence commitment to Kuwait, coupled with the setting of Anglo-Kuwaiti relations on a post-imperial path, left unresolved the thorny issue of the future status of the British protected states in the Lower Gulf. Britain's attempts in conjunction with other regional powers, not least Kuwait itself, to foster co-operation and unity between the nine states will be addressed in the following two chapters.

3 The failure of the federal idea in the Gulf, 1950–68

From the second half of the nineteenth century, amalgamating contiguous territories had become a standard feature of British imperial policy whether in Canada, Australia, or South Africa. While these experiments were largely successful, neutralizing radical nationalism (at least for a time) while facilitating the maintenance of close ties with Britain, similar attempts at nation-building in the non-European parts of the empire were markedly less so. Failed federations in Central Africa, the West Indies, South-East Asia (Malaysia), and South Arabia after 1945, to say nothing of the moribund Indian federation of the 1930s, not surprisingly made Britain chary about adopting a policy of closer association for the states of the Lower Gulf. As the British Ambassador in Abu Dhabi recorded: 'federations have not proved to be durable and the British have earned themselves a dismal reputation recently as their architects'.[1] The divisions and rivalries which so characterized the Lower Gulf, and had even resulted in a brief war between Abu Dhabi and Dubai in 1948, appeared to make the British protected states particularly poor candidates for federation. Individually, however, they were so weak few could conceive of them surviving in a state of separateness. In 1949, rumours that Britain intended to sponsor a federation of Persian Gulf Shaikhdoms reached the ears of the Iranian government.[2]

Despite disabusing the Iranians, reports of a prospective federation resurfaced the following year. Shaikh Abdullah Salim of Kuwait quizzed his Political Agent, H. G. Jakins, about a Damascus broadcast on this subject,[3] while the *Iraqi Times* ran a story that Oman, Kuwait, Bahrain, along with the 'neighbouring tribal regions of the Persian Gulf area', would be welded into a single Arab state.[4] While expressing the view that the closest relations between the various Shaikhdoms was 'most desirable', he recorded that there were no immediate plans to unite them all under a single government. Moreover, the Political Resident, Sir Rupert Hay, was able to confirm that 'While we might try to work towards a federation of the Trucial Coast Shaikhdoms . . . I do not think a federation of all the Gulf Shaikhdoms will be practicable for a very long time to come'.[5] Hay expanded on these themes in correspondence with the Secretary of State for Foreign Affairs.[6]

Local jealousies, coupled with geographical factors, he felt, militated against the achievement of a genuine federation of all the Gulf Shaikhdoms. Although he did favour the creation of a Gulf council which would co-ordinate such matters as education, health, and postal services, Hay was sceptical about the prospects of any kind of political union under a central authority. As regards the general approach which Britain should adopt towards the Shaikhdoms, Hay advocated the preservation, and even enhancement of their internal autonomy, while at the same time maintaining control of foreign relations and the right of intervention to 'prevent gross maladministration or preserve law and order in a serious emergency'.

The Foreign Office concurred with Hay's analysis. There was recognition of the functional advantages of co-operation between the Shaikhdoms, but an equal awareness of the practical problems in sponsoring closer political ties: in particular, scepticism was felt over the chances of joining Kuwait, Bahrain, and Qatar with their less developed counterparts along the Trucial Coast.[7] In his reply to Hay, the Secretary of State agreed with the Political Resident's conclusions, going so far as to express doubt about whether a form of political federation should even be adopted as an objective of policy unless there were a 'spontaneous desire' for it among the Rulers themselves.[8] The Secretary of State was more positive about a federation of Trucial States which he believed would 'ultimately provide the best hope of political and economic viability'. Earlier, C. M. Rose of the Foreign Office's Eastern Department had predicted that in the event of a future British withdrawal of protection from the Gulf States, 'the only way in which they would be able to preserve their independence would be by adopting 'some form of federal organization'.[9] When the Quai d'Orsay made enquiries about rumours of a federation of Gulf States, Rose felt able to respond that, although they were without foundation, Britain did see considerable advantage in encouraging the States to consult together in matters of common interest.[10] With such aims in mind, the British backed the formation of the Trucial States Council in 1952 consisting of all seven Trucial States: Abu Dhabi, Dubai, Ajman, Umm al Qaiwain, Ras al Khaimah, Fujairah, and Sharjah. The Council, which (in theory) met twice a year, gave the Rulers a voice in British-sponsored development schemes and, despite the lack of 'an organizational working routine', did establish a framework for co-operation and consultation.[11]

Hay remained sceptical about the chances of fostering unity. Referring to discussions on nationality at the second meeting of the Trucial States Council in May 1952, the Political Resident insisted that the time was 'not ripe for the creation of a federal administration which would deal with the issue of passports and naturalization certificates on behalf of all the Trucial States jointly', justifying his views on the grounds that it would be impossible to recover the expenses of such an administration from the States concerned'.[12] With such a lack of enthusiasm from the top, it is not surprising that the Council made little progress towards bringing the

Trucial States together. Recalling in March 1953 that the Council had not met for nearly a year, D. A. Greenhill of the FO's Eastern Department bemoaned that 'such a gap can but delay the achievement of our goal of co-operation between the Shaikhs and that the value of any progress made last year may well have been reduced'.[13] Although a meeting was held in Sharjah towards the end of April 1953, Hay reported that 'little concrete was achieved'.[14] Shortly before stepping down as Political Resident, Hay, while supporting the 'maximum co-ordination' between the Shaikhdoms, opined that 'so far as the major Shaikhdoms are concerned there is . . . no hope of establishing any kind of political federation'.[15]

Hay's successor, B. A. B. Burrows, was more positive about the Trucial States Council, arguing that it forced the Rulers to face problems that concerned them all, as well as instilling in them 'a corporate sense which, owing to the distances between them, the lack of communications and their natural jealousy' had been conspicuously absent in the past.[16] Indeed, the years immediately following the establishment of the Council witnessed a marked easing of tension on the Trucial Coast, especially between the two principal states, Dubai and Abu Dhabi.[17] A practical demonstration of this development was the attendance of the fourth meeting of the Council, held towards the end of 1953, by all seven Rulers. The Council was far from fulfilling the role of a consultative, let alone an executive body, however. The main reason for this, as the future Political Agent in Dubai, C. M. Pirie-Gordon, explained, was that 'the idea and practice of free discussion in semi-formal assembly is outside the ken of all the participants while a degree of mutual distrust renders them inhibited from speaking freely in the presence of each other'.[18] Pirie-Gordon noted that the only real exception to this rule was provided by Shaikh Saqr of Sharjah whose 'welcome interventions and ready comprehension of the various points at least gave some semblance of discussion to what would otherwise have degenerated into a mere monologue by the Political Agent'. Although Pirie-Gordon refused to be discouraged by the apathy which pervaded the meeting, he did assert that the Council was unlikely to come alive until its deliberations reached a stage where their outcome had 'some effect for good or ill on the various states concerned'. Pirie-Gordon was able to report progress at the fifth meeting of the Trucial States Council, however.[19]

With the exception of the ailing Shaikh Said of Dubai, all the Rulers attended. Said's absence proved fortuitous since Shaikh Rashid 'relaxed from the inhibiting presence of his father was able to play a full and valuable role in proceedings'. Even Shaikh Shakhbut of Abu Dhabi, whose bearing at his only previous appearance was described by Pirie-Gordon as 'sphinx like', made a number of interventions. Although these were 'almost without exception to express opposition and dissent from opinions by his colleagues', Shaikh Zaid explained his brother's irascibility with reference to a quarrel that they had had on their way to the meeting. Pirie-Gordon recorded that Zaid had taken the opportunity 'privately to identify the State of Abu Dhabi wholeheartedly with the proceedings and decisions of the Council whatever its Ruler might have said to the contrary'. The Political Agent was noticeably more cautious in his assessment of the subsequent meeting of the Council at the end of 1954.[20]

While Pirie-Gordon noted that much useful ground had been covered, he conceded that 'we should be flattering ourselves if we considered that we had in anyway succeeded in persuading the Rulers that the Council was for their benefit and that their attendance was otherwise than as a courtesy to the Political Agent'. With the exception of the Ruler of Fujairah, who valued the meetings as a symbol of his equality, the other six 'without exception would be relaxed if the institution could be quietly abandoned'. To justify his hypothesis, Pirie-Gordon cited the fact that no Ruler had ever asked when the next meeting would be, or even referred to past meetings. On the other hand, several Rulers had indicated their unwillingness to express themselves openly in front of their colleagues. The inference that Pirie-Gordon drew from this was that Rulers wished not to be held too literally to opinions and decisions reached during Council discussions. Summing up the achievements of the Trucial States Council in its first three years, the new Political Agent in Dubai, J. P. Tripp, admitted that it had become 'little more than a "talking shop"'.[21] The creation of the Council, nonetheless, did rekindle speculation, especially in Iran, about a possible federation of Gulf States.[22] In keeping with earlier Foreign Office opinion, the Permanent Under-Secretary of State, Sir Harold Caccia, confirmed that, while Britain did not oppose any political or economic association between the states, the possibility of the Rulers ever agreeing to form a federation was remote.[23] The debate over federation was reawakened in the aftermath of the 1956 Suez crisis.

The British Ambassador in Iraq, Sir Michael Wright, advocated a profound reassessment of Britain's approach to the Gulf. 'If we take no new line', he argued, 'we shall be accused of clinging to the past', justifying this view with reference to the strength of Arab nationalism and what he perceived as a growing belief that the British position in the Gulf was anachronistic.[24] To counteract these dynamics, Wright advocated the creation of a federation of Gulf States, coupled with a possible future association with the Baghdad Pact.[25] Political Resident Bernard Burrows did not share Wright's analysis, describing the idea of federation as 'purely fanciful'.[26] 'The Gulf States', he explained, 'are intensely parochial. Their interests and economic circumstances are different one from another and they have in many cases intense jealousies of their neighbours.' Burrows also felt that the Aden Protectorate provided a salutary lesson in the difficulties of trying to federate traditional states.[27]

In the mid-1950s, the Governor of Aden, Sir Tom Hickinbotham championed the idea of rationalizing the disparate territories of the hinterland. His specific proposal centred on the creation, in the first instance, of two federations, one each in the Eastern and Western Protectorates.

Hickinbotham envisaged that these developments would lay the foundation for the eventual federation of both Protectorates with Aden colony. The Governor's plans however, were not only attacked in broadcasts from Cairo, but also subjected to intense scrutiny in Britain. Foreign Secretary Harold Macmillan expressed concerns over the implications for Hickinbotham's scheme on British strategic interests in Aden. 'If we want to hold on there', he urged,

> surely better to leave the local Sheikhs and Rulers in a state of simple rivalry and separateness, in which they are glad of our protection and can, where necessary, be played off one against another, rather than to mould them into a single unit which is most likely (and indeed seems expressly designed) to create a demand for independence and 'self-determination'.

Prime Minister Eden added his voice to the debate, expressing fears about the 'growing agitation' which Hickinbotham's proposals were causing. Britain's abortive attack on Egypt in November 1956 dealt a further blow to Hickinbotham's plans: having roused the ire of the Arab world, Britain could not afford to expose itself to further odium by pursuing the federal project. Moreover, the new Governor of Aden, Sir William Luce, did not share his predecessor's enthusiasm for federation. 'So far', he mused, 'there has been no really effective support for federation among the Rulers and any attempt to impose it upon them could only bedevil our relations with most of them, and so weaken our influence with them.' Applying the Aden exemplar to the Persian Gulf, Burrows concluded that 'The commotion caused by our proposals to federate the States of the Aden Protectorate should perhaps also be a warning against undue zeal in this direction at the present time'.[28] While recognizing that federation might possibly be advocated by 'the younger elements in the Gulf States', Burrows maintained that it would 'never appeal to the Rulers and older and more responsible people'.[29] In the FO there was general acceptance of Burrows' views on the impracticality of promoting a federation, one official going so far as to urge the eschewal of any '"grand design" for the whole Persian Gulf'.[30] The former British Ambassador in Egypt, Sir Humphrey Trevelyan, also entered the debate not merely dismissing federation as 'out of the question', but also downplaying the prospects for schemes of joint administration.[31] Al-Thani ambitions, however, provided new impetus to the incipient links between the states of the Trucial Coast.

In the late 1950s, there were several dynastic matches involving members of the Qatari royal house, the most significant of which was the marriage between Shaikh Ahmed and Shaikha Miriam, the daughter of Shaikh Rashid of Dubai.[32] Ahmed assiduously cultivated his father-in-law by extending generous grants of money to him and his followers. It was also rumoured that Ahmed had offered to finance various development projects, including a piped water scheme. The Political Agent in Dubai, D. F. Hawley, remarked that, following a visit to Doha in February 1959, Rashid had shown little concern over the financial implications of the many new ideas and projects which had occurred to him or he had agreed to.[33] In particular, he had demonstrated insouciance over the recurrent costs inherent in Dubai's new airport.

Apart from the al-Thani 'Austrian type' marriage policy, as one FO official termed it,[34] Qatari influence was extended through educational contacts: members of the Qatar Education Department made a number of visits to the Trucial States, while Sharjah was provided with three teachers. Moreover, the head of the Qatar police, Cochrane, visited Dubai and offered assistance to their police force. Speculating on the reasons for the growth of Qatari interest in the Trucial States, Hawley offered a number of possible explanations.[35] The obvious aim was to increase the influence of Qatar over the Trucial States. Hawley also suggested that Qatar was attempting to outflank its principal competitor, Abu Dhabi, by obtaining allies east of this Shaikhdom. Shaikh Ahmed's own ambitions, which included a strong desire to succeed Shaikh Ali as Ruler of Qatar, might also have shaped his actions: he might have reasoned that a popular external venture, possibly even leading a federation of Trucial States, would enhance his chances of becoming Ruler. Finally, Hawley conjectured that, in seeking to penetrate the Trucial States, Qatar might be working in league with Saudi Arabia. The Head of the Arabian Department, R. A. Beaumont, added that the limited life expectancy of Qatar's oil reserves meant that it was a 'race against time' if the Qataris were to establish their hegemony on the Trucial Coast.[36]

Whatever Qatar's true motives, its actions were not welcomed by the British. Hawley saw the Qatar Education Department, itself strongly influenced by Egypt and Syria, as a disruptive presence. '[T]here has been', he reported, 'a considerable deterioration in the atmosphere in the schools since the Qatari delegation arrived and the emphasis laid on Arab nationalism and the struggle against imperialism has greatly increased'.[37] As these comments suggest, Hawley was especially worried that Qatar's efforts to penetrate the Trucial States would be at the expense of British influence. He advocated a policy which encouraged the Trucial States Rulers to 'stand on their own feet', and, while not discouraging the acceptance of aid, to be 'on their guard against undue influence being brought to bear'.[38] W. J. Adams (Second Secretary, FO) drew attention to the fact that the 'chronic weakness' of Shaikh Rashid's character made the Qatari task much easier, and called for the Secretary of State to impress upon the Dubai Ruler the importance of a 'robust and independent outlook in dealing with outside influences'.[39] Hawley had already anticipated this problem and suggested that it could be controlled by the channelling of external aid through the Trucial Council. It was left to the Acting Political Agent in Qatar, R. G. Giddens, to put some much needed perspective on the

Qatari initiatives. While agreeing that Shaikh Ahmed was pre-occupied first and foremost with the succession, Giddens opined that distribution of gifts derived essentially from a desire to 'flaunt his comparatively enormous wealth – an opportunity which does not exist elsewhere in the Gulf'.[40] Giddens also felt that if Ahmed's real intention was to penetrate the Trucial States, the gifts of money and technical aid would have been larger and more widespread.

Despite Giddens' scepticism, further evidence of the Qatari charm offensive was not slow in materializing. During a visit to Beirut in 1960, Shaikh Ali took the opportunity to cultivate fellow Gulf Rulers. Not only did he exchange calls with Shaikh Zaid of Abu Dhabi, but also offered the latter the use of a number of cars.[41] When Zaid attempted to return the vehicles, Ali insisted that he accept them as a gift and as a token of Qatar's desire to settle outstanding issues with Abu Dhabi. Ali sedulously observed protocol with respect to visits from other Gulf dignitaries, exchanging calls with Shaikh Abdullah of Kuwait and making sure that he was at the airport both to greet and see off the Kuwaiti Ruler.[42] Ali was also described as going further than protocol demanded by meeting the Ruler of Bahrain's uncle, Shaikh Abdulla, at the airport. Despite Ali's attempts to cultivate his fellow Rulers, the Abu Dhabi Ruler, Shaikh Shakhbut, represented a perennial block to integration.

In conversation with the US Consul General in Dhahran, Walter K. Schwinn,[43] Donald Hawley cast doubt on the prospects for federation on the grounds that 'Shaikh Shakhbut, secure in the knowledge that he will soon have a handsome income from oil, is disposed to object to virtually any proposal involving co-operative action on the part of the Rulers'. Hawley concluded from this that progress towards the federal goal could only be made by excluding Abu Dhabi. For his part, Schwinn was fearful that Shakhbut, unwilling to see the formation of a rival unit, 'might attempt by bribes or threats to induce one or another of the lesser states not to participate in the federation, thus frustrating it'. The US Consul General was unreserved in his criticism of the British for allowing this situation to develop:

> Had the British acted more positively in the past to create a federation among the Trucial States, even at the cost of arm-twisting, the present situation might have been avoided. As matters now stand, federation of all the Trucial States seems likely to remain an iridiscent [*sic*] dream or, at best, a truncated and ineffectual affair subject to constant intrigue and plotting.

The Political Resident was equally pessimistic, Schwinn's successor, John Evarts Horner, reporting that 'Sir William Luce expressed scepticism that federation is a feasible project, mainly perhaps because of the virtual impossibility of inducing Shaikh Shakhbut of Abu Dhabi to participate, and the poverty of the other Rulers'.[44] Luce himself told the FO that the idea of creating a viable political structure through association 'breaks down on the hard facts of geography and population. . . . The most ardent federalist would boggle at the task of making any political or military sense out of such a situation.'[45] In a similar vein, a Foreign Office brief for forthcoming discussions with the US State Department articulated the view that the Gulf States were 'too scattered and lacking in common interests to have the making of a federation, nor could such a federation defend itself if it came about'.[46] In contrast with the views of Hawley and Luce, however, the FO did not discount the possibility of some form of unity being achieved if the Trucial States came under the domination of Abu Dhabi.[47] The State Department itself was of the opinion that Bahrain, on account of the expected exhaustion of its on-shore oil reserves, would promote the formation of some form of Persian Gulf political entity funded largely by the wealthier states, principally Kuwait and Abu Dhabi.[48] The FO, however, expressed doubt about the genuineness of Bahrain's interest in associating itself with its neighbours. One official observed that

> In its present xenophobic mood . . . Bahrain will want full independence, rather than association with other states, which would be seen as a come-down. The Bahrainis would possibly swallow association with Kuwait, under continued British protection, but a link with Qatar, for example, would be anathema.[49]

Another official considered that, despite Abu Dhabi's growing economic ascendancy, the Gulf Rulers would 'continue jealously to guard their individual independence' and 'persist in their mutual bickering'.[50] The conclusion which was drawn was that Britain might find the Rulers 'increasingly embarrassing protégés well beyond 1970'.[51] Kuwait, however, offered a possible way out of this dilemma.

Kuwait had already shown its interest in the Trucial States by providing the Ruler of Dubai with a loan to carry out harbour improvement works and by supplying teachers from its Education Department for schools in the Lower Gulf.[52] Towards the end of 1963, Abdul Aziz Masaeed, a Kuwaiti publisher who owned three leading titles, told the British Ambassador in Kuwait, Noel Jackson, that he favoured a federation of Southern Gulf States under the hegemony of Kuwait, adding that economic convergence between the different states would facilitate this goal.[53] Although Jackson was initially sceptical about the extent to which these views were shared by the ruling family of Kuwait, they soon received endorsement from the influential Minister of Finance and Trade, Shaikh Jabir al-Ahmad. He expressed the view to Jackson that the smaller Shaikhdoms were a 'complete anachronism in the modern world' and that they should be instructed by HMG to federate.[54] 'When the Trucial States had got together', he concluded, 'they should join Qatar and Bahrain, and eventually Kuwait would be willing to join and help them all.' When Jackson highlighted the difficulties inherent in Jabir's approach, principally the reluctance of the Gulf Shaikhs to merge their interests in this way, he merely brushed the Ambassador's reservations aside. In explaining the origins of Jabir's views, Jackson posited that he was echoing Abdul Aziz Masaeed's ideas uncritically. That he was urging HMG to apply pressure on the Trucial States Rulers that the al-Sabah themselves would have balked at, even thirty years earlier, was a source of surprise for Jackson; he recalled that Jabir's father, Shaikh Ahmad (r. 1921–50), 'bitterly resented even the most called-for advice, however tactfully offered'.[55] Although the FO agreed that the Gulf Rulers would take exception to the type of compulsion which Jabir was suggesting,[56] it did record that, since he was the most important figure in Kuwaiti politics after the Amir, his interest in the Southern Gulf was significant.[57] Indeed, the FO had already considered the desirability of involving Kuwait in the affairs of the Gulf.

D. P. Gracie, who had been set the task of weighing up the advantages and disadvantages of tying the fortunes of Kuwait more closely to those of the other Gulf States, was strongly in favour of increasing Kuwaiti participation.[58] The main problem in achieving this, he observed, was that '"pep-talks" by Abdullah Salim to other Rulers . . . are little better received than similar approaches from us'. To overcome this tendency, Gracie advocated 'not periodic frontal attacks, but infiltration over a period'. In particular, he recommended that the government of Kuwait make available the services of oil, legal, and financial experts to advise on specific projects on the Southern Gulf States. As regards possible problems presented by inter-state rivalry and ill-feeling, Gracie speculated that 'Kuwaiti money will be a powerful salve to pride in the Trucial States, if not in Bahrain and Qatar'. Although Gracie recognized that Kuwait had been subjected to the pull of Arab nationalism, he did not see this as an impediment to Kuwaiti involvement in the Trucial States. 'We have', he opined, '. . . a strong interest in seeing that new ideas come to the Gulf not from the UAR but from Kuwait, whose rulers would . . . never willingly consent to lose control of their own affairs to Cairo'.

Gracie's views were not accepted uncritically in the FO. Following discussions with the Political Resident, J. A. Snellgrove (First Secretary, FO) drew attention to the fact that experts and teachers from Kuwait were in fact largely non-Kuwaiti, often Egyptians and Palestinians.[59] He also indicated that Kuwait had little real interest in sponsoring development in the Trucial States in the face of competing demands for its investment from other Arab countries. Certainly the Rulers of both Dubai and Ras al Khaimah complained about the inadequacies of the Kuwaiti aid programme.[60] Snellgrove concluded that it would be 'wrong to force both Kuwaitis and Trucials into a co-operation neither desired'.[61] From his vantage point in Dhahran, US Consul General John Evarts Horner was even more forthright, asserting: 'It is hard to imagine any scheme less realistic than federation of British Gulf protectorates headed by Kuwait'.[62] An alternative solution to the problems presented by the Gulf States was provided by Sir William Luce.[63]

Luce kept faith with the orthodox view that the continued stability of the Gulf, on which the smooth and increasing flow of oil on reasonable terms depended, rested on the British presence. Nevertheless, he recognized that Britain's special position was likely to be a source of 'increasing embarrassment' both in the United Nations and in Britain's relations with other Arab countries. As such he turned his mind to finding a 'valid long-term alternative method of securing stability of the area'. He dubbed his proposed solution 'Arabian Peninsula solidarity'. In his opinion, this area had the potential for solidarity because of its geographical cohesion and social compatibility; he also believed that oil wealth ensured the necessary financial strength to promote development and prosperity for the whole Peninsula. Because of its size and strength, the cornerstone of Luce's scheme was Saudi Arabia. Quite apart from the problems associated with long-standing territorial disputes, Luce did accept that it would be difficult for the small Gulf Shaikhdoms to deal with Saudi Arabia on equal terms. To overcome this snag, he urged a federation of the Trucial States which he described as a 'prerequisite of solidarity'. He also believed that such developments would assist in ensuring that change in the Gulf States would occur in an evolutionary, rather than a revolutionary way. 'One of our difficulties', he mused,

> is that while our protection and the presence of British Forces in the area help to maintain the stability of the present regimes, they also reduce the incentive to the Rulers to move with the times by insulating them to some extent from the forces of reform and progress. It might be possible to reduce this dilemma if we were able to present to the Rulers the concept of a gradual transition from the Pax Britannica to Arabian Peninsula solidarity on the lines I am advocating.

Luce's views did not receive unqualified support from other British representatives in the area. While seeing the attractiveness of Arabian Peninsula solidarity, Britain's Ambassador in Jedda, Colin Crowe, perceived that it would founder on the rock of Saudi territorial ambitions. He also questioned whether Saudi Arabia would be willing to deal with the Gulf States on the basis of equality. 'I doubt if a federation of these states would meet the case', he continued, 'since I do not think we could expect the Saudis to acquiesce in the formation of a federation, one of whose principal objects would be to consolidate such a federation against possible future Saudi encroachments.'[64] Having regard to Kuwait's important political links with both Cairo and Baghdad, Jackson had reservations about whether the Amirate would ever consider forming part of an organization of Arabian Peninsula states. He also pointed out that

Kuwait would not wish to see an expanding Saudi role, partly because of its own ambitions in the Lower Gulf, and partly because it did not welcome the prospect of Saudi control of the area's growing revenues.[65] Despite Kuwait's mounting interest in the Southern Gulf, it was Saudi Arabia which provided the impetus for drawing the Gulf States closer together. Before this could happen, the disruptive influence of Shaikh Saqr of Sharjah had to be tackled.

During the twentieth session of the Trucial States Council at the end of December 1964, Shaikh Saqr was keen to forestall an offer made by King Feisal the previous month to provide assistance with development, for fear of giving offence to the Arab League and to Cairo. Summarizing the meeting, H. G. Balfour-Paul (Political Agent, Dubai) contrasted the 'frequent interventions (not many of them helpful) from the Ruler of Sharjah' with the 'bearded silences of Ajman, Fujairah and Umm al Qaiwain'.[66] Shortly after the Trucial States Council meeting, Balfour-Paul confronted the wayward Shaikh, warning him of the dangers of throwing in his lot with Nasser.[67] Saqr had done little to mend his ways by the time of the twenty-first meeting of the Council in March of the following year, extolling the virtues of financial aid from the Arab League. Referring to the workings of the Trucial Council, Balfour-Paul bemoaned the fact that 'of the seven Rulers, the co-operative are inarticulate and the articulate unco-operative'.[68]

A visit to the Gulf by Nofal, the Assistant Secretary-General of the Arab League, merely fuelled Saqr's truculence. Not only did Saqr enthusiastically embrace the offer of Arab League aid, but also brazenly admitted to the Minister of State at the Foreign Office that he had given his formal consent to the opening of a League office within his territory. In Luce's mind, Saqr had unmistakably revealed his hand: 'The Ruler of Sharjah, after years of flirtation with the UAR, has now decided to cast his lot with the Egyptians in the expectation that they will build up his position at the expense of his neighbour the Ruler of Dubai.'[69] Britain's apprehension about the spread of revolutionary forces in the Gulf was shared by King Feisal.

Fearful that the long-standing divisions between the leading states would provide an opportunity for Nasserite subversion in the region, King Feisal impressed upon the Rulers of Bahrain and Qatar the desirability of meeting with a view to resolving their differences.[70] Feisal suggested Shaikh Shakhbut of Abu Dhabi also attend the putative meeting. The problem remained of finding a neutral venue. Much to Britain's relief the idea of using a British warship, though considered, was soon rejected. Feisal favoured Dubai and since its ruler, Shaikh Rashid, was agreeable plans proceeded on this basis. Held between 22 and 25 May 1965, the meeting, was attended by the Deputy Rulers (or Rulers' representatives) of Bahrain, Qatar, and Abu Dhabi, with Shaikh Rashid acting as host.[71] In addition to concurring on the need to co-operate in the interests of improving standards of living and maintaining the peace of the area, the Shaikhs also approved the creation of a Gulf currency to replace the Indian rupee, including the establishment of an Arabian Gulf currency board.[72] Moreover, the discussions facilitated reconciliation between the participating states, Shaikh Khalifah bin Hamad, the Deputy Ruler of Qatar, maintaining that 'a new and beautiful era of co-operation and amity' had been ushered in between his country and Bahrain.[73] As a demonstration of this newfound goodwill, an invitation had been extended to Bahrain's Deputy Ruler, Shaikh Khalifah bin Sulman, to visit Qatar. Although no invitation had yet been extended to the Deputy Ruler of Abu Dhabi, Shaikh Zaid, Khalifah bin Hamad was equally effusive about his talks with him.[74] Balfour-Paul went so far as to describe the May meeting as 'historic', justifying this hyperbole with the thought that this was the first time that the ruling families of Qatar, Bahrain, and Abu Dhabi had gathered to discuss common problems.[75] In a further boost to unity, Shaikh Saqr's divisive presence was removed at the end of June when he was deposed by leading members of his family on the grounds of his 'neglect of his subjects, misgovernment of the State, extravagance and his dissolute way of life'.[76] He was replaced by his more moderate cousin, Shaikh Khalid bin Mohammed.

At the May meeting, it was agreed in principle to hold further meetings. The groundwork having been done by the Deputy Rulers, the Rulers themselves met on 7 and 8 July 1965 in Dubai.[77] After the opening session, at which the text of the Arabian Gulf Currency Agreement was agreed upon and signed by the Rulers of the four states represented at the May meeting, the Rulers of the five smaller states attended all the remaining sessions. The July discussions gave the Rulers of Bahrain, Qatar, and Abu Dhabi an opportunity to get to know each other as a prelude to future co-operation. On his return to Abu Dhabi, Shaikh Shakhbut told his Political Agent that the meeting marked a 'turning point in the history of the Gulf'. Agreement was reached on the passage of Qatari vehicles through Abu Dhabi territory on their way to Dubai, and an embargo on air mail and air freight between Qatar and Bahrain was lifted. Although Luce reported that the Rulers of the four principal states were 'not greatly impressed' by their brethren from the five small Northern Trucial States, he did at least feel able to record that the four 'did what they could to make them feel part of the club'. Shaikh Ahmed of Qatar was especially solicitous and did much to cultivate Shaikh Saqr of Ras al Khaimah who was still smarting from the deposition of his kinsman, the Ruler of Sharjah.

Despite the undoubted ice-breaking which took place during the Rulers' two days in Dubai, the substantive achievements were more difficult to demonstrate. While it was agreed to establish a single committee to study matters of common interest, the Dubai meeting did not result, as Luce had hoped, in the creation of separate standing committees on such subjects as education, trade, and security. Luce's suggestion that the three oil-producing states contribute to the Trucial States Development Fund on the basis of fixed percentages of their annual oil revenues was also rejected.

Also, no positive step towards the establishment of a confederation in the form of a league of Gulf States was decided upon. Luce explained that

> There was a general feeling at the meeting that it was still too early to think in terms of such a league, the creation of which at this particular moment might have been regarded outside as being in direct opposition to the Arab League and might have become a focal point of attack by the latter on the Rulers as a group, with a consequent worsening of relations between them and the Arab League.

The positive glow which pervaded the July meeting could not conceal the fact that tangible results were slow in materializing. In August, the Deputy Political Resident, H. Phillips, reported that not only had the single committee, which had been agreed at Dubai, failed to emerge, but also there had been no ad hoc meetings of officials concerned in the various fields of interstate co-operation.[78] Although Shaikh Rashid of Dubai, Shaikh Khalifah bin Sulman of Bahrain, and Shaikhs Ahmed and Khalifah bin Hamad of Qatar did meet in Doha towards the end of July, there was no discussion of the disputed seabed boundary between Qatar and Bahrain.[79] Agreement over a common currency also soon foundered.

As early as June 1964, a Treasury official had predicted that 'Because of political jealousies there is a danger of the establishment of a number of small and relatively weak currencies in the Persian Gulf area.'[80] The Shah of Iran's angry reaction to news of the signing of the currency agreement in July 1965 was the trigger for such tendencies. Not only did he object to the term Arabian Gulf Currency, but also refused to recognize any currency with which Bahrain was associated.[81] Using the Shah's objections as a pretext, Shaikh Ahmed of Qatar announced his withdrawal from the currency agreement.[82] Instead, he proposed a separate currency for Qatar and Dubai which the five Northern Trucial States could also use.[83] The FO, not surprisingly, deplored this step which it described as 'contrary to the spirit of co-operation for the common good of the whole area proclaimed by the Rulers' communiqué of 8 July 1965'.[84] R. I. Hallows of the Bank of England, who had been involved in the negotiation of the currency agreement, gloomily observed that 'So far as the Arab States (excluding Kuwait) of the Gulf are concerned, the prospect of any form of political association between them appears more remote than ever'.[85] Fearful that the Indian rupee was in danger of devaluation,[86] Bahrain had already established its own currency in 1965 which Shaikh Shakhbut subsequently accepted in his state.[87] News that Umm al Qaiwain, Ajman, Sharjah, and Ras al Khaimah were proposing to form a new currency with Abu Dhabi merely underlined the fissiparous tendencies in the Gulf. Not only did Luce feel that the establishment of a second currency in the Northern Trucial States and a third one in the Lower Gulf did not make economic sense, he also argued that it could become 'a disruptive political force if it gets enough steam behind it'.[88] Attempts by the new Ruler of Abu Dhabi, Shaikh Zaid, to breathe life into the common currency project[89] foundered on account of rivalry between Bahrain and Qatar over the location of the prospective currency board's headquarters.[90]

Any hope of Kuwait taking the lead in bringing about a federation of Gulf States was also soon dispelled. Even before the July 1965 gathering, the Rulers of the southern states demonstrated an antipathy towards the Kuwaitis. Kuwait's attempt to assist Bahrain with the establishment of its own currency was firmly rebuffed by Shaikh Isa. An exploratory team despatched by Kuwait to the Lower Gulf fared little better. The frostiness with which Kuwaiti initiatives were received can be ascribed partly to a general feeling among the Rulers that they had never wanted Kuwaiti domination of the Gulf, and partly to fears over Kuwait's political orientation.[91] Commenting on the way things were going in Kuwait, Shaikh Isa had remarked that 'Kuwaiti "imperialism" might be used by the UAR as a stalking horse'.[92] In response to the Political Agent of Dubai's suggestion that the forthcoming meeting of Gulf Rulers should make friendly gestures to Kuwait, the Ruler of Qatar declared that 'Kuwait had proved itself the source of all the present troubles in the Gulf and that until it stopped serving deliberately as a stalking-horse for Egypt and Iraq a rapprochement was out of the question'.[93]

Concern to maintain Kuwait's development aid to the Trucial States prompted a more diplomatic response from the Bahrainis, although they agreed with the sentiments of the Qatar Ruler.[94] Notably the final communiqué of the July meeting made no reference to Kuwait. When the new Amir, Shaikh Sabah, indicated fresh interest in the Southern Gulf States, Luce expressed scepticism over whether the Rulers there would accept any form of federal union under the aegis of Kuwait.[95] On the one hand, Luce pointed out that the fragility of the moves to closer political integration made the building up of anything more than 'the habit of co-operation in practical matters of common concern' a distant prospect. On the other, he stressed that the Kuwaitis were not well-placed to take the lead in the Gulf: 'Kuwait has really nothing to offer the southern Gulf except money; she has neither military strength nor international prestige and her somewhat precarious position within the Arab world is not calculated to inspire confidence in her as a shield.' Luce doubted whether even Kuwaiti money could buy allegiance since the only area in which it would have any real impact was in the small, and politically insignificant, Northern Trucial States. Ill-feeling towards Kuwait was exposed when the Minister of the Interior in the Kuwait government, Shaikh Sa'ad, visited Bahrain towards the beginning of 1966.[96] The Deputy Ruler, Shaikh Khalifah bin Sulman, pressed his guest to ensure that any patronage given to Bahraini nationalists harbouring in Kuwait should be withdrawn 'in the interests of good relations between *all* the Gulf states'. Khalifah also criticized the Kuwaiti aid programme which he described as not merely favouring the 'have', rather than the 'have-not' states, but also being 'too conditional and too much influenced by the Arab League'.

With the momentum for Gulf co-operation foundering, the Political Resident pushed for a second Rulers' meeting.[97] At the beginning of 1966, he sounded out Shaikh Khalifah bin Sulman who welcomed the prospect but, no doubt recalling the rather unstructured first meeting, emphasized the importance of devising an agenda carefully in advance. During a subsequent discussion the Ruler, Shaikh Isa, gave his backing to the idea of a second meeting. Isa and Khalifah set about making preparations, favouring preliminary discussions between the Deputy Rulers of Bahrain, Qatar, and Abu Dhabi, along with the Ruler of Dubai.[98] Luce regarded this gathering as particularly important since the deputies were 'more inclined towards co-operation than their respective Rulers'.[99] Despite his support for the formation of a league or association of Gulf States, Luce studiously avoided taking the initiative, arguing that it was a question which the Rulers would have to handle 'in their own way and in their own time'. The Political Resident saw a second meeting of Gulf Rulers as an opportunity to build on the foundations laid the previous year, strengthen the habit of co-operation, and endeavour to ensure that matters of practical common concern were dealt with on a Gulf-wide basis. Nevertheless, he asserted: 'We want co-operation between the Gulf States to gain its own momentum and not to depend indefinitely on constant prodding from us.'

Luce's hopes for the organic growth of Gulf unity were frustrated by the recalcitrance of Shaikh Shakhbut. Reporting the Political Resident's views to the Prime Minister, Foreign Secretary Patrick Gordon Walker minuted: 'He is quite sure that so long as Shaikh Shakhbut is the Ruler, federation including Abu Dhabi, which is the only State with any substantial revenue, is out of the question, and there is no sign of his being ready to give any assistance to the other States.'[100] Luce had already been pushing for the removal of Shakhbut and replacement by his brother, Shaikh Zaid.[101] His case was strengthened by Zaid's stated preference for federation and the sharing of Abu Dhabi's oil wealth.[102] The choice facing Britain, insisted Luce, was between 'paying fairly heavily for a second-rate and incompetent federation', or accepting his case for a change of Rulers in Abu Dhabi.[103] There was some reluctance in the FO about taking such drastic action. Looking at the possible international repercussions of moves to depose Shakhbut, R. S. Crawford of the Arabian Department warned: 'It would seem unwise to add to our difficulties by giving the Afro-Asian members of the UN an easy entrée into the Gulf which they have not got at present.'[104] FO reticence notwithstanding, there was general acceptance that the Abu Dhabi Ruler represented an obstructive force with respect to moves towards greater co-operation among the Gulf States.

On the eve of the Minister of State's visit to the Gulf in May 1965, the FO explained that Shakhbut's 'chief disadvantage from the British point of view is not so much his bad government as his refusal to co-operate with his fellow Rulers in developing their States or laying the basis of an eventual Trucial States Federation'.[105] Shakhbut's ostensibly positive reaction to the July meeting in Dubai masked his reservations about committing Abu Dhabi to closer relations with his neighbours. '[W]hatever views one may hold about the desirability in theory of a federation of the seven and however different things might have been if there had been a Ruler of Abu Dhabi other than Shaikh Shakhbut,' intoned Luce disconsolately, 'we must accept that a federation covering the whole Trucial Coast is not a realisable project'.[106] Apart from his well-known reluctance to share his wealth, Shakhbut's attitude seems to have stemmed from, as Luce put it, 'his exaggerated sense of pride and importance' which dictated that 'Abu Dhabi should not be regarded as just another Trucial State but that it should be recognized as a full member of the senior club, along with Bahrain and Qatar'.[107] To symbolize this, Shakhbut sent his deputy to the Trucial States Council, rather than attending in person. Such displays of independence, Luce feared, threatened to destroy the Council and destabilize the area to the detriment of Britain's intended purpose of unity.[108] On a brighter note, Luce described the prospect of achieving a federation of the remaining six Trucial States as having been 'much improved by the departure of the late Ruler of Sharjah, with his intense dislike of Shaikh Rashid'.[109] Moreover, the Rulers of Bahrain and Qatar supported the idea of a convergence of the six on the grounds that their continued separation would be a weakness to the political structure of the Gulf which would be open to exploitation by hostile external forces.[110] They were also struck by the argument that with a federation of the six, these small states would only have one voice in the counsels of the Lower Gulf.

The accuracy of Luce's assessment of the Abu Dhabi Ruler's true feelings was not slow in materializing. As plans for a meeting of Deputy Rulers gathered pace, Shakhbut declared that co-operation with his neighbours was not in his interests and that consequently he would refuse to send his brother, Shaikh Zaid, to the meeting.[111] He also underlined his determination not to attend any gathering of Gulf Rulers. The immediate cause of his outburst was the continuing seabed boundary dispute with Dubai which Shakhbut accused of 'committing aggression on Abu Dhabi territory'.[112] Shakhbut's defiance unravelled plans to maintain the impetus for bringing the Gulf States together. Although the Bahrainis proposed to postpone the Deputy Rulers' meeting until 13 June, they were not prepared to proceed unless Shakhbut agreed to send a representative.[113] Fearing that Shakhbut would use the absence of an Abu Dhabi representative to claim that he was superior to his brother rulers and hence had no need to co-operate with them, Shaikh Isa insisted that if Shakhbut refused to send anybody to the meeting it would not take place.[114] Shaikh Khalifah bin Hamad went one step further, insisting that he would only attend if Shaikh Zaid represented Abu Dhabi with full authority from Shakhbut to take decisions.[115] It was left to Luce to report that since Shaikh Zaid was leaving for a lengthy visit to Britain and Shakhbut was unlikely to nominate an alternative representative, the gathering of Deputy Rulers, and consequently a full Rulers' meeting, would not take place.[116] In any case, Shaikh Khalifah bin Sulman, who had been a driving force behind recent initiatives, had, by this stage, lost heart.

On the eve of his retirement, Luce reviewed the prospects for closer association.[117] In his opinion, the weakest point in the political structure of the Gulf was the independent existence of the five petty Shaikhdoms of the Northern Trucial Coast which he characterized as 'poverty-stricken and too small ever to be viable entities'. The possibility of addressing this problem through a federation of all seven Trucial States, however, had been frustrated by the 'refusal of the Ruler of Abu Dhabi to participate in a federation or to share any part of his oil wealth, and the refusal of the other Rulers to federate without Abu Dhabi'. Luce also admitted that 'our recent experiences with federations elsewhere in the world have dampened our own enthusiasm for this particular solution'. Nevertheless, he identified the Abu Dhabi Ruler as the major impediment to progress in the Gulf: 'Shaikh Shakhbut is quite uninterested in co-operation with the other Gulf States, except on the rare occasions when it suits him, and his financial contributions to the development of the Northern Trucial States have been derisory in relation to his wealth'. Luce pinned his hopes on Shaikh Rashid of Dubai whom he described as 'a leader whose interests and aims are broadly in harmony with ours'. The Political Resident favoured the gradual establishment of Rashid as the dominant leader of the Northern Trucial Coast, with the hope that he could eventually absorb the whole area. The discovery of oil in commercial quantities in the Dubai seabed was seen as providing Rashid with the capability of 'buying the support of the people of the northern Trucial Coast, with or without their Shaikhs'. He was soon to have a rival, however.

The deposition of Shaikh Shakhbut in a palace coup at the beginning of August 1966 brought his younger brother, Shaikh Zaid, to the throne. At the end of 1964, Foreign Secretary Gordon Walker had vetoed any plan which would have required Britain to take the initiative in deposing the Abu Dhabi Ruler. He did, however, approve a more covert operation whereby Zaid would seize power having received a secret guarantee from the Political Resident that recognition and short-term military assistance would follow. The key advantage of this alternative scenario was that Britain would be seen to be responding to Zaid's initiative.[118] An opportunity to implement the plan presented itself by the visit of Zaid to London in mid-1966. During talks at the FO he was given the necessary assurances to act.[119] Rashid reacted angrily, denouncing the displacement of Shakhbut in which he saw the hand of the British. Balfour-Paul suspected that Rashid was attempting to discredit Shaikh Zaid 'in pursuit of his own ambitions in the Trucial States'.[120] Certainly Zaid set about assiduously cultivating the Rulers of the Northern Trucial States. Unlike the parsimonious

Shakhbut, he liberally distributed his state's wealth, giving the Ruler of Ras al Khaimah an immediate grant of money and telling the Rulers of the other northern states to come to him, rather than the other oil-rich states of the Gulf, whenever they needed funds. He also agreed to contribute £500,000 to the Trucial States Development Fund.

Although Zaid was clearly attempting to consolidate his position and extend the influence of Abu Dhabi, he genuinely appeared to favour closer relations with his neighbours. In conversations with Luce towards the end of 1964, Zaid had expressed the view that federation was a 'necessity', and that Abu Dhabi 'should provide the necessary funds'.[121] Zaid's accession increasingly came to be seen by the British as a mixed blessing with respect to integration in the Lower Gulf, however. 'The indications are', observed the new Political Resident, Sir Stewart Crawford, 'that Shaikh Zaid will prefer his relationship with the smaller Trucial States to be one of patronage rather than, as we would prefer, genuine collaboration'.[122] The Political Agent in Abu Dhabi, A. T. Lamb, cautioned that Zaid would not permit either the Trucial Council or its Development Office to play any part in the internal affairs of Abu Dhabi.[123] Commenting on this discouraging news, a Foreign Office official lamented that 'it is difficult to see how there can be much meaningful collaboration unless Zaid is willing to consider the problems of the area as a whole and to fit his policies into some kind of overall plan'.[124] Drawing these various dispiriting strands together, Balfour-Paul suggested that the Abu Dhabi Ruler's wealth, coupled with his determination to run his state his own way, 'may make the attempt to promote the elements of conciliary administration in the seven States even harder, in some ways, than they were in the days of Shaikh Shakhbut'.[125] Zaid's overbearing performances at the Trucial States Council were also causing concern, S. J. Nuttall (Assistant Political Agent, Abu Dhabi) referring to his conduct at the twenty-ninth meeting of the Council in August–September 1967 as 'deplorable'. Zaid's main crime was his obstructiveness towards the Trucial States Development Office. Accounting for the Abu Dhabi Ruler's behaviour, Nuttall remarked that

> the real reason for his opposition to any expansion in the functions of the TSDO was his realization that if it acquired Trucial States-wide authority in an increasing number of fields it would be more difficult for him to emerge eventually as the pre-dominant or even sole political authority in the area.[126]

'If Zaid is determined to reduce the Council to nothing more than an extension of his own development plans,' wrote Balfour-Paul indignantly, 'this conflicts with all our policies to date.'[127]

Despite Rashid's initial indignation at the circumstances surrounding Zaid's accession, he agreed to meet the Abu Dhabi Ruler before the end of the year in order to discuss, among other things, the boundary dispute between their two states. While a final settlement remained elusive, the two Rulers did agree to co-operate in security matters and look into the possibility of setting up a teacher training college for the Trucial States. Rashid was soon restored to good humour and declared himself optimistic about the chances of a further Rulers' meeting.[128] Shaikh Zaid's visit to Doha at the beginning of November appeared further to cement the collaborative atmosphere which was permeating the Gulf. The trip was described as a 'huge success from start to finish', with the al-Thanis having gone 'out of their way to impress and please'.[129] Although Shaikh Ahmed of Qatar subsequently played down the prospects of a further Rulers' meeting,[130] Political Resident Crawford was more hopeful, predicting that such a meeting would 'give a fresh impetus to Gulf co-operation'.[131] The disappointments which had followed in the wake of the July 1965 Rulers' meeting, coupled with the bitter experience of failed attempts to weld the flotsam of empire together elsewhere in the world, eroded Britain's attachment to the federal idea.

Referring to the prospective federation, the Head of the FO's United National (Political) Department, Sam Falle, expostulated: 'This proposal fills me with despair and it seems to me that we are creating yet another albatross as a worthy successor to the ill-starred Aden Federation and others elsewhere in the world.'[132] He went on to assert that the 'creation of a lovely new neo-colonialist federation would be manna from heaven for our enemies who would enjoy themselves inordinately at our expense.' Although more convinced of the aptness of unity in the Gulf, the Head of the Arabian Department, T. F. Brenchley, admitted: 'I certainly do not think that we should force federation through against local opposition as was done in South Arabia.'[133] In response to an enquiry from the Ministry of Power about the future of the Gulf States, the FO commented:

> we have often considered the possibility of federation but our present thinking is that it is only possible to approach it indirectly by encouraging co-operation in general terms and the 'development of common institutions and services' rather than try for any formal arrangement.[134]

Equally, P. R. Spendlove of the FCO's Commonwealth Policy and Planning Department observed that

> our experience in Asia and Africa in trying to do this leads one to suspect that in so far as the idea of fusing the Sheikhdoms is concerned the suggestion is self-deceiving rather than a practicable proposition. Essentially the idea depends on the extent to which it is possible to include within one boundary tribal groupings under the control of different Sheikhs. There seem to be many difficulties in this. . . . Are any Sheikhs in fact going to give up their present independence at our behest, only to place themselves in situations where they may become

> more subordinate than the traditional relations with the Arab communities in question suggests is practicable. What will bind them? And if bound, who will guarantee?[135]

Britain's disinclination to take the lead in prompting the closer association of the states of the Lower Gulf was underlined during discussions in London between the Kuwaiti Ambassador, Shaikh Salim al-Sabah, and the Secretary of State for Defence, Denis Healey. Although Healey agreed that the objective of linking up these territories was desirable, he felt obliged to tell Shaikh Salim that Britain's attempts to create federations had 'not been very happy' and that 'too obvious a pressure from an external European influence was likely to be counter-productive'.[136] In any case, the Cabinet Official Committee on Defence and Oversea Policy noted that since the 1965 high-point progress towards the creation of a single political unit had been 'slow and difficult'.[137] Not only had no further meetings taken place, but also the common currency agreement had been abandoned before implementation. The continuing rivalry between the Rulers of the principal states was demonstrated when instead of a single currency, two were adopted, one for Bahrain and Abu Dhabi, the other for Qatar and the Northern Trucial States. The Committee conceded that:

> reduction of the nine units to (effectively) four is the most we can hope for; either by a Dubai-led federation (or union) of the NTS [Northern Trucial States] or alternatively by a division of the five small states, with some uniting or federating under Dubai's leadership and others under Abu Dhabi's.

Even this was seen as fraught with difficulty since the small states could be expected to resist merger with their larger neighbours and insist on retaining their separate existence, if necessary appealing to Cairo for support. Although some level of regional co-operation on the basis of the existing Trucial States Council and Development Fund was envisaged, the Committee observed that a general federation or union seemed highly unlikely. It concluded that 'recent British experience elsewhere suggests that political association between reluctant units is an unsatisfactory feature of the decolonization process. The West Indies, Malaysia, Nigeria, Central Africa and South Arabia are not the most encouraging of precedents.' Relations between the Gulf States formed only one aspect of their evolution. Relations with their more powerful neighbours were also central to their future.

J. T. Fearnley of the FO's Oil Department remarked that whatever was achieved towards the promotion of closer association, it was 'unlikely to affect the requirement for some larger power, or combination of powers, to keep the peace and maintain the present stability in the area, not least so that the oil continues to flow and the investment remains assured'.[138]

Fearnley identified Saudi Arabia as the most promising candidate. 'The aim here would not be to hand over the Gulf States to Saudi Arabia,' he explained, 'but rather to achieve some arrangement which would ensure that separately or together the states continued to enjoy independence "guaranteed" by Saudi Arabia in the same sort of way that is guaranteed by Her Majesty's Government now.' Crawford advocated that British policy should work towards the promotion of a situation in which stability in the Gulf was maintained without a British military presence. He conceded that this involved 'considerations wider than the southern part of the Gulf, including, in the immediate foreground, the development of Iranian policy and the Iraq–Kuwait relationship, as well as, in the background, the relationship between the northern Arab countries'.[139] The Political Resident saw 'no alternative to putting our money on Saudi Arabia in the long-term as the state best able to provide the support which the Gulf States will need if they cannot count on us'.

By contrast, the British Ambassador in Iran, Sir Denis Wright, believed that future stability in the Gulf resided in 'Irano-Saudi co-operation rather than an exclusive Saudi succession'.[140] Nevertheless, Wright reported that the Shah was losing confidence in King Feisal on account of his growing conviction that Saudi Arabia would fall to Nasser. Consequently, the Shah was becoming increasingly convinced that he would have to 'go it alone' in the Gulf. Wright speculated that if the Shah failed to reach a settlement over Bahrain before Britain departed, he would take over the other disputed islands without prior consultation with the Saudis. Crawford was aghast at such possibilities. He estimated that if the Shah pursued a 'go it alone policy' in the Gulf, coupled with plans to seize islands, he would 'unite all Arabs against him and risk bringing closer the day of confrontation across the Gulf with hostile governments, whether Nasserite or other'.[141] Although in making these calculations Crawford was anticipating the day when Britain would leave the Gulf, he evidently perceived this would be sufficiently far in the future to permit a measured withdrawal and one which would facilitate the preservation of British interests. He drew a clear contrast with South Arabia where the insignificant nature of Britain's economic stake permitted it to take 'sizeable risks' with the stability of the territory by bringing to a precipitate end relationships with the rulers.[142] 'I do not think we could possibly take the same risks in the Gulf,' he asserted. The eventual termination of Britain's relationship with the Gulf Rulers, he continued, had to be handled with 'greater care' in order to ensure that there was a 'smooth transition from one security system to another'. The Political Resident envisaged that this was 'bound to be a lengthy and slow process' in which it was essential to keep the confidence of the Rulers and the governments of the other littoral states. 'We must be careful not to inflict shocks on them by abrupt changes of policy and we must try to carry them with us as our policy evolves', he urged.

Crawford was strongly opposed naming a date for British withdrawal.[143] First, he contended that such a strategy would 'frighten the Rulers and reduce their readiness to co-operate with us in developing their States to the point where they would no longer need our protection'. In the second place, he postulated that a commitment to withdraw by a particular date would

> give encouragement to all those who are dissident and in one way or another working against the existing Rulers. . . . More generally, activity and propaganda by the revolutionary Arab States would be encouraged and the chances of a smooth transition to a new security system after withdrawal would be hampered.

In addition, advance publicity risked removing 'any chance of settling any of the territorial disputes in the area before we left and therefore increase the chances of instability afterwards'. Crawford also feared that advance publicity on withdrawal would jeopardize the readiness of British expatriates to continue serving in the police. More generally, he felt that 'the situation in the Southern Gulf, which is developing in a reasonably satisfactory way already, should continue to evolve and get into a generally firmer state before any further major shocks are administered'. In making this recommendation, the Political Resident had in mind the state of agitation which Britain's imminent departure from South Arabia had engendered among the Gulf Rulers. Referring to recent assurances to the Rulers that forces would be built up in the Gulf to enable Britain to fulfil its commitments there following the withdrawal from South Arabia, the Political Resident concluded that 'An early indication that we had gone into reverse, even if related to a date some years hence, would destroy their faith in our good word'. In these circumstances, Crawford perceived the imminent visit of the Minister of State at the FO, Goronwy Roberts, to the Gulf as 'particularly timely'.[144] He recommended that Roberts use 'the most forthcoming and forward-looking formula possible to convince the Rulers of our determination to stay here until we are satisfied that there are . . . alternative arrangements for ensuring the stability of the area'. In this way, Crawford hoped that it would be possible to 'convince them that they can count on us for as long ahead as it is reasonable to look at present'. He also warned against pressing the Rulers too hard over strengthening their links with Saudi Arabia on the grounds that they would interpret this as a sign that Britain was trying to 'shuffle off' its responsibilities.

In conversation with the British Ambassador in Jedda, Morgan Man, Feisal confirmed that Saudi Arabia had 'no territorial designs on the Gulf States and wanted them to keep their independence'.[145] However, the King confessed he had warned the Rulers that Britain would 'not be staying in the Gulf for ever' and that consequently they should 'stop squabbling amongst themselves and form a cohesive unit against the tide of revolution'. Although Man emphasized Britain's determination to fulfil its commitments to the Rulers and rejected the idea of early withdrawal from the Gulf, Feisal perceptively commented that 'there was no guarantee that if we said one thing one day, we would not say something else the next'. The prophetic nature of the King's words were exposed by Goronwy Roberts' two visits to the Gulf, the first in November 1967, the second two months later.

The Rulers were looking to Roberts to set their minds at rest about Britain's intention to remain for the foreseeable future, their nervousness on this question having been fuelled by the unfolding South Arabian debacle and by less than reassuring noises that were emanating from a number of sources, including King Feisal and certain sections of the British press. Although the Deputy Political Resident, H. G. Balfour-Paul, realized that it would be unwise for Roberts to be drawn on precise dates (not least because of the risk of exposing Britain to future charges of breaking its word), he did hope that the FO Minister would be able to tell the Rulers that Britain expected to stay until the mid-1970s.[146] While he felt that it was too early to start talking about mini-states, much less the ultimate number of them, he did think it appropriate for Roberts to inform the Rulers of the larger states that Britain looked forward to their emergence on the international scene. Significant aspects of Balfour-Paul's proposals were reflected in the briefs prepared by the FO for Roberts' visit to the Gulf. 'It has . . . become extremely important,' asserted the FO, 'to convince the Rulers that HMG have no intention of abandoning their declared policy of maintaining an effective presence in the Gulf until the stability of the area has become such that our eventual withdrawal will not affect it adversely'.[147] On the question of bringing the Gulf States closer together, the FO confessed: 'we have been frustrated by inter-state rivalries and jealousies, and although we continue to preach the virtues of co-operation to the Rulers we no longer regard formal association as a realistic policy objective'.[148]

Roberts' visit to the Gulf and Iran took place in the first half of November 1967.[149] On his return he described his objectives as having been to reassure the Rulers that the British presence would continue as long as it was necessary to maintain peace and stability in the area, to urge the Rulers to accelerate the modernization of their administrations, and to encourage them to co-operate among themselves and resolve their differences. The dissemination of the first objective was, according to Roberts, 'welcome everywhere'. 'The Rulers have undoubtedly been very anxious especially in view of events in South Arabia', he added. Deviating from the FO brief, Roberts stressed: 'We must decide as soon as possible what form a closer association should take and, having decided, press forward with advice, encouragement and even pressure to this end.' Roberts was also keen to incorporate the larger neighbouring states into this pattern and in pursuit of this aim called in the Saudi and Kuwaiti ambassadors on his return to London for discussions.[150]

Crawford, however, remained sceptical, stressing the dangers of devising forms of association which he described as 'outside the realm of practical possibilities'.[151] Even so far as the more modest objective of promoting a Trucial States union was concerned, the Political Resident concluded that 'the smaller States will not merge themselves voluntarily in the immediate future and . . . there is no action open to us, within the framework of our general policy, to compel or encourage them to do so'.[152] Maintaining the logic of this position, Crawford argued strongly against bringing all seven Trucial States together.

> It would [he wrote] demand political and administrative skills from the participating States which they simply do not possess. It would leave unresolved rivalry between Abu Dhabi and Dubai. It would be at variance with Shaikh Zaid's refusal to allow any derogation from his sovereignty in Abu Dhabi and with his ambition that his State should cut a figure on the international scene.[153]

Instead he favoured the separation of Abu Dhabi from the rest of the Trucial States and the eventual grouping of the five small states under Dubai's leadership. Not surprisingly, Crawford saw little prospect of an association between the four principal states (Bahrain, Qatar, Abu Dhabi, and Dubai). 'Apart from the Rulers' mutual suspicions and rivalries . . . , and the absence of any will for association on their part,' he asserted, 'their States simply have not the political capability for operating the complex arrangements which organic association would be bound to entail.'[154] Crawford favoured a less ambitious approach in which the Rulers were brought together with a view to 'improving mutual understanding and co-operation.' This gradualist approach was torpedoed by the decision to withdraw from East of Suez in the wake of the devaluation of sterling.

In the light of his assurances delivered in November, Roberts' return to the Gulf just two months later to inform the Rulers of Britain's intention to withdraw from the Gulf by March 1971 came as a profound shock.[155] They were aggrieved by the lack of consultation and by the fact that no alternative security arrangements had been made.[156] The Ruler of Qatar's reaction was 'vehement', charging Britain with ignoring its responsibilities in the Gulf.[157] Qatar, Bahrain, and Dubai all objected strongly to a date of departure being included in the official announcement scheduled for 16 January. 'In the light of [the] South Arabian experience,' explained Crawford, 'they consider that this is bound to encourage subversive elements, frighten away foreign investors and increase difficulties all round.'[158] Shaikh Rashid reflected the dismay of his fellow Rulers when he condemned 'the decision, its timing and presentation and impending announcement of a date'.[159] Although producing a more measured response, Shaikh Isa of Bahrain fretted about the implications of Britain's departure for the economy of the island and for its position *vis-à-vis* Iran.[160]

In subsequent discussions, however, the full fury of the al-Khalifah became apparent.[161]

'To put it bluntly', remarked the Political Agent, A. D. Parsons,

> the Ruler and his brothers consider that they have been betrayed by an unvarnished volte face only two months after the reassurance of November 1967; and that they are being faced with the sudden and unilateral termination of 150 years of mutual relationship with no warning or genuine consultation.

They were 'highly sceptical of the chances of the Gulf States getting together to form a meaningful unity or of Iran allowing Bahrain to be included in any Gulf-wide mutual security system'. Shaikh Khalifah accused Britain of abandoning Bahrain to be 'kicked like a football between the players in the Gulf game'. Furthermore, the Gulf Rulers regarded the three or four years before Britain's departure as a 'derisory period' in which to resolve the disputes and claims which had lasted 'for generations', to create a defensive system amongst a set of states the largest of which was 'incapable of defending itself', and for Bahrain to construct the minimum defence force necessary for internal and external security. Worryingly for the future of Gulf unity, Parsons reported that it was clear the al-Khalifah were 'already thinking in terms of mini-statehood for Bahrain with a defence treaty with Saudi Arabia as the best and most practical of a bad lot of alternatives'. The British government's intention to announce publicly withdrawal rankled almost as much as the decision itself, the al-Khalifah fearing that it would create pressures which would not merely militate against the formation of a valid system to replace British protection, but also stimulate 'disturbances and terrorism in Bahrain on the Aden model'. Towards the end of January 1968 the mood in Bahrain had barely improved, Parsons reporting that the Ruler and his advisers were still in a state of 'bewildered resentment'.[162] Even at this early stage, the Political Agent recorded that the prevailing opinion was in favour of Bahrain's entry into the United Nations as a mini-state, coupled with a Saudi defence guarantee. Scepticism was felt towards closer association between the states of the Lower Gulf on the grounds that, such was the animosity between Saudi Arabia and Abu Dhabi, this arrangement would risk alienating King Feisal.

In Kuwait there was equal bewilderment. The Amir of Kuwait was 'stunned and surprised' by the sudden reversal of British policy, conveying uneasiness about the future of the states of the Lower Gulf.[163] These concerns were elaborated upon by the Kuwaiti Foreign Minister, Shaikh Sabah al-Ahmad.[164] Three years, he argued, was not long enough to permit the Gulf States to stand on their own feet. He did not accept the British premise that Iran was a source of stability and predicted that the Iranians would take action 'prejudicial to the Gulf States and to the interests of Her Majesty's Government'. In particular, he feared Iranian infiltration into the southern shore of the Gulf in order to establish a foothold on the Arab side. Ominously, Shaikh Sabah prophesied that British withdrawal would 'make way for Soviet influence, which was already spreading fast in the Yemeni Republic and South Yemen'. Underlying Kuwaiti fears was anxiety that the chaos left in the wake of a precipitate British departure would damage the security of Kuwait itself. As regards the popular reaction to the withdrawal announcement, the British Ambassador in Kuwait (G. G. Arthur) recalled that 'Nearly everybody was puzzled and severely shaken: the crucial if unacknowledged pivot of Kuwait's international existence was being taken away'.[165] One merchant told Arthur the British decision was the 'greatest misfortune Kuwait had ever suffered, far surpassing the war in Palestine', while a prominent banker predicted that after Britain's departure 'it would only be a matter of time before Kuwait was annexed to Iraq'.[166]

King Feisal's reaction to the reversal of British policy enunciated just two months earlier was calm and statesmanlike.[167] Saudi policy, he declared, 'welcomed co-operation with all her neighbours and would not object to any alliance especially among those in the South East from Abu Dhabi to Muscat'. For his part, Roberts assured the King that the British government wanted to do 'everything possible to prevent the emergence and success of revolutionary activity'. Although there was no intention to 'impose a system' on the Gulf States, Roberts committed Britain to assisting in the creation of 'the best possible successor system, both for external defence and internal security'. Shaikh Zaid of Abu Dhabi, who some months earlier had predicted that a swift British withdrawal would cause chaos in the Lower Gulf,[168] was quick to embrace this concept.

In conversation with his Political Agent,[169] A. T. Lamb, Zaid pledged himself to embark upon persuading the other Trucial Rulers 'to accept co-operation and togetherness'. His hope was that it would be possible to propose a programme which would ensure that the Trucial States could be 'developed as one unit in the eyes of the world capable of looking after itself when the time eventually came for HMG to withdraw its military forces from the Gulf'. Zaid emphasized the importance of impressing upon the other Rulers that 'whether the British withdrawal took place in three, five or ten years' time it was going to happen and they must begin organizing themselves now, not in six months' time'. He perceived the Trucial Council to be the appropriate 'unifying body'. While conceding that Trucial Oman could 'almost certainly exist and survive as a unit', the Abu Dhabi Ruler was keen to point out that 'a practical union between Trucial and Sultanate Muscat and Oman would ensure the continued existence of the whole of Oman'. Reading between the lines, Lamb cast doubt on the altruistic foundations of Zaid's thinking.

> There is [he wrote] . . . a qualification in his mind when he speaks of a practical union of Trucial Oman based on and operating through the

> Trucial Council. What he means here – and it is understandable in present circumstances that he is thinking principally of his own and Abu Dhabi's interests – is that he can only ensure the integrity of his own country if he has the whole of Trucial Oman under his control. He is asking us to back him to bring about, to a Zaidi design prepared with our assistance, a stable political and economic system in Trucial Oman which will safeguard Abu Dhabi's interests and, therefore, because of the immense wealth which is coming to him and which he is willing to spend in a Zaid-dominated Trucial Oman, also in the interests of the area as a whole.

No doubt hoping to attract British support for his designs, Zaid expressed confidence in being able to prevent the UAR from spreading dissension provided that he had a united Trucial Oman, plus the willing co-operation of the Sultan, behind him.

One possible impediment to Zaid's designs was Shaikh Rashid of Dubai who feared an Abu Dhabi takeover. Certainly, Zaid's perplexed reaction to the concept of sharing sovereignty did not augur well for genuine political co-operation.[170] Rashid was thought to prefer a loose form of association, possibly including Bahrain and Qatar, which would not merely allow him to maintain his close links with Saudi Arabia, but also to pursue his ambition of absorbing the smaller Trucial States into Dubai.[171] Crawford prophesied that closer association would 'come up against the serious problem of Rashid/Zaid rivalry'.[172] Equally, Zaid predicted that Rashid's apprehensions would make it difficult for him to co-operate with the other Trucial Rulers. Initially, however, the Dubai Ruler was in the vanguard of moves towards unity.

Towards the end of January 1968, he informed Crawford that he had had meetings with all the Gulf Rulers, the upshot being that the four principal ones had agreed on holding an early meeting in Dubai to consider the problems presented by the British decision to withdraw. Rashid justified such a meeting on the grounds that it was important for the Rulers to be seen by their people to be 'taking an energetic grip of the situation and were acting in unison'.[173] A more immediate reason for a gathering of Rulers was the need to discuss the possibility, already raised by the Rulers of Bahrain, Qatar, and Abu Dhabi,[174] of providing a financial contribution to the cost of Britain's forces in the Gulf in the hope of prolonging the British presence there. Although in public Crawford reacted cautiously to this prospect, informing Rashid that HMG would 'not wish to tie themselves either to staying indefinitely or to making their withdrawal subject to the veto of the Rulers', in private he told the FO that he supported the Rulers' proposal.[175] 'If we accept and thus can get away from the situation in which there is a fixed and final date for our presence here,' he expatiated, 'the whole political situation would be greatly eased.'[176] Injudicious remarks by Defence Secretary Healey, however, clouded the issue.

When questioned about the Rulers' offer during an interview with the BBC's *Panorama* programme, Healey dismissed it with the comment that

> I don't very much like the idea of being a sort of white slaver for Arab Sheikhs . . . I think it would be a great mistake if we allowed ourselves to become mercenaries for people who would like to have a few British troops around.[177]

Crawford was aghast at the Defence Secretary's bluntness, describing the possible effect of his words on the Rulers as 'catastrophic'.[178] 'Apart from feeling revulsion at terms used,' he explained, 'they will see it as totally at variance with statements made to them by the Minister of State on behalf of Her Majesty's Government in November that our military presence was based on our joint interest with the Rulers in the stability and peaceful development of the area.' The fact that no formal reply had been given to the Rulers merely exacerbated the affront. Crawford suggested that the only way of repairing the damage was to issue a public statement that the government was actively considering the Rulers' offer. Healey duly ate humble pie, apologizing for any offence he may 'unintentionally have given'.[179]

The Defence Secretary's earlier asperity notwithstanding, there was a growing consensus in opposition to acceptance of the Rulers' offer. Quite apart from potential problems surrounding command and control, the Arabian Department's Head, M. S. Weir, pointed out that it would be beyond the ability of the Rulers to offset the real costs of maintaining British forces in the Gulf[180] since the normally quoted figure of between £12m and £20m, which only covered foreign exchange expenditure, was in fact much higher.[181] Another official commented that 'it would be a mistake to get ourselves into the position of dependence on the Rulers which acceptance of the offer would imply'.[182] Summing up, the Permanent Under-Secretary of State at the FO, P. H. Gore-Booth, wrote:

> The important point is that, while we may regret the earliness of the date, and more especially its announcement, there is agreement on the general nature of the policy; and a limited extension paid for by somebody else does not really offer anything attractive politically.[183]

T. F. Brenchley of the Arabian Department had already noted that the Treasury had shown no interest in the offset idea while the MoD was strongly opposed to it.[184] In these circumstances, it is not surprising that Roberts' last minute attempt to revive the Rulers' proposal was firmly quashed by the Foreign Secretary, George Brown.[185]

The FO's use of military and economic arguments to justify the rejection of financial assistance from the Rulers[186] was not without its problems, however. Since they considered that the withdrawal decision was essentially a political one, the Chiefs of Staff were reported to be 'irritated' by this ploy.[187] The al-Khalifah were of a similar opinion,[188] the British rejection of the offset offer merely confirming them in their suspicions about the true motives behind British decision-making. Indeed, the Bahraini sense of betrayal remained unabated. The modification of policy to the extent that Britain would remain in the Persian Gulf until the end of 1971 did little to ease Bahraini worries. '[T]he emotion which is common to all and most strongly felt at all levels is fear of Iran coupled with a determination not to be taken over by any country', recorded Parsons. While Kuwaiti economic achievements were admired, the al-Khalifah looked upon the possibility of Kuwaiti leadership as 'a joke'. Fears about the power vacuum which Britain's departure would leave were compounded by uncertainties over the economic effects of the British decision. A loss of confidence on the part of foreign investors at a time when Bahraini development plans were beginning to come to fruition were especially worrying. Parsons concluded that all these considerations had led the al-Khalifah to the conclusion that Bahrain's only chance was to 'stand alone – buttressed if possible by a defence agreement or understanding with Saudi Arabia – as a full member of the United Nations'. The other states, however, pushed ahead with bringing their territories together, Britain's withdrawal decision providing the drive for unity with new momentum and urgency.

While M. S. Weir admitted that there could be 'no question of trying, or even being thought to be trying, to promote another "Whitehall Federation" on the lines of South Arabia', he did note that the Rulers' reaction to the shock of the withdrawal decision suggested that a number of them 'may be willing to contemplate surrendering part of their independence in return for the security which membership of a larger unit would offer them'.[189] Indeed, it took the shock of Britain's precipitate announcement of its intention to leave the Gulf to jolt the moribund federal idea back into life. The immanent and endemic rivalries which exemplified relations between the Gulf States had placed an apparently implacable obstacle to greater co-operation. Indeed, the mirage of unity at the time of the Dubai meeting of Rulers in July 1965 was soon exposed by the vexed question of creating a single Gulf currency. The high level of internal autonomy which the Rulers had enjoyed under British protection also militated against notions of pooling, or sharing, authority and responsibility. Growing British doubts about federalism in general, and its applicability to the Gulf States in particular, further undermined closer association. Ultimately, the drive for unity came from the Trucial States themselves, the resulting United Arab Emirates resting on an accommodation between the two leading states, Abu Dhabi and Dubai.

4 Unity and division in the Lower Gulf

The emergence of the United Arab Emirates

In view of the decidedly modest achievements in the field of co-operation over the previous couple of decades, the prospects for unity looked necessarily bleak following Britain's announcement at the beginning of 1968 of its intention to leave the Gulf within four years. To make matters worse, the region's two principal power brokers, Iran and Saudi Arabia, tended to hinder, rather than help, the drive for closer association among the protected states, not least because of their pursuit of unresolved territorial disputes. Although Iran's abandonment of its claim to Bahrain in May 1970 certainly eased tensions, William Roger Louis' claim that the resolution of this problem 'broke the deadlock over Qatar and the Trucial States as well as Bahrain itself',[1] is something of an exaggeration. Fearful of the Saudi reaction, it took over a year of agonizing for first Bahrain, and then Qatar, to edge towards a decision in favour of separate status. Equally, the principal proponent of unity, Shaikh Zaid of Abu Dhabi, continued to hope for a union of nine including Bahrain, not least to counter-balance the perceived disruptive influence of Qatar. While Bahrain's drift towards independence persuaded Zaid of the merits of a union of seven, rather than one of eight including the troublesome Qataris, the emergence of the United Arab Emirates in the second half of 1971 essentially rested on an accommodation between Zaid and Shaikh Rashid of Dubai which had been prefigured by their actions in the immediate aftermath of Britain's withdrawal decision.

Although the Political Resident, Sir Stewart Crawford, had earlier dismissed the idea that naming a date for departure would concentrate the minds of the Rulers on what had to be done for the period thereafter,[2] Abu Dhabi and Dubai were quick to react to the British policy change, announcing on 18 February their unification. Just a week later a hastily convened meeting of all nine Rulers took place in Dubai. However, it quickly became apparent that the rulers of the major states had different conceptions of how unity should be pursued.[3] Shaikh Zaid insisted that accession to the Abu Dhabi–Dubai union by the other states was the correct path to follow. Neither Shaikh Ahmed of Qatar nor Shaikh Isa of Bahrain were prepared to accept this premise. Ahmed was particularly incensed, fearing Dubai's absorption by Abu Dhabi to the exclusion of all other ties. Despite the palpable rivalry which pervaded the meeting, an agreement was signed by all nine Gulf Rulers which established certain principles for future co-operation on the basis of a Union of Arab Emirates (UAE).[4] First, it was agreed that there would be unification of foreign representation, which implied that the Union would form a single entity for international purposes. Moreover, the states committed themselves to organizing collective defence, including a joint duty to defend one another from external aggression.

The Rulers' ability to reach agreement was attributable in no small measure to Shaikh Rashid who was described by the Political Agent in Dubai, D. A. Roberts,[5] as 'manipulating the meetings and keeping his peers together by blurring the issues'. The most conspicuous example of this was in the tacit understanding not to force the issue of whether or not the Abu Dhabi–Dubai union subsisted, a question on which Rashid remained 'studiously ambiguous'. Another factor which militated against the breakdown of talks was the Rulers' recognition that if the meeting did not produce some kind of agreement, they would 'cut a poor figure and be exposed to public ridicule and anger'. Summarizing the results of the Rulers' gathering, Roberts observed that although Shaikh Zaid had gained vital support in the Buraimi dispute through agreement by all to come to each other's assistance in the event of aggression, doubt had also been cast on the Abu Dhabi–Dubai union. While Roberts saw the meeting and the resulting agreement as 'by no means negligible achievements', he was not sanguine about the chances of its implementation. 'No one who has had to deal with a meeting of the seven Rulers of the Trucial States', he remarked, 'is likely to be optimistic about the prospects of successful meetings of the nine Rulers of the Lower Gulf.' Nevertheless, Roberts felt able to conclude that 'the Rulers have taken one step forward and things can never be quite the same again'. The cracks which had been papered over so thinly during the February meeting, however, were soon exposed.

Shaikhs Isa and Khalifah of Bahrain were sceptical about the results of the meeting. They confessed to their Political Agent, A. D. Parsons, that they had only participated to avoid being the 'odd man out'.[6] With regard to the Dubai agreement, they were equally candid, admitting that they would 'play along with it for presentational reasons but would at the same time continue to pursue their preparations for their own alternative – mini-statehood'. A few days later, Isa confidently predicted that the agreement would 'run into the sand', and admitted that the only reason he had put his name to it was to prevent the meeting from 'breaking up in obvious disorder'.[7] Parsons observed that Isa and Khalifah were merely paying 'lip service to the desirability of Trucial States unity', and were 'clearly not prepared to stand up and be counted with Zaid'.[8] He ascribed this attitude partly to al-Khalifah tribal jealousy which resented any Ruler (in this case Shaikh Zaid) becoming 'too big for his boots'. Parsons went on to remark that Isa and Khaifah suspected Britain of engineering the Abu Dhabi–Dubai union, support for which they regarded as 'in some way a criminal offence'. Such was the level of suspicion that when Khalifah found Deputy Political Resident Balfour-Paul talking to Zaid in the latter's majlis, he made it sound as though he had 'stumbled on the Gunpowder plot'.[9] Problems with the Dubai agreement stemmed not merely from Bahraini scepticism, but also from Qatari dissimulation.

The main driving force behind the Dubai agreement was Qatar and its Ruler Shaikh Ahmed. The Bahrainis were convinced that his only real objective was to wreck the union between Dubai and Abu Dhabi and detach Rashid from Zaid,[10] a view shared by Sir Stewart Crawford.[11] Ahmed, Crawford speculated, may also have reached the conclusion that if the Abu Dhabi–Dubai union succeeded and attracted to it the other smaller states, Qatar would be isolated with nowhere to go except absorption by Saudi Arabia.[12] The inference which Crawford drew from this was that Ahmed might see Qatar's interest as best protected by 'preserving a multiplicity of small States in the Southern Gulf, with a loose union between them'. R. H. M. Boyle (Political Agent, Qatar) identified more sinister reasons for the Qatari actions, namely the guiding hand of Saudi Arabia.

In Boyle's opinion, Saudi Arabia had no intention of shelving the Buraimi issue and perceived the Union as a vehicle for pursuing their claims to this disputed territory.[13] 'The Saudis', he expounded, 'must feel that they can get nowhere with us over Buraimi, and hope that they will now be able to side-track us by dealing with Abu Dhabi through the other Rulers.' Indeed, Boyle conjectured that Saudi Arabia would exert pressure on the Rulers of Bahrain, Dubai, and Qatar to persuade Shaikh Zaid to accept a compromise over Buraimi, the *coup de grace* being that 'it would be better for him to agree now, while the British are still here, than to wait until 1971'. Although Boyle recognized that he was relying heavily on speculation, he did point out that Ahmed's 'quite extraordinary anger' over the Abu Dhabi–Dubai agreement was comprehensible if Saudi Arabia had been 'the prime mover' in sponsoring a wider union, with Qatar as its instrument. Other pieces of circumstantial evidence gave Boyle's theory further credence. Shortly after the conclusion of the Dubai agreement, Ahmed gave him notice that he intended to visit King Feisal shortly.[14] Crawford had also earlier reported that, along with Shaikh Ahmed, the main drive for agreement covering all nine states had come from the Saudi Ambassador in Kuwait.[15] The Political Agent in Abu Dhabi, A. T. Lamb, reported that Shaikh Zaid was haunted by the spectre of a 'Saudi dominated Lower Gulf with Abu Dhabi as the prize to be picked off by Saudi Arabia when it wishes'.[16]

In addition to the complications associated with the rivalries and differing priorities of the major Gulf States, problems also rose over the minor states. Shaikh Muhammad of Fujairah complained that Bahrain, Qatar, Abu Dhabi, and Dubai had dominated the February meeting and that the five others had been confronted with an agreement which they were only given about an hour to consider.[17] Consequently he regarded his signature as provisional and felt free to withdraw it if the future trend of events was not to his liking. Aside from the procedure, the Fujairah Ruler also disapproved of Ahmed of Qatar's suggestion that the five smaller states should be represented by a single ruler and have just one vote. 'The so-called big four', avowed Muhammad, 'were only big because they happened to have struck oil. This did not entitle them to more votes or to a more flattering description of themselves.'[18]

Taking into account the myriad difficulties which the Rulers' gathering had revealed, the FO was far from sanguine about the prospects for a workable nine-member union. D. M. Day (Assistant Private Secretary to the Foreign Secretary) dismissed the Dubai agreement as having been devised and announced with 'characteristic Arab lack of preparation'.[19] Although he accepted that a union of all nine would be a 'perfectly acceptable successor arrangement' after the British withdrawal, he identified the Bahraini plan for separate statehood and the apparent Qatari intention to wreck the Abu Dhabi–Dubai union as potential stumbling blocks. Day did, however, accept that independence for three of the four main Shaikhdoms (presumably Bahrain, Qatar, and Abu Dhabi) was 'equally viable' and 'perhaps more realistic'. The problems identified by Day were not slow in manifesting themselves.

Shaikh Isa openly admitted to his Political Agent, A. D. Parsons, that he believed the UAE would fail and that Bahrain's only possible future resided in independent statehood as a member of the UN.[20] Isa, however, found himself in an awkward position. On the one hand, he could not risk being seen to be 'crabbing' the UAE in the light of favourable public opinion in Bahrain and pro-union propaganda emanating from Cairo. On the other, he hoped that not much more time would be wasted on 'flogging the UAE horse'. Although Shaikh Khalifah bin Sulman had warmer feelings towards the UAE, both Ruler and Deputy Ruler regretted signing the Dubai agreement and were alarmed by the rivalries which had emerged on the Trucial coast.

With Britain's departure imminent, competition for the loyalty of the five northern states intensified. Shaikh Zaid's wealth clearly gave him an advantage in this regard. Shaikh Rashid complained bitterly that Zaid was using his money to seduce the Bedouin from their Rulers and threatening the latter that if they did not accept aid on his terms, he would deal direct with the people.[21] Although Crawford warned Zaid against such practices, Rashid claimed that they continued unabated.[22] If Zaid's aim was to draw the Rulers of the smaller states into the Abu Dhabi–Dubai union, his plan showed early signs of success. By the end of March 1968, he had obtained the Ruler of Fujairah's accession to the union, along with a commitment by the Ruler of Sharjah also to accede.[23] Although Zaid insisted that the unity of the Trucial States rested on the friendship of Abu Dhabi and

Dubai,[24] his actions had the effect of alienating Rashid. The Dubai Ruler came to the conclusion that Zaid was seeking to establish himself as the 'King' of the Trucial States, a view shared by Shaikh Ahmed of Qatar.[25] Zaid's approach to unity also threatened Ahmed's vision of a federation of all nine states. In keeping with his previously expressed views, Boyle surmised that Ahmed was acting in concert with, or under instruction from, Saudi Arabia, adding that 'the background to the whole matter is . . . Buraimi and the Saudi determination to dominate the region from Bahrain to the Sultanate [of Oman] after we are gone'.[26] Far from looking askance at growing Saudi sway, Boyle argued that 'If our influence in Arabia and economic interests in the Gulf are to survive, we must do our best to come closer to Saudi Arabia.' 'If we were able to reassure Saudi Arabia about our support for the UAE, and involve ourselves more deeply in it,' he continued, 'I feel we would be nearer achieving the continuance of stability in the Gulf, which all of us, not excluding Iran, so badly want.' In Boyle's opinion, Saudi Arabia would be less likely to interfere with a union of nine rather than one of seven, with Qatar and Bahrain on their own. He added that Iranian claims to Bahrain would be blunted if the state were incorporated into the UAE. Boyle did recognize, however, that his advocacy of a union of all nine Gulf States had been partly induced by the 'brain-washing' to which he was subjected by the Ruler and Deputy Ruler of Qatar.

A close union of the nine, however, did not fit in with Shaikh Zaid's vision for the future of the Gulf. 'It has been clear for some little time', observed E. F. Henderson of the Bahrain Residency, 'that the Ruler is absolutely determined to go for a unity of the seven in which he plays the dominant part'.[27] Zaid merely referred to the nine 'en passant',[28] and was only prepared to countenance a looser unity of all the states, with little or no relinquishment of sovereignty to the central authority.[29] With the exception of Boyle, who by his own admission was strongly influenced by the Qataris, British thinking tended to support Zaid's position. Following Crawford's discussions at the FO at the end of March 1968, it was agreed that Britain should 'discreetly' use its influence towards making the Union a loose confederation, linking Bahrain and Qatar with a more closely united Trucial States.[30] More specifically, and no doubt with the Abu Dhabi Ruler in mind, Henderson asserted that 'the Trucial Coast must be dominated by one man'.[31] This shift of emphasis contrasted with the policy outlined in mid-1967,[32] and confirmed in the immediate aftermath of the withdrawal decision,[33] of aiming for the independence of four mini-states – Bahrain, Qatar, Dubai, and Abu Dhabi – with the five smaller Trucial States attaching themselves to either Dubai or Abu Dhabi. While the FO conceded that this would be a 'sensible outcome', it admitted, no doubt drawing on the experience of failed federations elsewhere in the empire, that it would be counter-productive to try and impose such a system.[34]

Apart from reticence about taking anything that would constitute the initiative, a number of obstacles stood in the way of the achievement of Britain's chosen outcome for the Gulf. 'Only Zaid's aim corresponds with our preferred objective,' commented Crawford, 'but he is concentrating his activities in the Trucial States and doing nothing effective in the wider field.'[35] The Political Resident also chided Zaid for 'pressing too hard to get results and . . . trying to accomplish unity in much too short a time'.[36] Such an approach, warned Crawford, merely fuelled Shaikh Rashid's fears of being subsumed by Abu Dhabi, and Ahmed's suspicions that Zaid wished to wreck the Union. Moreover, the Head of the Arabian Department, D. J. McCarthy, remarked that 'If Zaid persists in his ambitions of dominating the other six Trucial States he will provoke a natural counter alliance of Qatar, Dubai, conceivably Sharjah and presumably Saudi Arabia. Both physically and politically he would then be encircled.'[37] Zaid, nevertheless, was in uncompromising mood and refused to conciliate Rashid whom he accused of having 'intrigued against Abu Dhabi with the Saudis and Qatar for 25 years'.[38] Described by the Political Resident as 'another move in his campaign to dominate the Trucial States', Zaid also increased the rates of pay for his own military forces, the Abu Dhabi Defence Force, to double those of the Trucial Oman Scouts.[39]

The rivalry between Abu Dhabi and Dubai, coupled with the lack of enthusiasm among the other states for a loose confederation (and outright opposition to it from Qatar), led Crawford to advocate a revision of British policy along the lines of support for the emergence of a federal union of the nine. Crawford, nevertheless, stressed that in order not merely to make the new structure workable, but also acceptable to the Rulers of Bahrain and Abu Dhabi, it would have to be simple, with the responsibilities of the federal government kept few in number. As a minimum, Crawford suggested central control of foreign affairs and defence.[40]

Support for Crawford's proposed change in policy came from the Political Agent in Bahrain, A. D. Parsons. Despite its long-held doubts, Bahrain had resolved to make a determined effort to get the UAE off the ground. Parsons advocated that Britain should adopt the same approach. Although he cautioned against giving the new structure the 'kiss of death by producing British expert writers of constitutions, etc', he was firmly of the view that Britain could be seen to be neither opposed nor indifferent to the UAE, justifying his comments with respect to Arab support for the Union.[41] Goronwy Roberts was sceptical, however, voicing concerns about the possible Iranian reaction to British sponsorship of a union of all nine states.[42] On the other side of the Gulf there was little need for such qualms since King Feisal had thrown his weight behind a union. Shaikh Khalifah of Bahrain, nevertheless, surmised that the King's support derived from his determination to prevent Zaid from becoming 'too big and powerful'.[43]

Despite Roberts' reservations, D. J. McCarthy provided a powerful defence of Crawford's policy modification:

> [T]he dangers of an open breach between Qatar and Dubai on the one hand and Abu Dhabi on the other (with the latter exacerbating local feelings by buying over the smaller Trucial States) argue strongly in favour of all the States forming a single effective organism and settling their quarrels within it, rather than fighting their battles as individuals and prolonging their present unviable fragmentation. We may not later have such a good opportunity of getting the States to sink their differences and establish at least a potentially stable central Gulf authority in succession to ourselves.[44]

Such arguments proved persuasive. In relaying the decision to the British Embassy in Tehran to accept Crawford's recommendations, the Secretary of State noted that inter-state rivalries made a close union of the seven Trucial States a distant prospect.[45] Since the four principal Rulers had agreed to make a simple union of all nine states their objective, he continued, it was incumbent on Britain to provide support. In keeping with Parsons' views, the Secretary of State asserted that 'The concept of a Gulf federation has received increasing support from the rest of the Arab world and for us to withhold our encouragement would expose us to attacks on the grounds that we were seeking to divide and rule'. If the Rulers failed in their efforts to secure a union of all nine, he speculated, they would 'fall back on a group of either eight or seven, with Bahrain and possibly Qatar as separate entities, or on a general system of loose co-operation'.

The obstacles to achieving unity were exposed when the Rulers met in Abu Dhabi on 25 and 26 May 1968 to discuss the implementation of the Dubai agreement. Shaikh Ahmed of Qatar was angered by Zaid's apparent unwillingness to abandon his aim of a close federation among the Trucial States to which Qatar and Bahrain could be associated.[46] To make matters worse the Rulers split into two groups with irreconcilable views.[47] On one side, Bahrain, Abu Dhabi, Sharjah, Ajman, and Umm al Qaiwan advocated the appointment of two experts to draft a constitution for the nine as a first step towards putting the UAE on a sound footing. On the other, Qatar, Dubai, and (less enthusiastically) Ras al Khaimah, had little time for such niceties and insisted that the meeting should choose a president and decide upon the site for the capital, which in their view should be Dubai. Although this second group were prepared to accept Shaikh Zaid as president, the Abu Dhabi Ruler refused to take up this post on the grounds that he could not lead a government whose framework and powers had yet to be determined. The ostensible cause of the breakdown of the May meeting was the second group's insistence that as a first step Dubai should be accepted as the capital of the Union, a position which Zaid refused to countenance. Crawford, nevertheless, identified the continuing rivalry between Qatar and Bahrain on the one hand, and Abu Dhabi and Dubai on the other, as the underlying reason for failure.[48] Divisions were sharpened by the positioning of Abu Dhabi and Qatar at opposite poles in the Arab world, the former keeping lines open to the United Arab Republic, the latter seeking to strengthen its links with its Saudi neighbour.[49]

The suspension of the Rulers' meeting following their failure to agree was clearly a poor augury for the next scheduled gathering in early July.[50] Crawford ascribed the disinclination to compromise to the fact that no single state possessed sufficient power and influence to impose its will on the others. The two states which had the greatest claim to leadership were Bahrain and Abu Dhabi: the former, though possessing half the Arab population of the Gulf States and being perceived as culturally the most developed, was hobbled by Iranian hostility to its membership of the Union; the latter, despite its wealth, was still comparatively primitive. 'The aim of each of the states is inevitably dominated by the search for its own security,' continued Crawford, 'but the circumstances of the Big Four, the threats to which they feel exposed, and their individual relationships with Saudi Arabia and Iran, all differ; in some respects their search for security drives them apart instead of pushing them together.' In spite of these divisive factors, the Political Resident did not conclude that the UAE was a lost cause. He justified his sanguinity in a number of ways. First, none of the States was confident of being able to stand alone. Second, although interest in the Union among the politically conscious elements of the Gulf States had waned, it could always be revived again by propaganda from Cairo, Baghdad, and Kuwait, where the governments had all expressed support for the UAE. Third, the concept of a union of all nine states continued to receive the powerful backing of King Feisal of Saudi Arabia. Finally, as Crawford put it, 'there is some realisation on the part of the Rulers that the alternative to success in establishing the UAE is a situation of confusion and instability which would serve them all badly'. Despite the failure of the Abu Dhabi meeting to reach agreement, the Secretary of State was also far from dispirited about the progress of closer association. 'In terms of the prospects of continuing stability in the Gulf after our departure,' he remarked, 'the promotion of a broad understanding between the Shah and Faisal is of greater importance than early and definite progress towards the establishment of the UAE.'[51] He expressed concern that 'Dramatic developments or public pronouncements over the nine may seriously endanger the present Iranian tendency to move towards an understanding with King Faisal'. In these circumstances, and provided that the movement towards closer association did not falter entirely or irrevocably, the Secretary of State saw no particular urgency in the Rulers reaching early decisions about the shape of the UAE. New life was breathed into the movement for union from an unexpected source, however.

Kuwait had been demonstrating increasing interest in the Lower Gulf, especially since the accession of the new Amir, Shaikh Sabah. Towards the beginning of 1967, the Kuwaiti Prime Minister, Shaikh Jabir informed the British Ambassador, G. N. Jackson, that his government was considering not merely offering the Rulers of the Lower Gulf the services of

Kuwait's embassies abroad, but also urging them to adopt the Kuwaiti dinar as a common Gulf currency.[52] In further conversations, Jabir explained that his proposals relating to diplomatic representation were aimed at the Trucial States, rather than Qatar and Bahrain.[53] The Amir himself claimed that Nasser had agreed to accept the Gulf as an area of Kuwaiti influence. Despite seeing the attractions of the Kuwaiti proposals, M. C. S. Weston (Second Secretary, Foreign Office) dismissed them as 'quite unacceptable to the Rulers of the Trucial States'.[54] 'The Kuwaitis', he expatiated, 'have to date behaved so tactlessly in their dealings with all the Gulf States that the latter would . . . take the view that the Kuwaitis are among the last people they would want to represent them abroad.'

Crawford was strongly opposed to the Kuwaiti initiative. First, he noted that the Kuwaiti idea of establishing a special paternalistic relationship with the Trucial States only could potentially frustrate the British objective of bringing all the Rulers of the Lower Gulf, including Bahrain and Qatar, into closer relations with one another.[55] The tendency[56] of the Rulers of the southern states to view the al-Sabah as 'arrogant and presumptuous upstarts', coupled with the fact that Kuwait was 'too weak and far away' for its primacy to be accepted, also counted against the Amirate's drive to extend its influence. Crawford also pointed out:

> there is a widespread suspicion in the Southern Gulf that, whatever may be said for the Al Sabah family, their Governmental machine is politically unreliable as a result of thorough penetration by Egyptians whose activities the Al Sabah, for fear of falling off the political tightrope they are trying to tread, are thought to be unable to curb.

That the Rulers of the Southern Gulf fervently believed the Kuwaiti educational system and the security service to be 'riddled with Nasserite influences', inhibited effective co-operation in these fields. As an indication of this, when the Ruler of Sharjah wanted to obtain replacements for a number of 'subversive' teachers, he turned to Saudi Arabia, rather than Kuwait. Referring to the political balancing act which the Kuwaitis were forced to perform in the Arab world, Crawford highlighted that Rulers of the Southern Gulf did not wish to be 'hauled onto the tightrope itself if they can avoid it'. Since the Saudis had taken a stand against revolutionary Nasserism, the Political Resident suggested that it would be to them, rather than to the Kuwaits, that the Southern Gulf would look for long-term leadership.

Although the new British Ambassador in Kuwait, G. G. Arthur, recognized that the Southern Gulf presented a 'natural outlet for an ambitious Amir who, for all his wealth, is too weak to make his mark in the Arab world as a whole', he stressed that the strategy 'ignores the facts of power, the imperatives of Kuwait's own defence policy, and the sensitivity of the lesser states of the Gulf'.[57] This final point was underscored by Crawford's observation that

> The distaste felt by the Al Sabah for the Al Thani of Qatar is reciprocated in full measure. The Al Khalifah of Bahrain, though superficially more tolerant, deeply resent the geographical accident that has suddenly made their Kuwaiti neighbours the richest family on earth: and they would rather die than be beholden to them.[58]

On the eve of Goronwy Roberts' trip to the Gulf in November 1967, the FO dismissed the ambitious Kuwaiti initiative relating to diplomatic representation and currency as 'unrealistic because Kuwait cannot hope to exercise anything like the same influence in the area as Saudi Arabia and Iran, nor would any form of Kuwaiti hegemony be acceptable to the Gulf States'.[59] Despite the failure of Kuwait to extend its formal influence to specific areas of government and administration in the Lower Gulf, it did play a key role in providing new momentum for the stalled discussions over the creation of the UAE.

The Gulf Rulers' announcement on 27 May 1968 that they would meet again at the beginning of July was reported to have aroused little interest in the Kuwaiti press since 'few people in Kuwait think much of the UAE's chances'.[60] This may have been the case at a popular level, but at a governmental one Kuwait's interest in the Lower Gulf remained undiminished. During the Ruler of Qatar's official visit to Kuwait in mid-May, the Kuwaiti Foreign Minister, Shaikh Sabah al-Ahmad, emphasized the Amirate's support for the UAE.[61] On 10 June, moreover, a weekly paper controlled by Shaikh Sabah's private secretary argued that, while Kuwait had taken no initiative in attempts to achieve unity, it had a natural duty to despatch an envoy to the Gulf to 'bridge the chasm'.[62] Shortly after the appearance of this report, the government of Kuwait resolved to 'break the log-jam and revive momentum' in the Union, despatching the Foreign Minister to the Lower Gulf for this purpose.[63] He put a number of proposals before the Rulers of the four major states, including postponement of the contentious issue of the location of the capital and the creation of a new body, the Council of the Union. The Ruler of Dubai declared the Kuwaiti intervention 'helpful'[64] and on the basis of Shaikh Sabah's recommendations the Gulf Rulers reconvened in Abu Dhabi on 6 and 7 July.

Thanks largely to preparatory work of the Kuwaiti Foreign Minister, the meeting was generally regarded as a success. Although the Rulers took no decisive constitutional steps, the type of breakdown threatened in May had been avoided, the possibility of the Union succeeding had been kept alive, and decisions were made on the first practical steps to be taken.[65] Moreover, the deterioration in relations between the principal Rulers, especially Shaikhs Zaid and Rashid, was arrested. The main area of contention was the composition of the Council of the Union. While Qatar favoured the nomination of Shaikhs, the Bahrainis pressed for a council consisting of officials on the grounds that this would give it a more genuinely representative aspect and that the work of the Council was of a type better suited to officials than to Shaikhs.[66] The Baharainis won the argument, though Qatar nominated its Deputy Ruler, Shaikh Khalifah bin Hamad, as chairman.

The customary rivalry between Bahrain and Qatar, which the controversy over the composition of the Council of the Union highlighted, coupled with the former's continuing scepticism towards union, were less encouraging signs to emerge from the July gathering. Shaikh Khalifah bin Sulman of Bahrain told the Political Agent, A. D. Parsons, that it was 'impossible to do business with people like the al Thani'.[67] He proceeded to say that the Qataris were interested only in 'dishing Bahrain' and that he saw 'no possibility of working with them on a long term basis'. Subsequently, Parsons[68] reported that

> It has become a stock joke amongst Bahrainis that it is impossible to find anyone in the island who believes in the Union. This is certainly true of almost every member of the Ruling Family as well as the senior merchant establishment and the top echelons of Government officials. This important stratum of public opinion has been unaffected by the apparent success of the latest Rulers' meeting. Its members take the view that the Rulers only succeeded in agreeing on matters which even they were unlikely to disagree, while all the bases of contention were swept under the carpet.

Although the officials, Shaikhs, and merchants favoured the idea of Bahrain becoming a mini-state, Parsons pointed out that

> the more intelligent of them are aware of the difficulties and dangers which would be involved if Bahrain tried to break away from the UAE at this stage, particularly in the light of the emotional attachment to Gulf unity of the younger generation of Bahrainis and of the support for the union from Cairo and other Arab capitals.

On the other side of the coin, however, all Bahrainis were united in their fears of Iranian intentions. 'Although they do not consider that the UAE would provide much more of a defensive shield against Iran than Bahrain would on her own,' observed Parsons, 'they still tend to feel that Bahrain would be more seriously isolated in the face of Iranian threats as a mini-state rather than as a component of a Union.' Pressure for Bahrain's inclusion in a union of all nine came from King Feisal who made it known that he would not support any other form of union.[69] Gulf unity, however, continued to be threatened by rivalry between Shaikhs Rashid and Zaid.[70]

The obvious bonhomie between the two Rulers immediately following Britain's decision to abandon the Gulf masked deep and enduring mutual suspicion. Rashid became increasingly preoccupied by the possibility of

Zaid dominating the Trucial States. These fears were kept alive by Zaid's actions, not least his apparent determination to build up his own army, the Abu Dhabi Defence Force (ADDF), without agreeing to either a co-ordinated defence policy, or an arms programme, or a measure of shared control. Crawford speculated that in such circumstances, Rashid would not merely press ahead with his own plans for a Dubai defence force, but also break off union discussions taking Qatar, and possibly Ras al Khaimah, with him. The Political Resident viewed such an outcome with dread since it raised the prospect of Britain spending the remaining years of its presence in the Gulf 'in a sterile round of mediation between Rulers increasingly resistant to advice'. 'In the end', lamented Crawford, 'we might leave behind a situation as disorderly as we found it 150 years ago.' '[E]ven if there were just a muddle', he concluded, 'this would be a very poor basis for stability after our withdrawal'. His fears were belied by decisions taken at the United Arab Emirates' Supreme Council held between 20 and 22 October 1968.

The Rulers reached agreement on the establishment of a union force for external defence, while recognizing the right of each state to have its own local armed forces. Crawford, nevertheless, doubted whether Zaid would be willing either to limit the size of the ADDF, or transfer to the union force the strike aircraft and other sophisticated equipment which he was in the process of purchasing.[71] On a brighter note, Crawford remarked that Shaikh Ahmed of Qatar had proved an 'active and successful' chairman of the Supreme Council, and that he and Zaid got on well. Shaikh Isa, on the other hand, remained 'unenthusiastic and sceptical about the Union'.[72] Summarizing the results of the meeting, nevertheless, Boyle was distinctly upbeat, describing the Rulers' more positive approach to union as a 'break-through'.[73] The Ruler and Deputy Ruler of Qatar were especially impressed with 'Zaid's attitude of frankness and co-operation'.[74] Shaikh Khalifah bin Hamad, however, questioned Zaid's sincerity, suspecting him of still hankering after a union of the seven Trucial States which flatly contradicted the Qatari position that only a union of the nine could provide stability in the post-withdrawal period.[75] At the other extreme, the Bahraini scepticism towards union remained strong.[76] Although Shaikh Rashid of Dubai had been positive about the results of October's Supreme Council meeting,[77] lingering doubts were fuelled by a visit to the Gulf by the former High Commissioner of the South Arabian Federation, Sir Kennedy Trevaskis. Ostensibly visiting the Gulf on business, Trevaskis was in reality on a fact-finding mission for the Conservative Party. In conversations with Shaikh Rashid of Dubai he did nothing to conceal his reservations about the future of the UAE, drawing parallels with the failed South Arabian Federation.[78] The much-vaunted visit of the Shah of Iran to Saudi Arabia in November 1968 did little to give the Union added impetus.

The Shah and King Feisal recognized their 'common interest in the stability of an area in which "other people" may intrude, when British influence came to an end'.[79] Beyond such bland rhetoric, there was little real substance to the two monarchs' talks. There was dismay among Gulf Rulers at the failure of the meeting to produce anything more concrete, the Ruler and Deputy Ruler of Qatar denouncing the final communiqué as 'weak and meaningless'.[80] The Shah's refusal to permit the insertion of a phrase relating to the 'preservation of the freedom of all the states of the area', was interpreted by Shaikh Khalifah bin Sulman as a sign that the Iranian ruler did not intend to relinquish his claim to Bahrain. The conclusion he drew from this was that unless Britain was prepared to countenance some form of defence agreement with the UAE, a union of nine would be out of the question. Boyle agreed that the negative results of the Shah/Feisal meeting would 'foreshadow the end of a union of the nine'.[81] From his vantage point in Dhahran, Saudi passivity in the face of Iranian intransigence was ascribed by US Consul General Dinsmore to Feisal's overriding concern to remain on good terms with Iran, a policy to which British and American pressure had in no small measure contributed.[82] Dinsmore postulated that Britain and America had done 'too good a job in selling this policy' because Feisal seemed determined to avoid doing anything which might cause offence to the Iranians.

The failure of the Shah/Feisal encounter to produce a breakthrough had the effect of stultifying progress towards union. In view of his close involvement with the UAE, the Kuwaiti Foreign Minister, Shaikh Sabah, was especially concerned, expressing regret that progress had been so slow.[83] In examining the root cause of the stasis,[84] Crawford stressed that 'the knowledge of the Iranian attitude has been directly or indirectly, the most important factor in causing progress over the Union to be slower than it should have been'. More particularly, he conceded that 'It is now almost impossible to find anyone in Bahrain who believes that the Union will work or who wishes to participate in an organization in which Bahrain is reduced to second-class status.' The Political Resident also pointed out that the incompatibilities among the principal Rulers had, if anything, grown. Summing up, he admitted that

> The preparations are moving slowly and without impetus: none of the Rulers, other than the Ruler of Qatar who originated the scheme, shows much enthusiasm for it and it has no active support from the public; the Rulers and their advisers have had useful experience of working together but this has not yet led them into making compromises on matters of real substance for the sake of the Union, or into settling their territorial disputes; no single one of the Rulers has emerged as a natural leader of the area as a whole. . . . If the Iranian claim were settled, the prospects would probably be brighter, but it might not be easy to head the Bahrain Government off seeking the alternative aim of progress as a separate mini-State.

Referring to British attitudes towards the UAE, Crawford acknowledged that

> Our own support, while genuine, has had perforce to be muted in the interests of our endeavour to coax the Shah into working generally for a cordial relationship with the Arab States of the Gulf, and more specifically, for a negotiated settlement of his claim to Bahrain and the smaller Gulf islands.

Despite his gloomy prognosis, Crawford still favoured backing the concept of union, arguing that a successful UAE would facilitate the achievement of Britain's principal objectives in the Gulf, the first of which he identified as 'to lay the foundation of an enduring and stable political system in the Southern Gulf to survive our withdrawal at the end of 1971'. The second objective, which Crawford suggested would also contribute to the achievement of the first, entailed effecting a 'smooth and peaceful military withdrawal in such a way as to maintain the goodwill of the Rulers and their peoples towards Her Majesty's Government and to maximise the prospects for the United Kingdom of a fruitful commercial and cultural relationship with the Gulf area in the period after 1971'. The fact that, on the one hand, the Union was supported by the leading Arab countries, and on the other derived from the Gulf Rulers' own initiative, thus neutralizing the stigma of being an 'imperialist plot', counted in its favour. Consequently, Crawford advocated that Britain should

> not only continue as now to promote its success by quiet support but also, if and when the Iranian claim to Bahrain is on the way to a settlement, should adopt a more positive attitude, urge the Rulers to move faster, play if necessary a more active role, in fact take more risks in favour of the Union than we are ready to take today.

Not surprisingly, Crawford's suggestion, which amounted to no less than a major policy change, was hotly debated in the FCO. D. J. McCarthy marshalled a number of cogent arguments against more overt and active backing by Britain for the Union.[85] Quite apart from the fact that British intervention would undermine the credibility of the union by giving it the appearance of an imperialist design, McCarthy pointed out that Britain's influence with the Rulers was 'steadily diminishing', and as such any success in overcoming their 'apathy and rivalries' would be necessarily limited. In reference to the Iranian claim to Bahrain, moreover, McCarthy indicated that 'So long as Iran remains opposed to the Union we should incur Iranian hostility'. On a purely practical level, he underlined the fact that if Britain pushed through the Union against the real aspirations of the Rulers, it would in all probability collapse after the withdrawal. McCarthy's emphasis on the need for the initiative to come from the Rulers themselves was answered by Abu Dhabi and Qatar.

Zaid and Isa, who met in Bahrain in mid-March 1969, agreed that little had been achieved over the previous year.[86] In an effort to provide new momentum, Zaid and Shaikh Ahmed of Qatar met later that month. Following the encounter, Zaid declared that the 'days of talk and delay were over'.[87] He stressed that at the next Supreme Council meeting a number of key decisions would have to be taken, not least on the site of the federal capital and the appointment of the president. Shaikh Ahmed echoed these sentiments, adding that he and Zaid saw 'eye-to-eye' on all federal matters.[88] The Political Agent in Qatar, Boyle, asserted that the Zaid–Ahmed talks indicated a 'decided change in UAE thinking on the part of the more important mainland Rulers' who now wished to see the UAE take 'more coherent shape'.[89] It soon became evident that such optimism was misplaced.

When the Rulers reconvened in Doha in May, differences were as deep as ever. The principal rivalry was played out between the old adversaries, Qatar and Bahrain.[90] Qatar refused to consent to a temporary capital in Abu Dhabi unless a decision on the construction of a permanent one on the Dubai–Abu Dhabi border was taken at the same time. While agreeing to the location of the temporary capital, Bahrain proved obdurate over the location of a permanent one. This in turn fuelled Qatari fears that Bahrain was attempting to secure the Union capital for itself. In part, Bahraini intransigence stemmed from the suspicion that the other main states intended to discriminate against Bahrain in the allocation of posts within the prospective Union.[91] The Qataris[92] accused the Bahrainis of blocking decisions which were within reach and doing so in a tactless and overbearing manner. The chief culprit in this regard was Bahrain's Director of Information and Foreign Affairs, Shaikh Mohammed bin Mubarak, whose manner Crawford described as 'rather that of an argumentative undergraduate than a senior government negotiator'. Shaikh Isa's fear that Bahrain would be blamed for the meeting's failure to achieve a breakthrough prompted him to despatch his Deputy Ruler to Saudi Arabia and Kuwait to mollify these powerful proponents of union. Shaikhs Ahmed and Khalifah bin Hamad, nevertheless, claimed that the other principal Rulers shared their view that responsibility rested with the Bahrainis.

Summarizing attitudes among the four major Rulers, the Political Agent in Qatar, E. F. Henderson, remarked that the only thing which seemed certain in their minds was that this latest impasse signified the end of a union of the nine.[93] The Deputy Ruler of Qatar accused Bahrain of sabotaging the union and announced that he would 'not waste another minute over any Union which included Bahrain', floating the idea of a structure incorporating Dubai, Abu Dhabi, and Qatar which the Northern Trucial States could subsequently join.[94] Henderson endorsed Shaikh Khalifah bin Hamad's suggestion, describing the creation of a union of nine as a 'hopeless task' unless Bahrain came to terms with Iran.[95] He also warned that 'if HMG presses for the inclusion of Bahrain now she may dissipate wholly her remaining powers of influence with the other big three'. In any case, Bahraini commitment to union, never very strong, was ebbing away. As A. J. D. Stirling (Political Agent, Bahrain) put it: 'Bahrain could not run the risk of being caught at the last minute with the Union in ruins and no alternative prepared'.[96] The Ruler and Deputy Ruler of Bahrain clearly prioritized the settling of the Iranian claim, which they perceived as the main obstacle to their country's future security, over progress towards the UAE.[97] Their underlying preference for mini-statehood also contributed to the Bahrain delegation's intransigence. Even Qatar, the progenitor of the union concept, showed signs of waning enthusiasm.

Shaikh Khalifah bin Hamad, once a firm supporter of unity among all nine Gulf Shaikhdoms, had come to favour a union of the seven Trucial States to which Qatar would attach itself in some unspecified way.[98] Khalifah's volte-face stemmed principally from mounting concern that a union of the nine would not evolve by the time of Britain's departure. Khalifah had also become convinced that the inclusion of Bahrain in any overarching structure for the Lower Gulf would be impossible, not least because of the ongoing Iranian claim. Powerful backing for Khalifah's new approach came from Shaikh Zaid who, in the aftermath of the Doha meeting, appeared to have reached the conclusion that the Union would not work if Bahrain was a member.[99] During several meetings at the FCO in the summer of 1969, he pressed his case for a narrower union.[100] Khalifah, who also had talks in London at this time, was said to have 'concerted his line very carefully with Shaikh Zaid'.[101] The Deputy Ruler of Qatar gave further substance to his objections to the inclusion of Bahrain,[102] emphasizing the Iranian hostility which Bahrain's inclusion would invite. Khalifah asserted that while Qatar and Abu Dhabi would contribute financially to the union, Bahrain would simply draw from it. Despite Bahrain's financial weakness, he predicted that Bahrain would seek to dominate the union by pre-empting jobs and higher education opportunities. Khalifah predicted that Bahraini internal disequilibrium would destabilize any union of which it was a part.[103]

Khalifah's arguments clearly had some resonance in the FCO, the Foreign Secretary informing the Bahrain Residency: 'we think that if Abu Dhabi and Qatar remain agreed and could persuade Dubai to go along with them the eight could now be a proposition while prospects for the nine seem very poor'.[104] Crawford, however, continued to press the merits of the original conception of the UAE.[105] He justified this position by stressing that none of the nine, including Bahrain with its larger and more Arab population, would be strong enough to stand on its own with any confidence. Equally, the Southern Gulf States would require Bahraini manpower in order to avoid dependence on 'potentially troublesome Northern Arabs'. Quite apart from the fact that the main outside Arab pressures favoured a union of all nine, Crawford was keen to indicate that the UAE as originally conceived would 'damp down rivalries that would otherwise recur not only within the Union but also between those inside it and those outside'. This is not to say that the Political Resident discounted the possibility of a union of eight, particularly in the light of the rapprochement between Shaikhs Zaid and Ahmed. On the other hand, Crawford identified the attitude of Saudi Arabia as a potential obstacle. 'The smaller the union,' he remarked, 'the more prominent Shaikh Zaid's role in it and the greater the risk that the Saudi Government would not support it.' The force of Crawford's arguments was underscored by the fact that the Saudis had consistently favoured a union of nine.[106]

Although Crawford[107] saw some sense in a yet narrower structure consisting of the seven Trucial States alone, not least because the existing institutions (most notably the Trucial States Council and the Trucial Oman Scouts)[108] provided a certain infrastructure, he was not in favour of this solution to the Gulf's post-colonial order. In addition to the likelihood of a Trucial States union foundering on the competitive rivalry of Shaikhs Zaid and Rashid, such a structure would be 'even more likely than a Union of Eight to arouse Saudi opposition, because of the greater prominence Shaikh Zaid would have in it'. An even smaller configuration consisting of the six Northern Trucial States led by Dubai was also rejected by Crawford on the grounds that it would be unacceptable to Shaikh Zaid who was 'clearly determined to cut a figure on a larger stage than Abu Dhabi'. Dependence on Zaid for financial support also militated against the poorer Trucial States accepting a union which excluded their principal benefactor. 'Whichever way things go,' warned Crawford, 'we should seek to ensure that the decision is seen to be that of the Arab Governments concerned and not of our contriving'. This advice clashed with the growing FCO conviction, despite McCarthy's earlier scepticism, that a more pro-active stance on behalf of the British government was required.

From his own conversations with visiting Shaikhs in the summer of 1969, Goronwy Roberts became convinced that the UAE was 'at a crossroads', and left to their own devices they would not achieve a viable union.[109] Failure, he averred, would lead at best to instability, at worst 'an Aden-style situation'. As a result of such considerations, he advocated that Britain should consider a 'much more active policy' to promote agreement, and in so doing not wait upon a solution to the Bahrain-Iran problem. This approach was supported by D. Slater (First Secretary, FCO) who feared that any slackening of British pressure would not only reduce the Rulers' enthusiasm for the scheme, but also be criticized by the Saudis who already felt that Britain was not doing enough to bring the UAE to fruition.[110] This latter concern was brought to the attention of Crawford by the Foreign Secretary who wrote: 'There are already plenty of people in the area who accuse us of doing too little for the Union while doing little or nothing themselves and we do not wish to give them any justification for their complaints.'[111] Indeed, in May the Kuwaiti Prime Minister, Shaikh Jabir al-Ahmad, had described the situation in the Gulf as dangerous and exhorted the British to 'bring more pressure to bear on the Rulers in order to make the Union work'.[112] When the British took a more pro-active stance during the fateful meeting of the Supreme Council in Abu Dhabi in October, the approach miscarried.

The importance of this gathering of Rulers was widely recognized. On its eve, Shaikh Khalifah bin Hamad of Qatar expressed the view that 'a further inconclusive meeting would kill the union stone dead'.[113] So far as the British were concerned, failure was also a dangerous option. 'Many countries outside the Union', predicted McCarthy, 'would probably conclude that the Union was finished and some of them, particularly the Saudis, would try to place a major share of the blame on us.'[114] As regards outside powers, Kuwait continued to urge the British to put more pressure on the Rulers so that their leisurely preparations for federation would be expedited. In an effort to assuage doubts about the necessity of union, Kuwaiti Foreign Minister Shaikh Sabah al-Ahmad bluntly told Shaikh Rashid of Dubai that 'whoever was in power in Britain in 1971, it would be too late to reverse the decision on military withdrawal'.[115] Sabah was also a staunch advocate of a coming together of all nine Lower Gulf Shaikhdoms. Although he felt that the omens for a successful meeting were good, ominously he detected a lack of warmth between Shaikhs Zaid and Ahmed[116] which prefigured the unhappy atmosphere within the Supreme Council.

Initially, the meeting went well, largely due to the willingness of the Bahrainis to yield on certain issues they had contested at Doha in May, most notably the location of the capital which, it was agreed, would be sited in Abu Dhabi as a temporary measure, while in the fullness of time a permanent capital would be built on the Abu Dhabi/Dubai border. Less helpfully, the Rulers confirmed a decision made by the Deputy Rulers in favour of the formation of a Cabinet. This was described by the Political Agent in Abu Dhabi, C. J. Treadwell, as 'a decisive factor leading to disarray in the Supreme Council'.[117] At midnight on 21 October, the first day of the meeting, Shaikh Zaid informed Treadwell of a plot hatched by Shaikhs Ahmed and Rashid to engineer Bahrain's removal from the Union.[118] Their chosen tactic was to provoke the Bahrainis to such an extent that they would have no option but to walk out. The principal reason they gave for adopting such tactics centred on the fact that Iran dominated Qatar and Dubai strategically and they refused to risk the consequences of Iranian hostility to a member state. Although Zaid was wholly opposed to Ahmed and Rashid's approach, he was at a loss to know how to respond. Neither was the Abu Dhabi Ruler necessarily well-equipped to act as mediator. Treadwell described him as a 'rambling conversationalist . . . unpractised in the art of directing debate. His is still a Bedouin passing the time of day with friends under a tree. He will never make a point in ten minutes if he has an hour to spare.'[119]

In pursuance of their aim of driving Bahrain from the conference chamber, Qatar and Dubai set about delivering a series of slights, especially relating to the distribution of portfolios in the prospective cabinet. The Bahrainis, however, frustrated these tactics by acting with restraint. Despite being offered only minor Ministries, they neither remonstrated, nor betrayed their sense of humiliation. Their patience was tested still further when Shaikh Khalifah bin Hamid declared that the allocation of Ministries should be binding on all members for all time. At this stage, Shaikh Saqr of Ras al Khaimah made an unexpected intervention, demanding the Ministry of Defence which had been provisionally earmarked for Abu Dhabi. He also refused to consent to a plan under which each Ruler would submit to Shaikh Zaid (as President) and Shaikh Khalifah bin Hamad (as Prime Minister) the names of three people whom they considered suitable for ministerial office. Even before this display of obstinacy on the part of the Ruler of Ras al Khaimah, the Foreign Secretary, Michael Stewart, had stressed that it was 'essential not only that any break-up should be clearly the Arabs doing, but also that we should not seem to have stood idly by when it threatened'.[120] Consequently, Treadwell was authorized to intervene to try and save the meeting from breaking up without agreement. As deadlock approached, Treadwell delivered a message from the Political Resident in which the importance attached to the achievement of the UAE was underscored. Emphasis was also placed on the disappointment which would be felt in the Arab world if agreement proved elusive. The message urged the Rulers to put the goal of unity before the pursuit of individual interests.[121]

Claiming that his intervention was unwarranted, Shaikhs Ahmed and Saqr walked out of the meeting. Saqr maintained that the British advice amounted to 'dictation to the rulers and offended their Arab dignity'.[122] Although Rashid remained, he declared his unwillingness to sign anything. Ahmed was persuaded to return to the conference table, but Saqr stayed away permanently. The Rulers disbanded without signing anything meaningful, an anodyne communiqué acting as an 'admission of present failure'.[123] Treadwell was of the opinion that the Iranian claim to Bahrain was the 'main factor inhibiting Qatar and Dubai from accepting membership of a Union which included Bahrain'.[124] Although Crawford concurred with this analysis, he disagreed over the extent to which Iran played a tangible behind-the-scenes role.

From his vantage point in Iran, the British Ambassador, Sir Denis Wright, reported that while the Iranians were clearly relieved that the Rulers' meeting had not made more progress, there was 'no direct evidence that the Iranians were responsible for the attitudes of Dubai and Qatar'.[125] Treadwell was inclined to agree with this analysis, asserting that 'despite adverse official reaction in Tehran to the Rulers' early successes, there was no hint that the Iranians were in any sense represented at the conference table'.[126] Crawford treated this claim with scepticism, preferring to place a conspiratorial interpretation on the behaviour of Ahmed and Rashid. 'We can assume', he remarked, 'that the Iranian position was known to the Rulers of Qatar and Dubai before the meeting and that it was in the knowledge of this that their tactics were fixed.'[127] Indeed, Crawford speculated that Rashid might have received explicit directions from Tehran, which he had visited at the beginning of October. What was not open to doubt was the Iranian government's public expression of regret at the decisions reached in the early part of the meeting and declaration that until the position of Bahrain had been settled satisfactorily Iran would not recognize the UAE. Crawford explained Saqr's dramatic intervention in terms of his fear of Iran given its claim to the disputed Tunb islands. Treadwell took a different line, relating Saqr's conduct to rivalry with Shaikh Zaid: by allying himself with the disruptive elements at the Supreme Council, Saqr perceived an opportunity to avoid involvement in a union which he feared would be 'dominated by an enemy'.[128] Saqr's sense of inferiority and suspicion was no doubt fuelled by the fact that Zaid made 'no pretence' of treating him as an equal. Support for Treadwell's theory was provided by the Political Agent in Dubai, J. L. Bullard, who, following an interview with Saqr, recorded that 'his real objection was to the part played by Shaikh Zaid in this episode and to the dominant position which Zaid threatened to assume in the Union'.[129]

The collapse of the Abu Dhabi meeting, coming as it did on top of the failed Doha gathering in May, clearly put the realization of the United Arab Emirates in jeopardy. On his return from Abu Dhabi, Shaikh Ahmed of Qatar informed his Political Agent that his people were now 'very much against the Union and glad that the last meeting reached no conclusions'.[130] He added that he was sure that the seven Trucial States wanted neither Bahrain nor Qatar. Zaid had also become disillusioned with the concept of an all-encompassing structure for the Lower Gulf. In the aftermath of the Abu Dhabi Supreme Council, Zaid fulminated that 'The UAE had failed not because of Qatari, Dubai or Ras al Khaimah obstruction, but because it was the wrong vehicle for the nine states'.[131] He placed the blame for 'encouraging the unity of such an odd assortment of peoples', squarely on British shoulders. Nevertheless, he did pledge himself to continue to work towards a union of as many states as possible.

Despite the discouraging results of the October Supreme Council, Crawford continued to press the merits of a union of nine as the best solution for the future of the Southern Gulf States.[132] On the one hand, he observed that the best alternative, a union of eight without Bahrain, had been damaged by the strained relations between its principal advocates, Zaid and Ahmed, as a consequence of the failed October conference. On the other, the behaviour of the Rulers of Sharjah, Ajman, Umm al Qaiwain, and Fujairah had indicated that 'their future was firmly fixed to Shaikh Zaid's star'. Backing for this contention was contained in Treadwell's report on the Supreme Council's proceedings. Referring to Ajman, Umm al Qaiwain, and Fujairah, he remarked: 'Politically orientated towards Shaikh Zaid's philosophies, and no doubt well paid by him for their allegiance, they represented solid voting strength on the side of Abu Dhabi.'[133] Despite the greater independence of mind displayed by Shaikh Khalid of Sharjah, there was 'reasonable confidence in Abu Dhabi that in any future association of Emirates he would be prepared to link his destiny with Abu Dhabi'.

No doubt with the recent failure of the Supreme Council in mind, the Foreign Secretary re-asserted the orthodox position that 'the will to unite must exist first among those concerned and cannot be imposed'.[134] Surprisingly, the initiative for renewed discussions over the UAE came from the wrecker of the Abu Dhabi meeting, Shaikh Ahmed. At the end of 1969, Zaid reluctantly consented to Ahmed's request for private discussions on the UAE, the two Rulers meeting at Resila in Abu Dhabi on 12 December. They agreed to suspend further negotiation for a union of the nine for up to three months in the hope that in the intervening period the impediment of the Iranian claim to Bahrain would have been removed. If the matter had not been settled by this time, Zaid and Ahmed accepted that they should abandon Bahrain and work for a union of the eight.[135] The sincerity of Ahmed's words can be called into question, however. Henderson had already described Qatar's attempts to maintain its leading position with respect to the union as a 'pretence'.[136] 'They seem to me', he continued, 'to be more and more losing control of their destiny; and we may perhaps find them doing not much more than catering for a state of independence while continuing to look over their shoulders to see if some form of Union could not be joined with safety.'

Apart from the traditional hostility towards Bahrain, Ahmed's opposition to Bahraini inclusion in the UAE stemmed from his fear of Iran. He described King Feisal of Saudi Arabia as 'no match for the Shah', and went on to assert that 'all the governments of the Arab world lined up together . . . could not face the Iranian forces'.[137] Despite Ahmed's disparagement, Feisal was not prepared to eschew involvement in the Gulf, and urged Shaikhs Ahmed, Rashid, and Zaid not to launch a union of eight while negotiations for a long term solution to the Iranian claim to Bahrain were close to resolution.[138] Support for Feisal's position came from an unlikely source.

At the beginning of 1970, Zaid had told his Political Agent that since he could neither risk alienating Qatar and Dubai (which were firmly opposed to Bahrain's inclusion regardless of the outcome of talks with Iran), nor frustrate the wishes of the people of the Trucial States who desired integration, he favoured pressing ahead with a union of eight.[139] He later claimed that he had deliberately misled Treadwell about his intentions in case it had been leaked to Qatar and Dubai that he was against abandoning Bahrain at a time when the uncertainty over its status would have given them an excuse to break with him.[140] With the Iranian threat receding, Zaid stood firm. In talks with the Deputy Ruler of Qatar, he stood by Bahrain, brushing aside Khalifah bin Hamad's arguments in favour of excluding it from the UAE.[141] Although the Ruler of Bahrain proclaimed a union of nine to be the best political solution for the Lower Gulf, neither he nor his government were prepared to continue to play a subordinate role. Indeed, the lifting of the Iranian shadow served to embolden the Bahrainis.

The expedient of a plebiscite to determine the wishes of the Bahraini people in the face of the Shah's resurrection of Iran's historical claim to Bahrain was not one which was supported by the British. Taking into account the fact that the Bahraini Arab community of around 165,000 was divided almost equally between Sunni and Shia Arabs, to say nothing of the small Iranian community of 7,000, A. D. Parsons argued strongly against a plebiscite. The determination of popular will in this way, he argued, would 'be likely to lead directly to major civil disorder, to the necessity for the intervention of British forces and perhaps to the collapse of the regime and to our being forced to make a disorderly withdrawal'.[142] Crawford was equally sceptical about the prospects of a plebiscite, not least on account of the likely reaction of Shaikh Isa who would see in the suggestion 'an intention on our part to weaken his position' with the result that Britain's influence over him would be endangered.[143] Stressing the importance of détente between the Arabs and Iranians for the future stability of the Gulf, Foreign Secretary Stewart recognized the importance of reaching a settlement before British departure from the region. In keeping with Crawford and Parsons, nevertheless, he was doubtful about a plebiscite on the grounds that not only would the Bahrain government 'come under bitter attack from Arab opinion everywhere for putting the "Arabism" of Bahrain in question', but also such an expedient would in all likelihood 'spark off demonstrations and lead to major violence'.[144] Although the Shah had pledged not to pursue his claim to Bahrain with force, he did insist that he could not relinquish the Iranian claim 'except through internationally recognized processes'.[145] In an attempt to break the impasse, Ambassador Wright managed to persuade the Shah to turn to the United Nations to determine the will of the Bahraini people.[146] On 9 May 1970, the Security Council endorsed the resulting UN mission's report that the vast majority of Bahrainis wished to live within an independent Arab state, thus allowing a reasonably dignified withdrawal by Iran of its claim.

With a resolution to the Iranian claim imminent, Crawford had predicted that the accommodating attitude of the Bahrainis would give way to an insistence that they be treated on the basis of equality with the other three principal Shaikhdoms, especially over the distribution of ministries.[147] Crawford's analysis proved accurate, the government of Bahrain refusing to acquiesce in the unequal treatment of Bahrain which, under the shadow of the Iranian claim, they had accepted at the Abu Dhabi meeting in October.[148] In discussions with British officials in the Gulf, Shaikh Isa and his advisers asserted that 'after two years' experience it was clear to them that UAE in its present form was a non-starter and that continued efforts to establish it could only delay consideration of more practical alternatives and endanger political stability'.[149] In further talks towards the end of August 1970, Shaikh Isa told the Foreign Secretary's personal representative, Sir William Luce, that, owing to lack of progress, the Bahrain government had lost patience with the UAE and now felt the island should 'go for separate independence, particularly as there was no longer any danger from Iran'.[150] A month earlier during talks at the FCO, Shaikhs Khalifah bin Sulman and Mohammed bin Mubarak had had the opportunity to express similar sentiments to the Foreign Secretary himself.[151]

Bahrain's new found assertiveness materialized at a meeting of Deputy Rulers held in Abu Dhabi at the end of October 1970. Not only did the Bahrainis refuse to accept the establishment of the permanent capital on the Abu Dhabi–Dubai border, but also vociferously pressed the case for representation in the prospective Union Council to be on the basis of the population size of each territory. Neither this, nor Bahrain's modified proposal that a census be held before the expiration of the four-year period envisaged for the provisional constitution, proved acceptable to Qatar which persuaded the other Shaikhdoms, with the exception of Sharjah and Abu Dhabi, to vote against. Following this rebuff, the Bahrain delegation not only abstained from voting for the remainder of the meeting, but also at its conclusion proclaimed their disinclination to participate further in discussions 'before ensuring that the Constitution guarantees the rights of the people of the Union, particularly in so far as the representation of the people in the Union Council is concerned'.[152]

Both the other Rulers and the British appear to have perceived the failure of the October gathering as sounding the death-knell for a union between all nine states of the Lower Gulf. Shortly after the collapse of the Deputy Rulers meeting, Treadwell opined: 'We can now be really certain that the Union of the nine has failed and it can only be a matter of time before Bahrain declare themselves free to go their own way'.[153] In a similar vein, the Foreign Secretary, Alec Douglas-Home, concluded that 'there is no further prospect of progress with a union of nine'.[154] At the conference of Political Agents in November, it was agreed, if only because of the differences between Bahrain and Qatar, that a union of nine 'could be excluded as a real possibility'.[155] Although Zaid clung vainly to a union of the nine, the Rulers of Dubai, Sharjah, and Ras al Khaimah regarded this concept as 'dead'.[156] The Bahrainis, who proved resistant to compromise over representation, were equally sceptical about the prospects for the UAE. 'They are likely', prophesied Political Agent Stirling, 'to continue their move towards separate independence, while publicly framing their policy to allow as far as possible for various Arab and Iranian susceptibilities and for protestations of willingness to join a "proper" Union whenever it might come into being.'[157] Indeed, while Bahraini faith in the UAE had evidently evaporated, there was a strong concern to avoid incurring the blame for its demise.[158]

The return of a Conservative government in Britain on 18 June 1970 may have had some bearing on the precipitate collapse of the Union. Within days of the change of government, the Political Agent in Qatar, E. F. Henderson, remarked:

> I naturally expected the sheikhs to be overjoyed with the British election result, but their joy surpassed my expectation. This raises the very real danger that if they are not pushed soon into Union they will assume they need do nothing as the new British Government will solve all their problems for them. I have not heard their views on this point; but I have seen their mood of euphoria, and six months or so ago Khalifa [bin Hamad] told me if the Conservatives formed a government all would be well and Union would not be necessary. I naturally said if that happened Union would be just as important, but he brushed this aside.[159]

Certainly the Kuwaitis, who over the previous two years had assiduously promoted closer association in the Lower Gulf, claimed that uncertainty over whether or not Britain would retain a presence in the Gulf had discouraged the Rulers from working wholeheartedly for Union.[160] The Kuwaitis also blamed the British for being 'too soft on the Rulers'.[161] Certainly, the FCO remained chary about taking the initiative in the drive for integration.

In May 1970, the Parliamentary Under-Secretary of State, Evan Luard, urged that there had been 'no moment when strong pressure from ourselves was so badly needed as in the next few weeks if we are to preserve the area from disintegration, with all the danger of penetration from outside'.[162] Foreign Secretary Michael Stewart endorsed this, recommending that 'now the Bahrain/Iran exercise has been concluded satisfactorily, we should exert the maximum pressure on the Rulers to arrange an early meeting at which practical decisions over the union can be taken, and we should make suggestions as to how these decisions might best be achieved'.[163] FO mandarins, however, resisted these arguments.[164] For instance, the Head of the Arabian Department, A. A. Acland, drew attention to the fact that Britain's capacity to bring pressure to bear on the Gulf Rulers had always been 'rather less than it might appear to be on the basis of a rigorous application of the Exclusive Agreements'. 'Recently', he added, 'it has been further limited by a new factor, the realization by the Rulers that the decision to withdraw militarily by the end of 1971 is probably irreversible'. In these circumstances, they sought, and took, British advice 'less and less'. Even if Britain were in a position to force the Rulers into a union, Acland doubted the value of an imposed structure: 'A successful Union which will survive our military withdrawal from the Gulf can only be brought about if the Rulers enter into it willingly with a genuine desire to make it work'.

In his valedictory despatch shortly before stepping down as Political Resident, Crawford added his own voice to the growing scepticism about the Union's prospects:

> I must admit to being a pessimist about the chances of genuine federal union of the nine States, from knowledge of the strains that exist between many of the Rulers, of the difficulty the Political Agents and I have had in trying to infuse into life their discussions, and of the lack of public support for the scheme. Even if outside pressure compelled the Rulers to bring a federal union into being, I fear that it would later collapse when the stiffening provided by our presence was withdrawn, the adequate human skills available for running it were exposed and the problems it would have with its neighbours became difficult. From the point of view of promoting long-term stability, its surviving on these terms would probably prove a delusion. A more realistic aim would be a reversion to the pre-1968 prospect of mini-States, including a union of six or seven on the Trucial Coast, and all united by confederal and consultative machinery.[165]

Fresh impetus, however, came from the Saudis and Kuwaitis. At the beginning of 1971, a mission led by the Kuwaiti Foreign Minister, Shaikh Sabah, and Prince Nawwaf of Saudi Arabia, attempted to breath new life into the increasingly cadaverous union project. Differences between Bahrain and Qatar over not only the siting of the new capital, but also the representation for the four principal Shaikhdoms, proved insurmountable.[166] In contrast with the prominent role accorded Kuwait, in particular by Robert L. Jarman in the eventual emergence of the UAE,[167] the Kuwaiti–Saudi mission actually increased the number of points at issue.[168] The Qataris even accused the mission's proposals of being 'slanted to the Bahraini point of view'.[169] To make matters worse, the main regional power broker, the Shah of Iran, made it clear he would frustrate the formation of the union unless his requirements over the disputed Gulf islands were satisfied.[170] It was Bahrain's decision to achieve separate independent status which sounded the death-knell for the union of the nine.

Although Bahrain had been a somewhat unenthusiastic participant in the unity ideal, it tended to shy away from setting out its claims for independence for fear of attracting the odium of its neighbours. As the time for Britain's departure from the Gulf drew inexorably closer, however, Bahraini qualms gave way to a determination to settle the country's future. Citing pressure from educated opinion in Bahrain, Shaikh Mohammed bin Mubarak informed the Minister of State for Foreign and Commonwealth Affairs, Joesph Godber, that his government had decided to seek independence.[171] There had already been strong indications that if Bahrain opted out of the union, Qatar would follow suit.[172] It came as little surprise, therefore, when Shaikh Khalifah of Qatar made known that his state would wish to follow Bahrain in a declaration of independence.[173] In discussions with Luce, the Amir of Kuwait and Shaikh Sabah both expressed scepticism about a union of nine, pinpointing differences between Bahrain and Qatar as the main impediment. Although Britain continued forlornly to extol the virtues of a union encompassing all the states of the Lower Gulf, the unreality of this objective was becoming self-evident. 'The basic problem in achieving a Union of nine', admitted Luce, 'is the old enmity between the ruling families of Bahrain and Qatar'.[174] During discussions with Shaikh Zaid in early February, he urged that 'an alternative grouping should be held in reserve for consideration if agreement on a Union of nine proved unattainable'.[175] Luce's final attempt to salvage the UAE through a meeting of Deputy Rulers represented little more than an attempt to placate King Feisal who remained wedded to the idea of a union of nine.[176] The animosity between Bahrain and Qatar was underlined by the refusal of either state to attend the proposed Deputy Rulers' meeting.[177]

While British policy-makers accepted the moribundity of a wider union, they remained convinced of the need to bring the Trucial States together, not least because of the non-viability of the five smaller states.[178] Following his tour of the Gulf in early 1971 to inform the Rulers of British decisions regarding future policy, Luce had reported that 'the little five strongly desire a Union and know that their chances of survival without one are slender'.[179] Fearing that Zaid would dominate a smaller number, Feisal still favoured a union of all nine Gulf Shaikhdoms.[180] Although the Saudi King remained wedded to this idea in public, Ambassador Morris in Jedda recorded that his advisers (and possibly the King himself) had come to realize that a smaller Trucial States entity was the best possible solution for Saudi interests.[181] Accounting for Feisal's intractability, the UAR Foreign Minister's Chef de Cabinet, Muhammad Riad, remarked that 'he did not want to be blamed in the future for what might happen in the Gulf and indeed wanted all the blame to rest on Britain'.[182] Accepting this risk, Foreign Secretary Douglas-Home stressed the need to encourage Shaikhs Zaid and Rashid to make progress to a union of seven, while putting pressure on Bahrain to make an early announcement on independence.[183] The Defence and Oversea Policy Committee had already agreed that 'a Union of seven or six appeared now to afford the best prospect of a political settlement to meet our minimum requirements'.[184]

Although Shaikh Rashid had hinted to a BBC correspondent in April 1971 that Dubai might 'go it alone',[185] less than three months later he agreed to join with the Rulers of Abu Dhabi, Sharjah, Ajman, Umm al Qawain, and Fujairah in forming the United Arab Emirates. Rashid's constant fear had been that Shaikh Zaid, with his superior wealth, would be able to exert an excessive influence over the five smaller Trucial States, allowing him to outvote Dubai on matters in dispute. The provision in the new constitution permitting Abu Dhabi and Dubai to exercise a veto in the Supreme Council may have allayed Rashid's concerns. The influence of his senior adviser, Mehdi Tajir, was also important at this crucial stage. Demonstrating a strong strain of pragmatism, Mehdi told Rashid that 'while Zaid, with his money, might be able to go it alone, Dubai, which only had the support of Iran, could not and might find itself an enclave in a Union of Six'.[186] Mehdi's intervention would appear to have been decisive in persuading Rashid to set aside his reservations and throw in his lot with the other Trucial States. While Zaid was prepared to set aside old feuds with Rashid for the sake of unity on the Trucial Coast, he proved more unforgiving with respect to Qatar. He accused the Qataris of setting out to hinder the development of the union and speculated that, as one of eight, the Qataris would 'embark in the same way on a course of obstruction and domination'.[187] Not surprisingly, he expressed the view that 'a union of seven would be preferable to one of eight unless the latter included Bahrain'.[188] With Bahrain sceptical about union, and Qatar assuming the status of a pariah, the other Lower Gulf States (with the exception of Ras al Khaimah) announced the formation of the United Arab Emirates on 18 July. This clearly left the status of Bahrain and Qatar unresolved.

A day after the establishment of the UAE, pressure was applied by the Political Agent in Bahrain for purposive action to be taken. Stirling bluntly told the Bahrainis that they were 'in danger of missing the boat in applying for UN membership', and that they should not be deterred by King Feisal who was 'most unlikely to be actively hostile if Bahrain declared for separate status'.[189] Despite unpromising signals emanating from Riyadh,[190] Shaikh Mohammed sought an audience with Feisal. As Stirling had predicted, the Saudi King, although clinging disconsolately to a union of all nine Lower Gulf Shaikhdoms, conceded that the Bahrainis were 'free to do as they pleased'.[191] Fortified with this knowledge, the Ruler informed the Political Resident that, on the advice of the State Council, he had decided to terminate the special relationship with Britain and submit an application for membership of the United Nations on 16 August. It was with considerable reluctance and foreboding about the future that Shaikh Isa did this. 'He knows', explained the Political Resident, G. G. Arthur, 'that he has lost his shield from the hard realities of an uncertain future in the Persian Gulf'.[192]

Predictably, Qatar expressed its wish to follow Bahrain into independence.[193] As early as February, Henderson had backed 'an independent Qatar as the likeliest horse . . . in view of current outstandingly bad relations with Abu Dhabi'.[194] Following the by now ritual visit to King Feisal, the Qataris gave notice of their intention to terminate the special relationship with Britain. Shaikh Ahmed's refusal to leave his villa near Geneva and return to Qatar delayed the process for a number of days. The relevant documents were eventually flown out to him and signed on 3 September.[195] In keeping with Bahrain, Qatar also concluded a Treaty of Friendship with Britain under which the two parties agreed to 'consult together on matters of mutual concern and in time of need'.[196] The assumption of independent status by both Bahrain and Qatar, along with the establishment of the UAE, left the future of just one Shaikhdom in the balance.

Shaikh Saqr of Ras al Khaimah decided to stand outside the UAE, giving unequal representation among member states under the provisional constitution and the Abu Dhabi–Dubai right of veto in the Supreme Council as his reasons.[197] Shaikh Zaid provided a different interpretation. '[I]n the bad old days when Zaid and Rashid were not at one', he told Arthur, 'the Ruler of Qatar and Rashid had used the Ruler of Ras al Khaimah as a cat's paw. This had given Saqr an exaggerated idea of his own importance'.[198] In any case, Saqr's uncompromising stance on the disputed Tunb Islands, which were also claimed by Iran, would have made him an uncomfortable bedfellow in the new political structure for the Lower Gulf, particularly since the Shah had vowed to destroy any union which claimed sovereignty over 'Iranian' territory.[199] While recognizing the ultimate desirability of Saqr joining the UAE, Douglas-Home conceded that 'it would be a complicating factor as regards the islands problem if Ras al Khaimah were to join now'.[200] 'We do not want the Ruler of Ras al Khaimah to join the UAE until we know how and when the islands problem is likely to be settled', agreed Arthur.[201] In discussions with officials at the US Embassy in London, the Head of the FCO's Arabian Department, A. A. Acland, mused that it was 'quite convenient' that Ras al Khaimah had refused to join the union since it would be easier for the British to deal 'peremptorily with an isolated Saqr than with a seventh member of federation'.[202]

An opportunity to put Acland's theory to the test soon presented itself when, at the eleventh hour, Saqr attempted to retain his special treaty relationship with Britain. The Political Agent in Dubai, J. F. Walker, felt able to rebuff the Ras al Khaimah Ruler's request. Not only would it be inappropriate to treat one Trucial State differently from the rest, he asserted, but also imminent military withdrawal dictated that Britain could not provide long-term protection.[203] For good measure, Walker also stressed that Britain wished to avoid any accusation that it was seeking to maintain Ras al Khaimah as a base in the Gulf. When Saqr complained that Britain had abnegated its protecting role by failing to prevent the occupation of the Tunbs by Iranian forces on 30 November, his protests were swept aside. Referring to the termination of Britain's treaties with the Trucial States on 1 December,[204] the Political Resident asseverated that 'no reasonable man could expect us to eject the Iranians by force only to abandon the islands for recapture by Iran the next day'.[205] Furthermore, Arthur reminded Saqr that he had been telling him for more than a year that the Shah intended seizing the islands. As these comments suggest, Britain had foreknowledge of Iranian aims.

As early as March 1968 US Ambassador to Britain, David Bruce, was reporting that the FO believed Iran would occupy the disputed islands once Britain departed the Gulf.[206] At the beginning of 1971, the British Ambassador in Tehran, Sir Denis Wright, affirmed that the Shah 'intended to occupy the islands with or without the agreement of the Rulers'.[207] Following his visit to the Gulf to explain Conservative Party policy, Luce recorded that the Shah's attitude towards the islands had 'hardened' and he had 'once again made clear beyond all doubt that he intends to have these islands and now believes that the only solution is to seize them'.[208] The Shah had explicitly informed Foreign Secretary Home, during face to face talks in July 1970, that if the Rulers did not come to terms over the islands he would take them by force.[209] Not surprisingly, Home predicted that if Shaikh Zaid pressed ahead with the UAE in the absence of a settlement of the islands dispute, the Shah would 'almost certainly seek to take the Islands by force just before or just after the formal establishment of the Union'.[210]

Although this was the anticipated result, British policy-makers were conscious of the need to avoid Arab opprobrium. Any deterioration in Anglo-Iranian relations, it was felt, would be temporary and not affect Iran's basic orientation towards the West. On the other hand, it was feared that any loss of influence among the Gulf Arabs risked being permanent.[211] Certainly Shaikh Zaid had warned that 'if Britain handed Abu Musa over unilaterally it would be impossible for [the] proposed Federation of Trucial States to have relations with the UK or to accept British officers in its defence forces'.[212] In such circumstances, the British maintained negotiations for the remaining months of their treaty obligations while surreptitiously preparing for an Iranian occupation should they fail. Home also argued the merits of speeding up British military withdrawal on the grounds that 'The presence of these forces in the Gulf at the time when the Iranians seize the Islands without opposition will inevitably make it appear that we are colluding with Iran.'[213]

Initially, it appeared that the resolution of Iran's claims to the island of Abu Musa would be as protracted and intractable as those relating to the Tunbs. Shaikh Khalid of Sharjah, fearing a hostile Arab reaction to handing over the island, insisted upon his sovereign rights. Khalid even told the US Consul General in Dhahran, Dinsmore, that he feared for his life if he yielded 'Arab' territory to Iran.[214] As Britain's departure grew near, Luce worked furiously to achieve a settlement. Khalid's obduracy was softened by new generous terms proposed by the Shah.[215] In addition to offering Sharjah financial assistance for a period of nine years, he also agreed that exploitation of oil resources off Abu Musa would be conducted by a company designated by Sharjah on the basis of a 50/50 split of oil revenues. Furthermore, the Shah expressed a willingness to limit the area of Abu Musa occupied by Iranian forces.

Unlike Shaikh Khalid, Shaikh Saqr of Ras al Khaimah remained intransigent, refusing either to agree to voluntary cession of the Tunbs, or to accept Iranian money for them. This deadlock, FCO Minister of State Godber told the Cabinet, made it 'virtually certain that the Shah would take control of the islands in his own time'.[216] Recognizing this danger,

Luce had already entered into clandestine discussions with the Shah over the timing of an Iranian takeover of the islands.[217] Despite the fact that the Defence and Oversea Policy Committee had previously expressed its unwillingness to 'endorse a course of action which entailed conniving at an Iranian seizure in our present treaty relationship to Trucial States',[218] it was agreed that 30 November would be the date for the landing of Iranian forces on Abu Musa and the Tunbs. Prior to this Kuwait, Saudi Arabia, and the UAR would be briefed by Britain on the terms of the islands settlement, a final attempt being made to persuade Shaikh Saqr to cede the Tunbs to Iran and join the UAE on 28 November.[219]

The UAR reaction to the news was strong on the grounds that the islands settlement would arouse Arab anger, while that of Saudi Arabia and Kuwait was more reserved.[220] King Feisal's muted response no doubt stemmed from the partial account he received from Ambassador Morris who, after relaying the terms of the Abu Musa agreement, merely noted that no similar accord had been reached over the Tunbs.[221] As regards Kuwait, Foreign Minister Sabah had previously dismissed the difficulties over Tunb Islands with the comment that 'many Gulf Arabs had traditionally considered it Persian'.[222] The death of one Arab and three Iranians during the occupation by Iran of the Tunbs served to inflame opinion, however. Kuwait condemned the British, while Iraq went so far as to sever diplomatic relations. Rioting also broke out in Ras al Khaimah and Sharjah.[223] With feelings running high, the Deputy Ruler of Sharjah was wounded by an unidentified gunman following the announcement of the agreement over Abu Musa.[224] Exploiting the sense of confusion, the former Ruler, Shaikh Saqr, led a coup attempt at the end of January 1972 in which Shaikh Khalid was killed.[225] To make matters worse, Shaikh Saqr of Ras al Khaimah was implicated in the Sharjah plot.[226] Although foiled by other members of the ruling family, the coup was a clear manifestation of instability following the British withdrawal. Julian Amery (Minister for Housing and Reconstruction) even speculated that Sharjah would have seceded from the federation if the coup had been successful.[227] Still reeling from events in Sharjah, the Lower Gulf was rocked by another coup, this time in Qatar.

On 22 February, Doha radio reported that Shaikh Khalifah bin Hamad had assumed the position of head of state and Amir of Qatar in place of Shaikh Ahmed, who was accused of being concerned only with realizing 'personal benefits at the expense of the homeland'.[228] Indeed, in an effort to cement his position, Shaikh Khalifah transferred Ahmed's income into the general budget. Although Khalifah's seizure of power appeared to have the support of powerful elements, not least the ruling family and the army, his actions poisoned relations with the UAE. The former Ruler of Qatar's father-in-law, Shaikh Rashid of Dubai, was especially incensed, commenting that 'Khalifa already had all the power in Qatar and Ahmed never stood in his way'.[229] So virulent did Rashid's criticisms become that Khalifah, fearing military action on the part of the UAE to restore Ahmed to power, appealed to Saudi Arabia for support.[230] Khalifah also launched regular tirades against the UAE in general and Shaikhs Zaid and Rashid in particular. On one occasion, he accused the Union of being 'no Union at all', justifying his comments by pointing out that it was 'split by petty differences' and 'Zaid had no authority to pull it together'.[231]

Despite the subjective nature of Khalifah's critique, it did appear to have some basis in reality. Britain's Consul-General in Dubai, J. F. Walker, reported a groundswell of criticism among the Northern Trucial States of Abu Dhabi's 'management (or non-management) of Union affairs'.[232] There was also dissatisfaction over the siting of government departments and the capital in Abu Dhabi itself. The former Political Agent and subsequently Britain's first Ambassador in Abu Dhabi, C. J. Treadwell,[233] recorded gloomily that 'The UAE is a federation of seven disparate States controlled by ruling families whose one common characteristic is an inability to comprehend the meaning of modern political government.' He also pointed out that, since Shaikhs Zaid and Rashid were the 'cornerstone of the Union', the UAE would be destroyed if they were ever to fall out. Ominously, Treadwell noted that in temperament they were 'as different as chalk and cheese'. While recognizing that the UAE stemmed from the decision in February 1968 of Zaid and Rashid to unite, Treadwell asserted that 'without our guidance, coaxing, encouragement and plain interference, it would all have come to nothing'. In the three years of 'wrangling, inertia, equivocation, and skulduggery' which it took the Rulers to abandon a union of nine, claimed Treadwell, the British did much to bring Zaid and Rashid together. In this respect, Treadwell's insistence that the UAE was in part a 'British federation' is justified. Nevertheless, the two Rulers of the principal states had strong reasons for pushing through the concept of unity among the Trucial States. For Zaid, unity afforded him the opportunity to play a major role in the Gulf beyond the borders of Abu Dhabi, while for Rashid, fearing Dubai's reduction to a mere enclave on the Trucial Coast, saw in co-operation with Zaid the possibility of moderating his influence over the five small emirates. As pragmatic men, moreover, both Zaid and Rashid recognized the impracticability, and indeed danger, of separate independence for these tiny states. Despite Zaid's determination to extend union authority and Rashid's equal resolution, especially following his assumption of the prime ministership in 1979, to resist the same,[234] the two men belied Treadwell's dire predictions, managing to preserve the basis for a working relationship. Despite its tortured inception, the UAE, bolstered by oil wealth, proved to be a success story among a litany of British failures in closer association.

5 Conflict and co-operation

Anglo-American relations in the Gulf from the nationalization of Anglo-Iranian Oil to the Yemeni revolution

Anglo-American relations since 1945 have exercised an enduring fascination for historians of British decolonization and international relations more generally. In the aftermath of the Second World War, the emphasis, unsurprisingly, tended to be on the closeness and intimacy of the relationship between Britain and America. With the opening of official records on both sides of the Atlantic from the 1960s, however, a different picture began to emerge which stressed that Britain and America were, in Christopher Thorne's memorable phrase, 'allies of a kind'.[1] D. C. Watt suggested that American pressure on the British and other European empires artificially hastened decolonization, rendering the transition from colonial rule to independence more problematic than otherwise would have been the case.[2] Although more recently the theme of Anglo-American co-operation has been re-stated, attention has been paid to the unequal nature of the relationship.[3] Drawing on the theme of co-operation and applying it to the Middle East, Ritchie Ovendale contends that the 1958 Anglo-American intervention in Lebanon and Jordan 'marked the assumption by the United States of Britain's traditional role in the Middle East'.[4] 'It was America in Britain's place', he concludes. 'But this is what Britain wanted.'[5] Ovendale's interpretation is open to question, however. Indeed, the tameness with which Britain accepted American leadership, and the alacrity with which America assumed this leading role in defending Western interests, is doubtful. Britain clung on tenaciously to its assets in the Persian Gulf and southern Arabia, while America demonstrated little interest in actively supplanting the British. Only in situations where Britain could no longer provide area security did America tend to become more heavily committed. Equally, the post-war reverses in the Middle East did not engender a defeatist attitude on the part of the British. 'As the British were gradually forced out of Iran and Egypt,' observes Tore Petersen, 'they tried to regain lost ground in those countries by expanding their influence to the Persian Gulf and even into Saudi Arabia proper.'[6] By so doing, they clashed with competing American interests.

Following his visit to the Gulf in early 1952, Sir Roger Makins described the nature of Anglo-American relations there as 'not really satisfactory'.[7]

'There are no common political or strategic aims in the area, nor is there even consultation on matters of the first importance', he fulminated. Justifying this peroration, Makins pointed out that the agreement between the United States and Saudi Arabia over control of the military base at Dhahran had been concluded without consulting, or even notifying, the British. America's insistence on the appointment of a consul in Kuwait, despite British scepticism on this point, was indicative, in Makins' opinion, of the failure of the United States to appreciate the nature and implications of Britain's special position in the Gulf. Referring to oil matters, Makins perceived a similar lack of mutual comprehension. '[T]he degree of consultation on major matters of policy which is necessary if the [oil] companies are to maintain their position does not appear to exist', he recorded. Summing up his findings, Makins concluded:

> The interests of both countries in the area are similar and very great: yet American activities tend on the whole steadily to weaken the British position in the area without increasing the American position very much. If the process is allowed to continue, the joint interests of the two countries and of the other Western Powers will be gravely prejudiced.

Without explicitly referring to Iran's contemporaneous nationalization of the Anglo-Iranian Oil Company (AIOC), it seems likely that Makins comments were informed by Anglo-American divisions during this drawn-out crisis.

AIOC's refinery at Abadan in southern Iran was the largest in the world, while taxation of the Company's profits provided valuable revenues in the context of Britain's drive for post-war economic recovery. Not surprisingly, Britain investigated ways of reversing the nationalization, including the use of the military force. The Truman administration, however, was implacably opposed to a resort to arms and favoured negotiations instead. In a letter to Prime Minister Attlee shortly after the nationalization, Truman not only referred to the 'serious implications of this explosive situation', but also underlined his concern that 'no action should be taken in connection with this dispute which would result in disagreement between Iran and the free world'.[8] In spite of US views, plans were made to invade Abadan following the expulsion of British workers from the oilfields on 20 September 1951. Truman, nevertheless, reiterated his opposition to military action which prompted Attlee to inform the Cabinet that 'in view of the attitude of the United States Government, [he did not] think it would be expedient to use force to maintain the British staff in Abadan'.[9]

The early months of 1953, however, marked a turning-point in the crisis. With Mussadiq apparently flirting with the communist-inspired Tudeh, or masses, Party, the President and his Secretary of State, John Foster Dulles, worked for the Iranian premier's overthrow. 'First and foremost in their minds', notes Moyara de Moraes Ruehsen, 'was a desire to prevent Iran from going the same way as China.'[10] While recognizing the significance of these Cold War concerns, Steve Marsh places considerable emphasis on Mussadiq's peremptory rejection on 20 March of British proposals to settle the dispute put to him a month earlier. By so doing, argues Marsh, Mussadiq 'publicly showed that there was little prospect of him ever signing an oil settlement', which left the Eisenhower administration 'only with the option of working with a new government in Iran'.[11]

Although the coup d'état which unseated Mussadiq in August 1953 owed much to Anglo-American co-operation, tensions between the two countries resurfaced during negotiations to create an oil consortium in place of Anglo-Iranian's former exclusive position in Iran. Shortly after the coup, Prime Minister Churchill cautioned that 'In present circumstances, it would be easy for the Americans by the expenditure of a relatively small sum of money to reap all the benefit of many years of British work in Persia.'[12] In many ways Churchill's fears were realized since American companies were granted a forty per cent stake in the consortium which emerged. 'In a demonstration that Western leadership in Iran had passed from London to Washington,' contends Mary Ann Heiss, 'US interests dominated the negotiations.'[13] Steve Marsh describes Anglo-Iranian, which only received a forty per cent share in the oil consortium, as a ' sacrificial pawn in the end game designed to protect the Anglo-American Special Relationship'.[14] Equally, he also points out that 'larger considerations of the Special Relationship and an unwillingness to commit to the Middle East dictated that the Americans could not break with Britain over the Anglo-Iranian oil crisis.'[15] Moreover, Mark Gasiorowski has refuted the suggestion that the US government perceived support for Britain in overthrowing Mussadiq as an opportunity to open Iran to American oil companies.[16] In particular, he demonstrates that the Truman and Eisenhower administrations saw the participation of US companies in the Iranian oil industry in a post-Mussadiq Iran as essential to the maintenance of stability in that country and in keeping the Soviets out. Putting the AIOC's forty per cent of the consortium in perspective, furthermore, J. H. Bamberg has remarked that 'the final terms of the settlement represented a great recovery from the situation which in early 1953 looked a virtually lost cause for the Company'.[17] A more blatant example of American activities weakening the British position in the Gulf is provided by the disputes over the Buraimi oasis.

Supported by the US-owned Arabian American Oil Company, King Ibn Saud of Saudi Arabia in August 1952 moved forces to the disputed Buraimi oasis area which was also claimed by Abu Dhabi and Oman. Since the Arabian American Oil Company held an exclusive concession in Saudi Arabia, an extension of Saudi control to other potentially oil-bearing parts of the Arabian Peninsula was clearly in its interests. The US government, which enjoyed military facilities at the Dhahran airbase, also tended to overlook Saudi expansionism. The British, whose interests on the Arabian peninsula were focused on the small Gulf Shaikhdoms, could not afford to be similarly indulgent. If Saudi adventurism went unanswered, Britain feared, its standing in the eyes of the Gulf States under its protection would suffer. This attitude led President Eisenhower to snap: 'surely the British would not maintain that every mile in every borderline in the whole area would be a matter of British prestige'.[18] Secretary of State Dulles, who described Britain and France as 'millstones around our neck' following his tour of the Middle East in May 1953, 'could not see that British prestige could be as important as the US relationship with King Ibn Saud'.[19] Indeed, Dulles felt that Saudi Arabia was intrinsically more important to America than the Persian Gulf States were to Britain. Reflecting British opinion, by contrast, the Permanent Under-Secretary of State at the FO, Sir Ivone Kirkpatrick, told Dulles in December 1955 that 'To throw a small Arab State to the wolves for the American reason, which was with respect, that the Saudi government would be annoyed if we did not, was entirely wrong.'[20] With such considerations in mind, British forces had evicted the Saudis from the oasis in October 1955, following failed arbitration proceedings during which the Saudis had been accused of bribery.

The expulsion had taken place without prior warning to the United States. This approach was very much in line with Prime Minister Eden's sentiments expressed in Cabinet a few weeks earlier. Having observed that British interests, and experience, were greater than those of the United States, he proceeded to draw the conclusion that

> We should not therefore allow ourselves to be restricted overmuch by reluctance to act without full American concurrence and support. We should frame our own policy in the light of our interests in the area and get the Americans to support it to the extent we could induce them to do so. Our policy should be based on the need to help our acknowledged friends and allies, such as Iraq, and the Trucial States on whom our oil depended.[21]

Buraimi remained a running sore in Anglo-American relations in the Middle East, however. In his discussions with Dulles in December 1955, Kirkpatrick had expressed his bewilderment at the US approach to the problem:

> Although Saudi Arabia seemed to be at best a neutral state on the Nehru model and at worst pursuing a Russian policy by the purchase of arms, antagonism to the Northern tier, and anti-Western activity generally, the United States Government were supporting the Saudis in their drive to absorb the small pro-Western States of South-East Arabia.[22]

At a lower level, FO mandarins told staff from the US Embassy in London of their concern at the way in which the British and American governments 'seemed to be working on entirely different planes in regard to South-East Arabia'.[23] Relating Buraimi to wider issues of Anglo-American relations in the Middle East, Tore Petersen argues that the dispute 'eventually contributed to the rupture of the Atlantic alliance during the Suez crisis of 1956'.[24] 'It may be that the United States attitude to us in the Middle East dates from our refusal to give up Buraimi', Eden mused in early 1957.[25]

The grudging acceptance of the fait accompli presented to the Americans at Buraimi was not repeated a year later when Britain, in collaboration with France and Israel, launched a military assault on Egypt following a prolonged stand-off resulting from Nasser's nationalization of the Suez Canal in July 1956. American ire at British unilateralism had already been raised by attempts in December 1955, against American wishes, to persuade Jordan to join the Baghdad Pact.[26] 'It was precisely this pattern of unilateral actions that exhausted American patience, and made Eisenhower take forceful countermoves during the Suez crisis', asserts Petersen.[27] The President and his Secretary of State, John Foster Dulles, were particularly concerned that British actions risked not only alienating newly independent nations, but also handing the Soviets a propaganda victory. 'For many years now', Dulles told the National Security Council,

> the US has been walking the tightrope between the effort to maintain our old and valued relations with our British and French allies on the one hand, and on the other try to assure ourselves of the friendship and understanding of the newly independent countries who have escaped from colonialism. . . . Unless we now assert and maintain this leadership, all of these newly independent countries will turn from us to the USSR.[28]

'At all costs the Soviets must be prevented from seizing a mantle of world leadership through a false but convincing exhibition of concern for the smaller nations', concurred Eisenhower.[29] The President's annoyance boiled over into fury by the British government's duplicity in colluding with France and Israel while keeping the US in the dark. 'Nothing justifies double-crossing us', fumed Eisenhower.[30] Deploying diplomatic and economic pressure, the US forced an Anglo-French ceasefire followed by humiliating withdrawal. The impact of the Suez episode on Anglo-American relations in the Middle East has provided a variety of interpretations.

John Charmley remarks upon Britain's 'total subservience' to America in the wake of Suez, 'not so much the forty-ninth state as a satellite state'.[31] Pursuing a parallel line of enquiry, W. Scott Lucas argues that 'to restore the Anglo-American "alliance", Britain paid the price of permanent subservience to American policy'.[32] Likewise, Muhammad Abd el-Wahab Sayed-Ahmed contends that from the time of Suez, 'the American government assumed the role of the sole legitimate guardian of Western interests in the area against Soviet attempts to penetrate the region'.[33] In the aftermath of Suez, Congress passed a resolution, the so-called Eisenhower doctrine, to provide Middle Eastern nations with military and economic aid designed to help them maintain their national independence. It was this development, argues Douglas Little, 'which made Washington the senior member of the Anglo-American partnership in the Middle East'.[34] According to Steven Z. Freiberger, the doctrine demonstrated that 'The United States had taken the final step in reversing its relationship with the United Kingdom in the Middle East by replacing it as the dominant power'.[35]

A different interpretation is given by Ray Takeyh. He suggests that the Eisenhower doctrine provided the basis for the 'rehabilitation of Britain and resumption of close Anglo-American co-operation'.[36] Consequently, he departs from the conventional view that following the Suez crisis, the US sought to displace the British. 'Far from seeking to supplant Britain,' he argues, 'Eisenhower hoped to restore British power and employ it against Egypt.'[37] Takeyh justifies this assertion by noting that since the US administration had come to see Cairo's policies as 'prime obstacles to the implementation of the containment doctrine in the Middle East', it was inclined to 'seek assistance from all corners'.[38] In Takeyh's opinion, the Americans hoped that their increased role in the Middle East would be an 'interim measure', and that British participation would 'eventually reach its pre-Suez levels'.[39] As regards Britain's attitude towards its role in the Middle East after Suez, Nigel John Ashton stresses that 'the British did not retreat from the maintenance of what they considered to be important positions in the area by force', justifying his remarks with reference to military intervention in Jordan in 1958 and Kuwait three years later.[40] Referring specifically to the approach of Eden's successor, Harold Macmillan, Ashton remarks that although the new Prime Minister 'would never again push Anglo-American differences over the Middle East to the point of rupture, he would equally not trim British strategy in the region to suit the US administration'.[41] In identifying a continuing patchwork of conflict and co-operation between the two powers, Ashton perceives 'a large measure of continuity in Anglo-American relations in the Middle East before and after the Suez Crisis'.[42] Responding to Peter Hahn's claims that Suez 'destroyed all vestiges of Britain's influence in the Middle East',[43] Petersen underlines the fact that it 'still had a major voice in the affairs of Jordan and Iraq (until 1958), and along the Persian Gulf'.[44] Although Suez cannot be viewed as anything other than a reverse for Britain, it neither extinguished British influence in the Middle East, nor led to a transfer of power in all instances to America. This was especially so in the Persian Gulf where Britain, while seeking American support, resolutely defended its traditional role.

At the beginning of 1957, the Ruler of Bahrain asserted that in the Gulf context Americans should 'confine themselves to trade and commerce but not to enter into local politics', adding that it would be a 'mistake' for any third party to impinge upon the special relationships which Britain had established with the Gulf Rulers.[45] In the light of such a ringing endorsement of the British presence, an FO official observed: 'I do not think any of the PG Rulers would welcome US participation in our political responsibilities in the Persian Gulf.'[46] Despite this, he did suggest that the United States should be consulted about 'changes of policy and day to day tactics'. The head of the Eastern Department, D. M. H. Riches, gave the following coruscating response: 'The Americans are ignorant and impossible in colonial or semi-colonial situations in the M[iddle] E[ast]. We should enlighten their ignorance but not give them responsibility until we are quite sure they will shoulder it.'[47] Writing to the Political Resident, Bernard Burrows, Riches confirmed that 'we should certainly not wish it to appear that we were being ousted in any respect by the Americans.'[48] The FO had also prepared a stout defence of Britain's role in the Gulf for the Bermuda conference between Eisenhower and the new British Prime Minister, Harold Macmillan.[49] When Eisenhower pressed Macmillan to make concessions on Buraimi, the Prime Minister pointedly refused to 'betray our friends'.[50]

With the exception of the vexed question of Buraimi, the consensus was that the United States was unlikely to press for a major modification of the existing arrangements in the Gulf. American self-interest was seen as the key to this attitude. Nevertheless, there was concern that Britain would come under pressure from US representatives to modernize its relationship with the Gulf States. Secretary of State Dulles's recent minatory statement that he did not want to see the US fighting for colonialism anywhere[51] was seen as especially relevant in this context. To counteract any US pressure, the FO recommended a response which stressed that any serious modification in Britain's exclusive treaties would 'probably lead to a free-for-all among the expansionist . . . Middle Eastern states during which the present precarious balance might be upset and British and United States interests in the Gulf would suffer'.[52] Subsequently, Burrows avowed: 'Americans are particularly prone to the fallacy that one must have a "dynamic" or "forward-looking" policy, but in an extremely conservative society such as this an attempt to bring people into line with modern ideas too quickly is likely to result only in chaos and disaster.'[53]

Although the FO sought public US support for 'the maintenance of something resembling the present general situation in the Gulf', it was equally keen to avoid giving the impression to the Rulers or their peoples that 'we are merely surrendering some of our local influence to the Americans'.[54] John Denson of the FO also pointed out that the simmering territorial disputes involving Saudi Arabia limited the extent of US support for the British position in the Persian Gulf. 'It is . . . clear from recent statements by Mr Dulles before Congress and by Mr Hoover[55] to HM Ambassador at Washington', he wrote, 'that the United States is not willing to commit herself to any guarantee which would safeguard HMG's interests and the interests of the Persian Gulf on whose behalf we are acting against the threat of Saudi territorial expansion. In other words we can expect no help from the United States.'[56] The conclusion which Denson drew from this was that Britain would have to rely on US self-interest, especially its fifty per cent stake in Persian Gulf oil, in securing American acquiescence in the British presence.

Despite accepting the difficulty of extracting a commitment from the US to guarantee the existing position in the Gulf, A. R. Walmsley of the FO's Eastern Department believed that it was necessary in the light of the 'decreasing weight' of Britain's influence in the Middle East and in the 'world at large'.[57] The British Ambassador in Tehran, Sir Roger Stevens, had already proclaimed that 'we shall get no assistance from the United States Government in maintaining or advancing our position in the Gulf on its present ill-defined basis'.[58] For his part, Burrows rejected any notion of an American 'guarantee' for the Trucial States, or of Britain's special position there, on the grounds that this would in itself 'go a long way to undermining that position'.[59] 'Our intention in asking the Americans for a guarantee was not to invite them to take over from us,' clarified Denson, 'but merely to use their influence to deter the Saudis.'[60] Riches had already dismissed the possibility of securing a US guarantee, declaring that 'understanding and therefore moral support . . . is the maximum we can hope for'.[61] This conclusion was reiterated by Foreign Secretary Lloyd in his report to the Cabinet on the results of the Bermuda conference. 'It must also be remembered', he continued,

> that the United States are committed to support Saudi Arabia whose interests are in many cases in conflict with those of our protected Rulers, while any apparent increase in United States power in the Gulf would be interpreted locally as a diminution of our own and the net result might be the weakening of the Western position as whole.[62]

The degree of American support for the British position in the Gulf was soon to be tested.

On 14 July 1958, the pro-British Hashemite monarchy in Iraq was swept aside in a bloody revolution. In his memoirs Macmillan described this event as 'destroying at a blow a whole system of security which successive British Governments had built up'.[63] Alarm at the possible consequences of the Iraqi revolution, especially for other pro-Western regimes in the region, soon spread to America. Due partly to anticipated domestic political difficulties, and partly to fear of being seen to be colluding with the British, President Eisenhower was reticent about Macmillan's grandiose plans for ambitious joint Anglo-American intervention in order to shore up Western interests in the Middle East.[64] Indeed, US intervention in Lebanon the day after the Iraqi revolution was unilateral prompting for Macmillan to quip to the US President: 'You are doing a Suez on me.'[65] In order to discuss the growing crisis, Foreign Secretary Lloyd visited Washington between 17 and 20 July. 'One of the most reassuring features of my talks here', he enthused to Macmillan,

> has been the complete United States solidarity with us over the Gulf. They are assuming that we will take firm action to maintain our position in Kuwait. They themselves are disposed to act with similar resolution in relation to the Aramco oilfields in the area of Dhahran ... They assume that we will also hold Bahrain and Qatar, come what may. They agree that at all costs these oilfields must be kept in Western hands.[66]

Belying earlier British fears, Secretary Dulles assured Lloyd that 'it would be foolish for the US and the UK to move into Lebanon and Jordan and not plan at the same time to hold other areas of greater intrinsic value.'[67] While recognizing the importance of bolstering Jordan and Lebanon, Eisenhower told Macmillan that 'we must also, and this seems to me even more important, see that the Persian Gulf area stays within the Western orbit'.[68] Behind the scenes, however, other voices expressed doubts about a military occupation of the oil fields. During a conference with the President, Allen Dulles, CIA director and brother of John Foster, asserted that 'oil concessions should be adjusted to Arab nationalism,' adding 'we should make a deal with the new Arab groups'.[69] Allen Dulles' views were well-received by Eisenhower who agreed that 'we must win them to us, or adjust to them'. He also expressed scepticism about military intervention, stressing that 'the use of force will outrage the Arabs'.[70] The Assistant Secretary of State for Near Eastern Affairs, William Rountree, was of the same mind.

In a memorandum to the Secretary of State, he emphasized that unless a military occupation of the oil fields was requested by the relevant governments 'it would be likely to provoke the most adverse political reactions not only on the part of the local populations but also from the ruling families concerned. Strikes and sabotage might well threaten petroleum production which is currently proceeding normally'.[71] Rountree also pointed out that the situation in the oil-bearing states of the Arab Gulf did not justify immediate military intervention. In assessing the arguments against the provision of US assistance for a British military operation in the Gulf, the National Security Council Planning Board noted that 'If armed force must be used to help retain this area ... the benefits of any actions in the direction of accommodation with radical Pan-Arab nationalism will be largely lost and US relations with neutral countries elsewhere would be affected.'[72] A Special National Intelligence Estimate came to a similar conclusion, adding the apocalyptic possibility that 'In the event of British use of force, the US might find itself confronted with a Soviet threat aimed at frustrating the British action.'[73] The legality of using American troops in support of the British was also questioned. 'If we were to send troops to Kuwait, solely on the basis of a request from the British (and particularly if the Government of Kuwait objected),' opined the State Department's legal adviser, 'our position would be doubtful, to say the least, under international law.'[74] The FO itself conceded that 'We shall discount the value of American help in regard to Kuwait; their innate prejudices and their public opinion will make them unreliable when it comes to the point.'[75]

It is highly questionable, therefore, whether the US government would have sanctioned assistance for British military intervention in the oil fields of the Persian Gulf in anything other than the most extreme of circumstances. Fear of inflaming Arab opinion in general, and alienating America's friends in the region in particular, engendered a cautious attitude among US policy-makers towards military intervention. Indeed, despite Lloyd's euphoric report of his visit to America in the immediate aftermath of the Iraqi revolution, the subsequent debates about the possibility of US backing for a British military operation actually served to weaken Anglo-American solidarity on the Gulf. At the beginning of 1960, nevertheless, the Political Resident, Sir George Middleton, expressed his keeness to keep the Americans 'in cahoots', as he put it, on the grounds that Britain's troubles in the past had been due, in part, to a lack of communication leading to mutual misunderstanding.[76] Consequently, Middleton reported that he had been keeping in close touch with the US Consul General in Dhahran, as well as US navy personnel. He also suggested that the US Consul in Kuwait, Talcott Seelye, be kept abreast of British military plans for the defence of Kuwait. The FO expressed some disquiet over Middleton's remarks: there was concern that any leaks from the US Consulate would alert Kuwaitis, ever-wary about external influence, to Britain's co-operation with the Americans. A related worry was that British plans would receive too wide a distribution were they to be forwarded to the State Department by the US Consul.[77]

The optimistic picture of Anglo-American co-operation given by Middleton was short-lived. A little over a year later, the MoD admitted that 'no actual plans for coordinated action, let alone joint action, exist'.[78] Worse still, the British had no details of unilateral American plans for the Persian Gulf.[79] For Sir Frederick Hoyer Millar (Permanent Under-Secretary at the FO) this state of affairs was not merely unsatisfactory, but also potentially dangerous in the event of a sudden emergency arising in the area. 'It is really rather ludicrous', he fulminated, 'that there should be an American Admiral stationed at Bahrain alongside a British Admiral (and a British Brigadier) both of them apparently working in water-tight compartments and not having much idea of what the other is doing.'[80] An added degree of uncertainty was introduced by the recent inauguration of John F. Kennedy as President. In an unguarded moment before his election, Kennedy had told Sir Winston Churchill's private secretary, Montague Browne, that 'the British have made such a mess of things in the world and especially the Middle East that the best thing they can do is to keep out of it in the future'.[81] The renewal of the Iraqi claim to Kuwait in June 1961[82] provided a tangible test for Anglo-American co-operation in the Gulf.

Discussing the possibility of American assistance in defending Kuwait two days after Iraqi premier Qassem's declaration on 25 June that Kuwait was an 'integral part' of Iraq, an official of the FO observed: 'The United States authorities have shown increasing reluctance even to discuss military plans for the area. The State Department have been most careful to avoid any commitment that the United States Government would support the United Kingdom Government if the latter took action in Kuwait.'[83] The US State Department itself expressed the fear that American entry into the dispute would merely 'goad Qasim to new intemperance'.[84] Despite such unpromising signals, US support for possible British intervention in Kuwait was sought.

With the Suez precedent firmly in mind, the British Cabinet was in agreement on the importance of receiving 'clear and public support' from the United States for British military intervention in Kuwait.[85] Foreign Secretary Home justified its request for 'full political support' by stressing: 'The importance of Kuwait to the Western World is such that . . . we cannot take the risk of allowing Qasim to seize it unopposed'.[86] In reply, the US Secretary of State, Dean Rusk, stressed: 'We understand the depth of your obligation, we agree that the independence of Kuwait must not be destroyed by force, and we are prepared to render the full political support you request.'[87] Rusk even offered to send a small naval force, known as the 'Solent Amity', to the Persian Gulf. The Secretary of State also promised to prevail upon Saudi Arabia, with which Britain had no diplomatic relations, to mediate in the dispute. Furthermore, America put its diplomatic weight behind Britain, especially in the United Nations.

America's co-operative attitude, despite the earlier unpromising signals, is explained by Nigel Ashton with reference to the US economic stake in Kuwait.[88] Fifty per cent of the KOC was owned by the American concern, Gulf Oil. Ashton contends that the US administration 'undoubtedly came under pressure from Gulf Oil executives, who wanted to make sure their investment was secure'.[89] He goes on to say that 'The interests of Gulf Oil provided a powerful reason for the administration to back British intervention in Kuwait if there was any possibility at all of an Iraqi invasion.'[90] The State Department, however, rebuffed any suggestion from Gulf Oil executives that direct military assistance would be given to the Ruler of Kuwait with the comment that 'USG in no repeat no way wishes to undercut British position in Kuwait'.[91] The US Consul in Kuwait, furthermore, was told to impress upon Gulf Oil's general manager America's 'support both of British primary responsibility and of such British action as required [to] preserve Kuwait's independence, and that US will avoid usurping British role with [the] Ruler'.[92]

Despite initial US backing, Ashton argues that doubts about the operation soon began to materialize. These focused on whether there really was an imminent Iraqi military threat to Kuwait. The US embassy in Baghdad was unable to verify any of the claims made by its British counterpart. On 4 July the American Ambassador, John D. Jernegan, reported that there was still 'no direct evidence that Iraqi armor has been moved south from [the] Baghdad area'.[93] Three days later, Assistant Secretary of State for Near Eastern Affairs, Phillips Talbot, asserted that 'the British have placed more force in and off Kuwait than was justified by the magnitude or even the seriousness of the Iraqi threat'.[94] By mid-July, Jernegan assessed that the danger of an Iraqi attack on Kuwait had all but past.[95] Projecting into the future, Jernegan mused:

> Department undoubtedly realizes that long-term weakness of British position (and our own so far as we are involved) lies in unnatural character of Kuwait as [a] state, character of its rulers, and social injustices of concentration [of] so much wealth in minds [hands?] of [a] few people in [the] middle of [an] area crying out for economic development.[96]

Nevertheless, it is important to guard against exaggerating the degree of Anglo-American disunity at this early stage in the crisis. Reporting the views of his British counterpart, Jernegan noted that 'Trevelyan remains firmly of opinion, as I do, that [it] is of first importance to get British troops out of Kuwait just as soon as way can be found to give reasonable assurances [of] maintenance [of] Kuwait's independence'.[97] 'Much as I dislike the prospect of continued presence [of] British troops in Kuwait,' Jerngan added,

> I am forced to agree that their presence may very well be only thing which prevents Qassim making [a] grab. Prize is so tempting and his relations with other Arabs already so poor that he may well think successful seizure would be worth price of Arab League displeasure, which most probably would manifest itself only in words.

It was not until the end of the year, when renewed Iraqi threats to Kuwait provoked a British response, that significant Anglo-American fissures opened up.

In December 1961, Jernegan communicated that 'Although Embassy has no solid indication of impending Iraqi military action against Kuwait, there are widespread reports in Baghdad that Qassim intends to move against the shaikhdom soon.'[98] Despite the sketchy nature of the Iraqi threat, British military assets in the region were put on alert. Phillips Talbot warned that 'the recent British actions tend to erode the principal political bulwark to Kuwait's security, namely, Arab League support for Kuwait's independence'.[99] He described Qassem as playing:

> a cat and mouse game with the British, hoping to wear them (and the UK treasury) down by a series of scare gestures which will make it increasingly clear to the rest of the world and the Arabs in particular that Kuwait is, after all, only a British colony.[100]

'While British determination to defend Kuwait must be clear at all times', he surmised, 'we believe that a positive US affirmation of an intention to participate in this defense would be unnecessary and would probably strengthen Iraq's case for greater Soviet assistance and weaken Kuwait's posture as an independent Arab country.'[101] The US Ambassador Iraq also expressed misgivings.[102]

'It appears to me', wrote Jernegan, 'that in leaving initiative to Qassim we are in grave danger [of] being drawn into costly and politically disastrous situation over Kuwait.' He admitted to being disturbed by the prospect of 'British troops fighting Arabs on Arab soil with moral and political (if not military) support of US'. 'Even another precautionary landing of British forces', continued Jernegan,

> would play right into hands of Qassim (not to mention Soviets) who would trumpet this as new "proof" of "bogus" nature of Kuwaiti independence. Re-entry of British would also be politically retrograde step which would make mystery [mockery?] of concept of Arab League responsibility for protection [of] Kuwait and would place Jordanians and Saudis in even more invidious position than they now occupy.

The Ambassador saw nothing less than 'major and continuing fin[ancial] contribution to develop other Arab states (particularly oil have-nots such as Jordan and UAR) will in long run save Kuwait from total absorption by one of its neighbours.' Jernegan concluded: 'The West can no longer afford present policy of reliance on British military protection, which seems to be most attractive one to greedy short-sighted Shaikhs.' In a separate despatch, he returned to some of these themes, arguing that 'Kuwait, lacking many of [the] normal attributes [of a] sovereign state, must earn its place in [the] Arab world thru [*sic*] generous and imaginative use of its disproportionate financial resources.'[103] Jernegan's strong views stimulated debate within America's decision-making establishment.

President Kennedy's Special Assistant for National Security Affairs, McGeorge Bundy, described Jernegan's views as 'persuasive',[104] while Secretary of State Rusk recorded that his Department had been 'impressed by the cogency' of the arguments presented by Jernegan.[105] The US Ambassador in Cairo, John S. Badeau, was more sceptical: 'While I agree with Ambassador Jernegan that reliance on British protection of Kuwait places UK and US in increasingly difficult position, I see no alternative which under present circumstances would adequately guarantee preservation [of] Kuwait's independent status and UK and West's interests there.'[106]

Nevertheless, Badeau did concede 'I agree that greater involvement of other Arab states, particularly UAR, would be desirable, and believe formation [of] Kuwait fund for Arab development would be helpful in gradually building up greater Arab stake in future of Kuwait'. Similarly, the US Ambassador in Amman, William B. Macomber, urged that the

> best practical course available at [the] moment would be for USG [to] concentrate efforts on getting UKG [to] impress on Sheik of Kuwait need of launching in immediate future generous Arab area financial aid and support program. From vantage point here [it] would seem Kuwait's long-run chance [of] maintaining independence [is] not great, but prompt announcement [of] generous aid program of which Egypt and fertile crescent area states would be beneficiaries could result in all these states having vested interests in not allowing any one of their number obtaining entire Kuwait resources and buy time for Kuwait to make ultimate association (confederation or otherwise) arrangements of its own choosing.[107]

American scepticism about continued dependence on the British military guarantee for the preservation of Kuwait's independence, however, did not manifest itself in a desire to assume Britain's protecting role. Rather, the concern was to rely on the Arab powers themselves to fulfil this task, dangling the prospect of increasing quantities of Kuwaiti economic assistance as an incentive. By casting the aid net as widely as possible, as Macomber implied, Kuwait would provide the major regional powers with a strong interest in ensuring that rival powers did not establish a hegemonic position in the Amirate. Despite the apparent originality of US thinking, British policy-makers had reached not dissimilar conclusions.

As early as August 1961, the Cabinet Official Committee on the Middle East recognized that it was 'politically desirable that the Kuwaitis should be discreetly encouraged to increase investments in Arab countries'.[108] Echoing American views, the British Ambassador in Kuwait, John Richmond, observed that

> generous investment by Kuwait in her sister states is an essential complement of her reliance on the Arab League for support in the face of the Iraqi claim, and we can only gain politically at any rate, if £50m of the much publicised reserves is withdrawn from London and devoted to the Arabs.[109]

Moreover, as a Foreign Office official pragmatically remarked: 'We cannot really do anything whatever to stop the Kuwaitis from taking money out of their London reserves for this (or any other purpose).'[110] With the lessening of the Iraqi threat to Kuwait (and with it the prospect of British military intervention), following the overthrow of Qassem in February

1963, more traditional American attitudes towards the British presence in Kuwait resurfaced. In July, Rusk informed the US Ambassador in Kuwait that American objectives continued to be the 'maintenance, for [the] time being, of paramount UK position along the Persian Gulf and preservation of existing UK ties'.[111] Rusk went on to say that

> we recognize that western interests must be preserved primarily by UK actions and programs and that US role should remain essentially one of consultation, encouragement, and support with regard to such British policy as we believe will deal successfully with problems of [the] region.

Anglo-American co-operation in the immediate aftermath of Qassem's claim to Kuwait, to an extent, belied earlier British fears (expressed most articulately by Permanent Under-Secretary Hoyer Millar) on this matter. With this precedent in mind, the Political Resident in the Persian Gulf, Sir William Luce, recommended towards the end of 1961 that Britain should consider inviting other Western powers, most notably the United States, to take greater interest in the area.[112] Nevertheless, he pointed out that the Americans were 'content, and perhaps anxious' to leave the burden of maintaining stability to the British. In these circumstances, he speculated that a communist success in the Middle East was a necessary precondition for a possible Anglo-American undertaking to preserve the integrity of the Persian Gulf.

Luce's views, not surprisingly, provoked much debate in FO circles. On the one hand, there were reservations about involving the US too closely in the Gulf.[113] In particular, the fact that there were no American land forces in the Gulf was seen as limiting the practical advantages of joint military planning. US naval forces in the Mediterranean and South-East Asia, moreover, were seen as being too remote from the Gulf to be of any real assistance. Perhaps most importantly, continuing uncertainty over future British deployments rendered joint Anglo-American discussions, on anything other than a general level, premature. Indeed, the FO pointedly argued against US participation, military or otherwise, in British policy towards the Gulf.[114] Such sentiments were reinforced by US Ambassador to Saudi Arabia, Pete Hart's, view that the State Department 'would not be inclined to consider military co-operation even to the extent of reinforcing their squadron now in the Gulf'.[115] Elaborating on this, Hart explained that the State Department did not wish to give Abdul Karim Qassem the impression that the British and Americans were 'ganging up' on him for fear that this would push him closer to the communists.

On the other hand, the general feeling within the FO was that there was little chance of Britain shuffling its responsibilities onto the Americans or its other allies. As one official put it:

> I cannot see that any western power would want to take on tasks that from their point of view are now well performed for them by the British without embarrassment to themselves (this feeling is no doubt behind the Americans reluctance to make joint military plans with us).[116]

The British Embassy in Washington expressed similar views.

Despite indicating support for joint military planning, the British Ambassador, David Ormsby-Gore, suggested that the Americans were content for Britain to bear the responsibility for maintaining stability and security in the Gulf and that they would be 'reluctant to get involved in any of our local problems'.[117] D. A. Greenhill (Counsellor, British Embassy, Washington) speculated that the Americans would

> come down on the side of whatever policy they thought was most likely to maintain the British position in the area for as long as possible, so that it would remain . . . one of the few parts of the free world which they themselves do not have to keep thinking about.[118]

Greenhill also drew a subtle distinction between Saudi Arabia and the Gulf States. In the former, America had the greater part of its oil interests. This fact, coupled with the staunchly anti-communist stance of the Saudi Arabian government, encouraged the US to see the country as one of 'their' countries. By contrast, the Gulf States were regarded primarily as a British responsibility. As Greenhill put it: 'They [the Americans] assume that our aims in this area are extremely close to their own, and they seem quite prepared to let us take the lead in action in pursuit of those aims, and indeed also to co-operate with us as fully as possible unless such co-operation causes them embarrassment elsewhere.'[119] On a more cautionary note, Greenhill noted that Middle East oil production, both in terms of oil supply and balance of payments, was much more important to the British economy than the American. Nevertheless, when William Polk of the State Department's Policy Planning Council discussed the Persian Gulf with the FO a few months later, he fully concurred with the importance which the British placed on preventing a reduction in the number of independent oil-producing countries. Neither did he demur with the FO contention that despite the damage which British policy inflicted on its relations with the Afro-Asian world in general, and other Middle Eastern states in particular, there was no alternative to the British presence.[120] Despite this note of harmony, British and American policies diverged markedly following the Yemeni revolution in September 1962.[121]

On 27 September, Colonel Abdallah al-Sallal seized power in Yemen in an Egyptian-style military coup. With the assistance of Saudi Arabia and Jordan, however, the deposed Imam led resistance to the new Egyptian-backed republican government. Fearing that prolonged involvement would not merely destabilize the two Arab monarchies, but also presage an all-out war between Egypt and Saudi Arabia, the Kennedy administration favoured an early recognition of the Yemen Arab Republic, coupled with a disengagement plan designed to end outside interference in its internal affairs. Confounding the American government, Prime Minister Macmillan prevaricated over the question of recognition.

'[R]ecognition especially by you', Macmillan told Kennedy, 'would spread consternation among our friends throughout Arabia, and particularly in the Aden Protectorate where it would be assumed that Britain was not resolute enough to be dependable and that the United States was pursuing a separate policy'.[122] Privately, Macmillan confided: 'the Americans will risk paying the price (recognition) without effecting the purchase (Egyptian disengagement)'.[123] The British government rejected Kennedy's premise that its interests would be served by 'closing out the Yemeni affair',[124] preferring instead to prolong the internal conflict in Yemen. As Macmillan informed Kennedy, 'it would not suit us too badly if the new Yemeni régime were occupied with their own internal affairs during the next few years'.[125] This attitude stemmed from concern that the republicans would pursue Yemen's traditional irredentist ambitions towards Aden with renewed vigour, using the large Yemeni population there to further their aims. Robert W. Komer of the National Security Council, by contrast, gloomily predicted that 'the UK will end up having alienated the Yemen, thus exacerbating the very threat to Aden it would like to damp down'.[126]

Although the Governor of Aden, Sir Charles Johnston, accepted that in seeking to remove the Egyptian presence from Yemen Britain and America had similar objectives, he emphasized that the two allies disagreed on the method of achieving them.[127] 'One major fallacy in the American thesis seems to me to be the assumption that the only way of getting Nasser out of the Yemen is to give him complete victory', excoriated Johnston. Stressing that Britain should 'avoid following the error of supposing that recognition will make it easier for Nasser to go', Johnston concluded: 'such faith in Nasser's assurances would seem to me inconsistent with the scepticism and tough mindedness which are traditional in British foreign policy, more worthy in short of the State Department than of Whitehall'. Britain's refusal to fall into line with America in the aftermath of the Yemeni revolution supports Michael Kandiah and Gillian Staerck's conclusion that 'Britain was generally unwilling to compromise her external policy interests merely to suit the Americans'.[128]

British procrastination over recognizing the legitimacy of the Yemen Arab Republic resulted in the expulsion of the British legation in February 1963. 'I am sorry that the result is that you and me should now seem to be somewhat out of step in our Yemen policy,' Macmillan told Kennedy, 'but as I see it this is due more to differences in our circumstances than to divergence in objectives.'[129] The Yemeni revolution, however, exposed deeper fissures in Anglo-American relations. On the one hand, while Britain still saw Nasser as the principal threat to Western (specifically British) interests, America was prepared to co-operate with the Egyptian president, seeing him as an anti-communist influence in the region.[130] On the other, historians have identified systemic weaknesses in the concept of interdependence which had informed British policy towards America since the Suez war.

Interdependence, according to Nigel Ashton, was founded on a fundamental misapprehension of its meaning on either side of the Atlantic. While Britain viewed the concept as a 'partnership of equals', in the Kennedy era interdependence meant 'more central control, and that meant American control'.[131] 'Tensions were bound to arise', he contends, 'in a relationship that for one party was one of partnership and equality and for the other one of patron and client'.[132] In Ashton's analysis, Anglo-American differences in the aftermath of the Yemeni revolution were symptomatic of a 'crisis of interdependence' which revealed itself through a whole host of contentious issues in the winter of 1962–3.[133] In a similar vein, W. Taylor Fain stresses that 'Events in Yemen during the early 1960s reveal the fiction of the Anglo-American "special relationship" and the shortcomings of "interdependence"'.[134] Macmillan himself remarked: 'When I launched "interdependence" with President Eisenhower, I think he personally was sincere. But lower down the scale, his wishes were ignored. So it is with President Kennedy.'[135] While there is no denying that differences of perception about their respective roles contributed to the failure of Britain and America to harmonize policy over Yemen, in the Persian Gulf interdependence on the British model proved far more fruitful. Despite some American scepticism, US diplomatic and military support for Britain's Kuwait operation in mid-1961 revealed a degree of partnership. Far from seeking to assert American control in the Gulf, moreover, the US continued to support the British position there.

A State Department paper produced towards the end of 1962 stressed the importance of continuing to 'endorse and give political support to the special UK position in the Persian Gulf proper, recognizing that for the time being US interests can be best preserved by UK actions and programs.'[136] Nevertheless, the State Department did sound a note of caution, observing that Britain's military capabilities were insufficient to deal with an attack by a non-area power such as the Soviet Union. The conclusion was reluctantly reached that in a war situation, whether conventional or nuclear, 'the chief burden of preventing the USSR from reaching or attacking the Gulf oil area would fall on the US'.[137] Although the FO smarted from the State Department's (accurate) prediction that by 1970 British disengagement from the region would be entering its final stages, it did describe the paper as 'an encouraging recognition on the British role in the Persian Gulf'.[138]

Returning to a theme raised at the end of 1961, Sir William Luce advocated more than simply American acquiescence. Identifying the baleful influence of Nasser as the principal threat to British interests in the Gulf area, the Political Resident urged that Britain should 'strive for an agreed and concerted Anglo-American policy to build up the whole of the Arabian peninsula, including Jordan if possible, as a bastion against the expansion of Nasserism'.[139] To achieve this aim, Luce recommended that Britain and America should endeavour to make the Arabian Peninsula 'safe for evolution by exerting all possible pressures on the ruling authorities to adopt enlightened and progressive policies'. In sum, Luce envisaged the emergence of 'an Arab bloc of constitutional monarchy, of ever-increasing prosperity and providing ample opportunity, both political and economic, for the educated class'.

Luce's views did not find favour in the FO. One official not only doubted the extent to which Britain and America could influence the course of events in the free countries of the Arab world, but also expressed concern that the taking of sides in the regional power struggles would be 'at the cost of further alienating the Arabs and possibly driving them into the arms of the Russians'.[140] In a similar vein, another official warned that 'Open UK support of Rulers against Nasser runs the risk of weakening their popularity among their own peoples'.[141] Displaying a strong strain of pragmatism, the same official urged that Britain should avoid writing off either Nasser's importance as a barrier to communism or, to the extent that his interests and those of Britain converged, his readiness to acquiesce in the maintenance of British positions in Arabia. Distilling FO opinion, Deputy Under-Secretary of State Stevens told Luce that the best way of limiting Nasser's capacity to damage vital interests was neither to oppose him openly, nor depart from the stated British policy of non-intervention in Arab affairs. As regards the key question of Anglo-American co-operation in the region, Stevens was equally forthright:

> I do not think that there is any prospect of getting the present US administration to subscribe to the theory that we must work together to exclude Nasserism from the Arabian Peninsula. Their answer would be that Nasserism is another name for the upsurge of Arab nationalism and radicalism and that you can no more exclude it from evolving Arab communities than you can withstand a tidal wave.[142]

Stevens' analysis received support from J. E. Killick (Counsellor, British Embassy, Washington) who found it difficult to envisage the Kennedy administration making the radical shift in their policy necessary to pursue Luce's anti-Nasser crusade.[143]

Despite the scepticism which he had expressed towards the preservation of the British footholds in the Gulf in the aftermath of the Suez crisis (see Chapter 1), Stevens put the case for Britain's long-term presence in the region at a meeting with members of the State Department and the US Embassy in London. His justification centred on the continuing importance to Britain of Persian Gulf oil which, he argued, could be measured in 'decades rather than years'.[144] In a submission to the Cabinet Defence and Oversea Policy Committee, the FO conceded that if the United States took over Britain's responsibilities in the Gulf, there was 'no reason to suppose that Western interests would suffer'.[145] Nevertheless, the FO concluded that there was 'no foreseeable prospect of this occurring, given the absence of United States defence facilities in the area and the undoubted reluctance of the United States Government to take on a quasi-Imperial role'.

During a seminar at the Middle East Institute in Washington attended by members of the US administration and oil company representatives, P. R. H. Wright of the British Embassy defended the British presence in the Gulf. He told his audience that Britain had 'no intention of "disengaging" from the Gulf', stressing that the maintenance of the present position was 'a vital interest, not only of the United Kingdom, but of the Western world in general'.[146] Despite supporting Britain's continuing role, there was fairly widespread comment about the perceived anachronism of the British relationship with the Gulf Rulers. Wright responded by pointing out that the promotion of reform and modernization was limited by long-standing restrictions on Britain's ability to interfere in the internal affairs of the states.

Wright's robust defence of the British position in the Gulf indicates the degree to which Britain had clung tenaciously to its Middle Eastern interests after the Suez crisis. Britain's defence of Kuwait in 1961, coupled with the refusal to accede to American pressure over recognition of the Yemen Arab Republic, also cast doubt on interpretations which identify either the eclipse of Britain by America or British subservience to the United States in the Middle East. While Britain suffered a number of serious reverses, not least the successive nationalizations of the Anglo-Iranian Oil Company and the Suez Canal, it remained determined to preserve its remaining interests. The extent to which America wished to replace Britain is also open to doubt. In the immediate aftermath of the Suez crisis, the US role unquestionably increased, but, as Matthew Elliot points out, 'within a few years of Suez Britain had resumed the leading security role inside the Arab Middle East'.[147] Writing from Dhahran in 1964, US Consul General Horner mused that 'it is clearly in US interests that UK maintain its special relationship with Gulf Shaykhdoms, and retain its military forces in [the] area, hopefully long enough for shayhkdoms to acquire minimum competence to assume control of their own affairs'.[148] As America became more and more enmeshed in Vietnam in the 1960s, the importance attached by the US to the British presence East of Suez grew accordingly. This, and Anglo-American divisions over the eventual British decision to abandon its world role, will be examined in the final chapter.

6 The 'special relationship' and the withdrawal from East of Suez

David Reynolds has described the Anglo-American 'special relationship' as 'a device used by a declining power for trying to harness a rising power to serve its own ends'.[1] More specifically, he argues that the special relationship must be seen 'primarily as a stratagem of British diplomacy rather than as a metaphysical entity'.[2] In a similar vein, Geoffrey Warner identifies Britain's aim as being 'quite simply to harness the much greater military, political, and economic power of the US in support of its own objectives'.[3] Injecting similar realism into the debate, Ian Clark argues that 'the special relationship was viewed from London not as a romantic and sentimental ideal but rather as a pragmatic instrument for the attainment of British interests'.[4] Referring specifically to the Middle East, Matthew Elliot comments that while Britain wanted to 'use American political, military and economic weight in support of their own efforts to obtain treaties or economic agreements with Arab states', it also sought to 'deny the United States real control and to limit the advance of American influence'.[5] The self-interested nature of British calculations inherent in these interpretations complements the questioning by some of the US's hegemonic status in the Anglo-American relationship. 'Contrary to popular apperception,' observes Alex Danchev, 'specialness is not a matter of grace and favour. It is not in the gift of one partner, however strong. . . . It is a process – a process of interaction'.[6] In a similar vein, Alan Dobson points out that the USA 'had to compromise and accommodate her policies on numerous occasions and was not in a position to call all the shots unilaterally except in the Western hemisphere'.[7] Equally, John Dumbrell's analysis of the Cold War era and after has led him to conclude that 'the history of recent US-UK relations is not one of unremitting and absolute American domination'.[8] The British decisions, taken in spite of countervailing US pressure, to devalue sterling and withdraw from East of Suez can be seen in this context. In the mid-1960s, Britain also sought to harness American economic and financial power in the interests of preserving its overseas commitments. This utilization of American power for the pursuit of British interests had been anticipated during the Second World War by the future Prime Minister, Harold Macmillan.

Musing with Richard Crossman on the nature of Anglo-American relations from his vantage point at the Allied Forces Headquarters in North Africa, Macmillan declared:

> We, my dear Crossman, are Greeks in this American empire. You will find the Americans much as the Greeks found the Romans – great big, vulgar, bustling people, more vigorous than we are and also more idle, with more unspoiled virtues but also more corrupt. We must run AFHQ as the Greeks ran the operations of the Emperor Claudius.[9]

Macmillan's attempts, following the Suez crisis, to give practical application to his concept through the establishment of Anglo-American working groups to examine issues of common concern had foundered, not least on the rock of American 'determination to avoid establishing too exclusive a relationship with their British ally' for fear of alienating other NATO members.[10] On another level, to see the weaker, but more cunning, British manipulating the stronger, yet malleable, Americans, is too simplistic. The Johnson administration perceived the maintenance of sterling's value and the preservation of the British presence in the Persian Gulf and Far East as being vital to America's national interest, especially in the context of the Vietnam war. Referring to British and American relations at the time of Suez, Scott Lucas stresses that 'any "alliance" of British and American policies in the Middle East was conditional upon the temporary convergence of differing British and American interests in the area'.[11] In many ways, this tendency was equally true for the 1960s. In these circumstances, it is not surprising that Anglo-American relations were scarred by fundamental divisions.

Anglo-American differences surfaced over the question of US consular representation in the Southern Gulf. In view of American investment in the Trucial Coast and the increasing number of US citizens working there, the State Department requested permission to open a 'branch office' in Dubai.[12] The growing independence of the Gulf States was also advanced as a justification for this US proposal. To avoid giving the impression that America supported Saudi territorial claims in the Trucial States, the State Department recommended that the prospective office in Dubai be put under the supervision of their office in Aden, rather than the Consulate-General in Dhahran. The FO, however, felt disquiet.[13] On the one hand, there was concern that the opening of an American office would make similar requests from other countries difficult to refuse. On the other, the FO demonstrated scepticism over US claims that the opening of a Dubai office was justified by the level of American investment and the number of US citizens residing in the Gulf area. On a practical level, the FO felt that since Americans, like all other non-Muslim foreigners in the Gulf States, were under British jurisdiction, their consular needs were small and could reasonably be met by periodic visits from officers of the US

Consulate-General in Dhahran. The British authorities in the Gulf were in agreement with FO reasoning.[14]

The State Department, however, continued to press their case, using reports that the Arab League was opening an office in Dubai as an added reason for American representation in the area.[15] While conceding that the League would, in all likelihood, seek to establish a presence in either Dubai or Sharjah to administer future aid, the FO stressed its determination to block such a development: the establishment of a US office in the area, it argued, would complicate this objective.[16] Sir William Luce was in full agreement. 'The arrival of a US Consul', he stressed, 'would be bound to weaken our hand with the Rulers and make it more difficult for them to resist the Arab League or, of course, requests from the UAR and Iraq for consular representation.'[17] The Political Resident also set out to demolish the view that, since there were already large numbers of Egyptians in the Gulf in the form of teachers, the opening of a UAR office would do little to increase the risk of subversion. He pointed out that teachers' movements were comparatively circumscribed, and in any event they could be expelled if they ever became a security risk. Professional members of the Egyptian Intelligence Service, by contrast, would not merely enjoy diplomatic immunity, but would also be free to cover any part of the Trucial Coast. Not surprisingly, Luce favoured the continuance of the existing system which had the added advantage of providing Britain with valuable information as a result of the frequent visits by staff from the US Consulate-General in Dhahran. Opposition to a formal American presence on the Gulf coast was reinforced by the calculation that in the first six months of 1965 the Vice Consul, Dhahran, would spend only three days in the Trucial Coast dealing with strictly consular business.[18] Satisfaction among US citizens living and working in the area with the service they were receiving from Dhahran persuaded the State Department to leave the question in abeyance for the time being.[19]

If Anglo-American differences arose over US consular representation in the Gulf, they did too over the relations with Nasser. Ruminating on the long-standing British belief that the Egyptian President was the principal menace to stability in the Middle East, the Minister at the British Embassy in Washington, Sir Michael Stewart, warned that there was little prospect of persuading the Americans to bring pressure to bear on Nasser in the UK's interest.[20] Stewart was also at pains to stress that 'the United States are not prepared to take any risks with the US–UAR relations for our sake'.[21] As regards the British position in general, the United States demonstrated a determination to retain the British presence, US Secretary of Defense, Robert McNamara, impressing upon the British Ambassador, Sir Patrick Dean, and the Home Secretary, Roy Jenkins, that any substantial change in British Middle East policy during the following five years, as set out in the 1966 defence review, would be most unwelcome from the American point of view.[22]

In January 1966, Foreign Secretary Stewart and Defence Secretary Healey had travelled to Washington for discussions on the forthcoming defence review, including the decision to withdraw from Aden. A few months earlier, the United States had provided financial support for the ailing pound. The US administration perceived sterling as a 'crucial buffer, the first line of defense for the dollar, and a critical component in the Vietnam war effort'.[23] The concern was that if speculators turned their attention to the dollar, a whole series of unpopular economic measures, not least a rise in interest rates, deflation, and an increase in taxes, would be the result, thus undermining domestic support for the expensive commitment to Vietnam. In the summer of 1965, Secretary of the Treasury Fowler established a Special Study Group to examine ways in which the US could relieve pressure on sterling in order to provide Britain with the breathing space necessary to 'get its economy into shape'. This, it was hoped, would 'sharply reduce the danger of sterling devalution or exchange control or British military disengagement East of Suez or on the Rhine'.[24] McNamara had already impressed upon Foreign Secretary Stewart the central message: 'Don't pull out Britain because we can't do the job of world policeman alone.'[25] Indicating the drift of American thinking, the President's Special Assistant for National Security Affairs, McGeorge Bundy, had wanted Lyndon Johnson to intimate that 'a British Brigade in Vietnam would be worth a billion dollars at the moment of truth for Sterling'.[26] Although Bundy was overruled with respect to pressure for a British commitment to Vietnam, links were established between support for sterling and maintenance of Britain's role East of Suez.

In September 1965, Bundy reported that 'it took two talks for [Harold] Wilson to agree to the association between our defense of the pound and their overseas commitments'.[27] Indeed, the Prime Minister, during initial talks with Under Secretary of State Ball, had insisted that 'no clear link could be made between the US efforts to assist Sterling and a common approach to foreign policy'.[28] In subsequent discussions, Ball and the US Ambassador in London, David Bruce, explicitly stated that 'it would be a great mistake if the United Kingdom failed to understand that the American effort to relieve Sterling was inextricably related to the commitment of the United Kingdom to maintain its commitments around the world'.[29] Wilson eventually capitulated with the comment that he had expressed earlier reservations 'merely to make the record clear that the United Kingdom would not accept an additional demand for a United Kingdom contribution to Vietnam as a quid pro quo for US Government short-term assistance for Sterling'.[30] With Wilson's upcoming visit to Washington in mind, Secretary Rusk impressed on the President that 'in many areas (e.g. the Middle East) the UK can perform political security functions that no other nation can take over'.[31] During the visit itself in December 1965, Wilson explicitly recognized the importance which America attached to a continuation of British defence commitments and provided assurances that 'the British world-wide role would be maintained'.[32] US economic diplomacy had its drawbacks, however. Jeremy Fielding has criticized the Johnson Administration on the grounds that it 'saw financial aid as a means to help achieve the end result of sustained British global presence at prior levels rather than to solve the underlying economic problems'.[33]

In view of the American wish to preserve Britain's world role, it is not surprising that in advance of the January 1966 talks in Washington on the British defence review, the State Department produced a paper which strongly supported British intentions to build up military forces in the Gulf 'to a strength sufficient to meet local security problems, to reassure Iran, and to play a long-term stabilizing role in the region'.[34] During the discussions themselves, Secretary of State Rusk stressed that the US attached 'the greatest importance to Britain's retaining a world power role'.[35] 'It would be disastrous', he continued,

> if the American people were to get the impression that the US is entirely alone: they simply will not accept it. There are great strains now on this point and insistent questions are being asked by the American people as to what our allies are doing while we are in Vietnam.

The US administration was keen to make clear that in no circumstances would it be willing to contemplate taking over any of Britain's commitments. Indeed, this had been one of Rusk's constant refrains, reinforced by marked congressional aversion to further commitments.[36] MacNamara was of a similar opinion, warning that 'for the next year or two . . . anything which will smell of a British pull out will fatally undermine our domestic base on Viet Nam'.[37] Rusk also explicitly told the Foreign Secretary, George Brown, that

> If there is any thought that we might be able to take on your commitments when you left, as we did in Greece [in 1947], I must say at once that there is no sentiment in this country to take on additional commitments in any area.[38]

American diplomats in the Gulf were also sceptical of assuming a greater role in the Gulf, the US Consul General in Dhahran warning that 'we should avoid letting ourselves get into the position where we share responsibility for maintaining the present ruling families in power without the ability to exert a corresponding influence on their actions'.[39] Looking at the British presence from a Cold War perspective, a National Intelligence Estimate cautioned that 'A British withdrawal from the Persian Gulf would provide the USSR with some opportunities to expand its influence there.'[40] Following Foreign Office Minister Robert's visit to the Gulf to bolster nervous Rulers in November 1967, the Assistant Secretary for Near Eastern Affairs, Lucius D. Battle, breathed a sigh of relief:

> The evident British intention to soldier on in the Gulf is reassuring. We believe every opportunity should be taken to encourage them in this direction, since no power on the horizon is likely to replace the security and stability the British now provide.[41]

Not surprisingly, the announcement at the beginning of 1968 of Britain's intention to quit the Gulf by 1971 was greeted with disbelief in Washington.

Relations between President and Prime Minister had been far from smooth. Although Johnson's description of Wilson as a 'little creep camping on my doorstep' was apocryphal,[42] it does give a flavour of the relationship between the two men. Personal antipathy was complemented by divisions over Vietnam. Wilson's tendency to interfere over Vietnam infuriated the President. 'I won't tell you how to run Malaysia and you don't tell us how to run Vietnam', LBJ snapped during a transatlantic telephone conversation.[43] Wilson's refusal to commit British troops to Vietnam, motivated in part at least by domestic political considerations, also dismayed the President. During their Washington meeting in July 1966, LBJ told Wilson plaintively that 'a platoon of bagpipers would be sufficient, it was the British flag that was needed'.[44] The President also dismissed Wilson's efforts to promote a peace deal over Vietnam as a case of 'Nobel Prize fever'.[45]

On learning of British plans for total withdrawal from the Persian Gulf and Far East by 1971, Johnson gave full vent to his feelings:

> I cannot conceal from you my deep dismay upon learning this profoundly discouraging news. If these steps are taken, they will be tantamount to British withdrawal from world affairs, with all that means for future safety and health of the free world. The structure of peace-keeping will be shaken to its foundations. Our own capability and political will could be gravely weakened if we have to man the ramparts all alone.[46]

In subsequent correspondence, the President told Wilson that 'accelerated British withdrawals from its Far Eastern bases and from the Persian Gulf would create most serious problems for the United States Government and for the security of the entire free world.'[47] 'Americans will find great difficulty in supporting the idea that we must move in to secure areas which the United Kingdom has abandoned', he added.

Foreign Secretary George Brown, who had travelled to Washington to explain British policy, sampled American wrath at first hand. Brown admitted to having a disturbing and distasteful discussion with Rusk during which the latter expostulated, 'For God's sake act like Britain'.[48] Rusk went on to say that he believed Britain to be 'opting out of its world responsibilities', that confidence had been 'terribly shaken', and, perhaps most worryingly, that 'it was an end of an era' which Brown took to mean that the age of co-operation with the United States was over. Rusk was also incensed by what he perceived to be the lack of consultation which preceded the British decision, using the phrase 'the acrid aroma of fait accompli' to underline his point. Brown recorded that the Americans were more concerned about the British withdrawal from the Middle East than from the Far East: ironically in view of the impending Tet offensive the Americans justified this view on the grounds that they were anticipating a fairly early conclusion to the Vietnam War. In the US version of discussions between Brown and Rusk, the latter described British policy as 'a major withdrawal of the UK from world affairs' which would result in a 'catastrophic loss to human society'.[49] A State Department official chimed: 'You're not going to be in the Far East. You're not going to be in the Middle East. You're not even going to be in Europe in strength. Where are you going to be?'[50] Brown admitted to his colleagues that 'There really isn't any answer to that. We've not gone pacifist: we've gone straight neutralist.'[51] Summing up, he declared that 'this was the end of an era'.[52] On the other side of the Atlantic, Secretary Rusk and Defense Secretary Clark Clifford agreed that Anglo-American relations were entering a new phase since, as Clifford put it, Britain 'cannot afford the cost of an adequate defense effort'.[53]

The strength of the US reaction to the British decision to withdraw from East of Suez has been questioned by Matthew Jones who dismisses American protests as mere 'emotional appeals' which soon gave way to resignation and acceptance.[54] In a similar vein, Saki Dockrill asserts that 'although Washington objected to the timing of the British withdrawal, its military disengagement from East of Suez was something which the United States came to appreciate as part of the inevitable process of historical change'.[55] Certainly, the British decision to pull-out East of Suez did not come as a complete surprise to American policy-makers. Towards the end of 1965, the Assistant Secretary for Near East and South Asian Affairs at the State Department, Raymond A. Hare, predicted that 'With the evolving political circumstances and their own dwindling financial position in the world, the British will be forced in the coming years at least somewhat to withdraw their presence in the Gulf.'[56] A few months later, Under Secretary Ball informed the President that 'Britain cannot ask the British people to sacrifice wages and profits while still paying for a world role which, they tend to feel is more nostalgic that real'.[57] In early 1967, moreover, the Special Assistant to the President, Walt Rostow, recorded that the continuing defence review in Britain had 'coincided with a period of national soul-searching', with the result that 'more and more Englishmen are unable to find any real reason why their country should spend blood and treasure in far off places'.[58] To justify his downplaying of the American reaction to the British withdrawal decision, Jones indicates that the US government, increasingly assailed by its own economic difficulties, was disinclined to pay the price necessary to keep British forces East of Suez. 'By 1966–67,' he contends, 'growing awareness of American economic problems made the notion of offering open-ended support to sterling increasingly unattractive, while the US Treasury saw the financial stringencies now being introduced by London as necessary steps to avoid the perils of devaluation.'[59]

While it is difficult to dispute the administration's reluctance to provide an open-ended guarantee to sterling, Jones' interpretation can be questioned. The strength of the US reaction, especially on the part of Secretary Rusk and the President himself, is self-evident, the failure to reverse British policy an expression of American economic weakness and the limits of the 'special relationship' itself. The eleventh hour attempt by the US Treasury to stave off devaluation indicates not merely American concern at the economic repercussions of this action for the American economy, but also the importance which continued to be attached to Britain's defence commitments East of Suez.[60] Equally, the failure of the US to make greater efforts to prevent devaluation and withdrawal demonstrates the difficulties of tying conditions to economic assistance[61] rather than any disinclination to keep troops East of Suez.

The Prime Minister was unimpressed by US arguments presented by Johnson and Rusk.[62] As regards the charge of presenting the Americans with a fait accompli, Wilson responded that the Johnson administration had recently announced economic measures which would place an additional burden on Britain's balance of payments of some £100m. He also pointed out that since both countries were seeking to eliminate their external deficits, they should look to their own interests first. While recognizing that the United States was in a position to damage Britain economically, the Prime Minister concluded combatively that 'it should not be thought that we were not in a position to reply in kind'.

In the Cabinet discussion which followed, it was recognized that, if Britain acted in a way likely to stir American enmity, grave financial and economic consequences could result. In this regard, there was a clear realization that the United States 'did not need to take hostile action, but merely to refuse help'. On the other hand, the Cabinet agreed that:

> We should no longer adopt policies merely because the United States wished us to adopt them and out of fear for the economic consequences if we did not do so. The friendship of the United States had been valuable to us; but we had often paid a heavy price for it.

Echoing the views of the Prime Minister, his colleagues accepted that since the United States government was dealing with its balance of payments on the basis of self-interest, it could not complain if the British did likewise. As if to underline the fact that the post-war 'special relationship' would henceforth be on a somewhat lower plain, the Cabinet observed that 'there was no reason why our relations with the United States should not be at least as good as, for example, those between the United States and Germany'.

In further Cabinet discussions, ministers tended to downplay the impact of the British decision to withdraw from East of Suez on Anglo-American relations. Despite recognizing that the United States was more concerned about the Persian Gulf than the Far East, the Cabinet concluded: 'past experience had shown that, although her initial reaction to our policy changes might be sharp, she was unlikely to take retaliatory action against us in view of the common interests she had with us and our ability to damage her'.[63] Comforted by such sentiments, and fortified by Cabinet approval, Wilson resisted American pressure to reverse the decision to withdraw from East Suez. As regards the Far East and the Gulf, the Prime Minister told Johnson:

> it is absolutely clear to us that our present political commitments are too great for the military capability of the forces that we can reasonably afford, if the economy is to be restored quickly and decisively; but without economic strength, we can have no real military credibility.[64]

Despite Johnson's dire warnings of the consequences,[65] Wilson also relayed the Cabinet's conclusion to cancel the order for fifty American F111 aircraft.[66]

Despite American dismay, there was little enthusiasm for assuming the British position in the Gulf. Reflecting a widely held view, Assistant Secretary Battle remarked: 'the Western position in the Persian Gulf is almost entirely dependent on the British presence. There is no politically feasible way for the US or any other Western power to step in with an equally effective presence once the British are gone'.[67] Not surprisingly, there was a concerted effort to tie the British to the Gulf, even after their formal departure. The State Department eagerly asserted its hope that the military withdrawal would not mean an end to Britain's special political position in the area and that Britain would continue to extend technical co-operation and advice, especially to the smaller states.[68] In a similar vein, Hal Saunders of the National Security Council Staff declared: 'Our reasoning is that the British, even if they may have to pull their troops out, can still do a lot to encourage new political and economic relationships in the Gulf. They have influence and the experience where we do not.'[69] It was also reported by the British Embassy in Washington that the Americans believed in 'a continuing need for constructive and mutually helpful association of smaller states in the Gulf with the UK', and would be taking 'appropriate opportunities to encourage the British to continue playing a meaningful role there after 1971'.[70] An opportunity presented itself in the form of Anglo-American talks in the State Department, during which the US side expressed the hope that Britain would maintain 'as large a "non-military" presence as possible' and would 'on no account' wash its hands of the area.[71] Several months earlier, Assistant Secretary Battle had impressed upon FO Deputy Under-Secretary Greenhill, and officers of the British Embassy, the American government's hope that Britain's presence and ties with the Gulf States would remain despite the phasing out of the military presence.[72]

The State Department was also careful to avoid giving the impression that the United States intended taking over any part of Britain's military responsibilities, and did not even wish to be seen to be consulting with the British over the future of the Gulf.[73] When Under Secretary of State Gene Rostow floated the idea of replacing the British military presence in the Gulf with a regional grouping, the State Department moved quickly to disown this initiative.[74] If tackled by the Ruler of Bahrain about American intentions towards the Gulf, moreover, the US Consul General in Dhahan, Art Allen, had been instructed not merely to express the hope that the Gulf States would maintain close relations with the United Kingdom, but also to discourage any proposal that the United States should take up Britain's protective role.[75] US officials also rebuffed tentative Qatari attempts, following the withdrawal announcement, to draw the Americans into the affairs of the Gulf States.[76]

During a meeting at the State Department on US-Bahrain relations shortly after the British withdrawal announcement, William Brewer of the Bureau of Near Eastern Affairs, noted that 'this is no time for the USG to assume new commitments. Our position is that the littoral states, not the USG, must replace the British presence by establishing new bases for co-operation.'[77] In a similar vein, Rusk stressed that the US government had no intention of replacing the British in the Gulf, expressing the hope that the 'littoral states themselves will seize the opportunity to resolve differences and to establish relationships mutually acceptable to them which will contribute [to] peace and orderly development in the Gulf region'.[78] The Interdepartmental Regional Group (IRG) for Near East and South Asia agreed that it was 'neither politically feasible nor desirable for the US to "replace" the British presence in the Persian Gulf', favouring instead the maintenance of as much of Britain's special role as possible, and the encouragement of greater political and economic co-operation among the Gulf States themselves.[79] At a subsequent meeting of the IRG, the defence member 'expressed concern over the dangers of our taking steps to "fill the vacuum," by selling arms to states with which we do not now have a military supply relationship, as the British withdraw'.[80] The US government went so far as to disavow publicly any intention to fill the vacuum created by the departing British.[81] When the Amir of Kuwait visited America at the end of 1968, he was informed that the United States had 'no plans to take the unique place the UK once held' on the grounds that the British position had 'developed under circumstances not existing today'.[82] It was for the people of the Gulf themselves to determine the future of the area, he was told.

For their part, the British demonstrated little interest in drawing the Americans into the region. The head of the Arabian Department, D. J.

McCarthy, observed that there were some 'fairly ham-handed customers among Americans in Tehran and at near top level in Washington'.[83] 'The risk of British information getting out through people such as these,' he expatiated, 'is simply not worth taking. The problems are too difficult and there is too much at stake to disseminate information on more than a need-to-know basis.' The only real advantage McCarthy could envisage in keeping the Americans abreast of developments in the Gulf related to their putative influence over the Shah of Iran. Even in this case, McCarthy expressed concern that the Shah would attempt to play the British and Americans off against one another if he got wind of close joint consultations. The impending change of administration in America, following the election of Richard Nixon as President, re-opened the question of Anglo-American discussions on the Gulf.

The hiatus between Nixon's election and President Johnson's departure from the White House gave considerable scope for confusion over American policy, ably exploited by a number of rogue figures within the US set-up in the Gulf. Admiral King of the COMIDEASTFOR, the US naval force in the Gulf, along with the Bahrain Petroleum Company (BAPCO) manager in Bahrain, Josephson, were reported to be building up false hopes among Gulf Rulers about US intentions.[84] Shaikh Isa of Bahrain even spoke confidently of an agreement having been reached between the Americans and King Feisal of Saudi Arabia on the Gulf. The US Ambassador in Jedda, Herman Eilts, was keen to play down such hopes.[85] He admitted that following the British announcement on withdrawal, Feisal had, on several occasions, urged the Americans to 'do something'. When pressed, however, the King was unable to be specific. In response to Feisal's representations, Eilts told him that in the US government's view it was for the Gulf States themselves, and particularly Iran and Saudi Arabia, to co-operate in making arrangements to provide security for the region. The Ambassador went on to say that there was 'no question of the United States taking over the British position and that the Gulf States should 'continue to look to Britain for advice and assistance' even after the departure of British forces. In conversation with his British counterpart, Eilts observed that Britain's position in the Gulf had been the result of 'unique historical circumstances' and that, as such, the US could not take it over, even if there were (which he doubted) any American inclination to do so. He also sought to disown King, whom he described as 'a very bad appointment'.[86] Although the British Ambassador in Washington, Sir Patrick Dean,[87] confirmed the suspicion that King's activities were unauthorized, he did indicate that there were elements within the Defense Department who wished to 'beef up' COMIDEASTFOR. These wishes, predicted Dean, would face strong internal opposition, especially from within Congress. He also pointed out that the US had to take account of possible Soviet reactions to any increase in its Gulf presence when formulating policy: any substantial expansion in US deployments in the Gulf could potentially give the Soviets an opportunity either to seek a corresponding increase in the area, or to exploit the US move for propaganda purposes.

In the difficult decisions which confronted the new administration, Dean bemoaned the fact that the State Department was no longer taken into British confidence about the future of the Gulf. 'The Americans', he explained, 'find our attitude difficult to understand in an area where as they see it, we both have such large common interests and where we are entering into a period of increasing uncertainty.' The lack of trust which the Americans perceived was attributed to some injudicious remarks made by the Under Secretary at the State Department, Eugene Rostow. With the exception of Rostow, stressed Dean, the State Department was good at keeping secrets, provided that it was made clear that information was for the Department's use only and not for US embassies abroad. The Ambassador then set about making a powerful case for closer consultation with the State Department on the Gulf. First, he drew attention to the fact that, since the best hope of resolving the Iranian claim to Bahrain was through the United Nations, American assistance would be required to carry negotiations through to a successful conclusion. With the impending withdrawal of British forces, moreover, Dean urged the FO not to forget that in future reliance would have to be placed on COMIDEASTFOR for the evacuation of Britons and for the protection of British interests generally. 'To freeze the Americans out now', he warned, 'may cost us much-needed goodwill in the future.' Finally, the Ambassador indicated that the garrulous Rostow was due to leave the State Department imminently.

Dean's views clearly influenced FO thinking. Even D. J. McCarthy accepted the case for informing the Americans more fully about the prevailing situation in the Gulf. Predicting a 'characteristic dog fight' between the State Department and the Department of Defense, he still urged the necessity of keeping any briefing to a 'very tight circle even within Washington'.[88] In reply to Dean, the Permanent Under-Secretary of State at the FO, Sir Paul Gore-Booth, accepted the need to have a 'full and frank' exchange with the Americans, but on the understanding that there would be no leak of any kind.[89] The Permanent Under-Secretary explained that past reluctance to take the Americans into British confidence over the Gulf had had less to do with Rostow's faux pas, than with the importance attached by the countries of the region, especially Bahrain and Iran, in maintaining absolute secrecy about ongoing and delicate negotiations. In these circumstances, Gore-Booth asserted that it was 'doubly important . . . that if there is any leak, it should not be from British or American sources'. Accordingly, when the relevant Country Director at the State Department (Bill Brewer) was given details of discussions between Iran and Bahrain they received very restricted circulation within the State Department. Other US government agencies were kept in the dark, removing the 'hideous possibility' of Admiral King being brought into the picture.[90]

In March 1969, G. G. Arthur, FCO Assistant Under-Secretary of State and a former Ambassador to Kuwait, travelled to America for talks with representatives of the State Department. In the aftermath of the British announcement of its intention to withdraw from the Gulf, Arthur had specifically told the Amir of Kuwait that he doubted whether he could in future rely on the United States.[91] In the briefing paper Arthur took with him, the FO noted that present indications were that the US was not contemplating taking over Britain's commitments in the Gulf.[92] Equally, Arthur was instructed to tell his hosts that Britain did not support an American take-over, favouring instead US expressions of interest, encouragement and backing. During the discussions themselves, Brewer confirmed that the US 'did not intend to, and nor indeed could they, take over the previous British role in the Persian Gulf'.[93] Although Brewer reported that the Nixon administration had not yet faced up to the future of COMIDEASTFOR, he stated that there were currently no plans either to increase or reduce the force's strength of one missile frigate and two destroyers.

A few months later, the Vice President of the Chase Manhattan Bank, Ian Michie, told the Deputy Political Resident during a visit to the Gulf that new proposals were emanating from the State Department along the lines that Britain should be encouraged to retain a presence in the region beyond 1971, even if this necessitated US financial assistance.[94] The Minister at the British Embassy in Washington, Sir Edward Tomkins, however, was able to refute Michie's contentions.[95] In conversation with White House staff, Tomkins learned that National Security Adviser Kissinger had only 'vaguely mentioned' the Gulf and appeared in no great hurry to refer the matter to the National Security Council. Since the NSC machinery was so 'clogged up' anyway, there was little chance of attention being turned quickly to the Gulf. This information was confirmed by Brewer who added that while the British decision to leave the Gulf had not been welcomed, it was now accepted; British efforts to ensure stability in the area by settling the future of Bahrain and building a Union of Arab Emirates were looked on with favour and America would only review the position if these arrangements collapsed and it looked as if confusion would follow in the wake of British withdrawal. Brewer disclosed that far from considering the possibility of financing a continued British presence, the Americans had not even reached a firm decision on the future of COMIDEASTFOR. If the possibility ever arose, he concluded 'it would be necessary to think long and hard about what purpose any naval presence whether US or British or both, would be designed to serve'.

The Vietnamese miasma, which had been choking American public life since the escalation of US involvement in the mid-1960s, influenced policy-making towards the Gulf. Michael Palmer points out that with public opinion profoundly divided over involvement in Vietnam, Nixon recognized that the American people were not prepared to accept additional commitments around the world.[96] In what became known as the Nixon doctrine, the President told reporters on 25 July 1969 that in future the nations of Asia would have to bear an increased burden with regard to their own defence. Iranian plans to sponsor a regional security arrangement in the Gulf were described by Ambassador MacArthur in Tehran as 'in keeping with [the] so-called "Nixon doctrine" that in the first place it is up to Asian nations to get together to assure their own defense rather than looking to us or other great powers to do so'.[97] Although the Nixon administration wanted to balance Iranian power by drawing Saudi Arabia into any regional security scheme,[98] the sparsely populated desert kingdom could only ever play a secondary, or subordinate role to its infinitely stronger neighbour on the Persian side of the Gulf. As Joseph W. Neubert of the State Department's Planning-Coordination Staff put it: 'Iran is the dominant regional power and an effective US policy in the Gulf must be built on co-operation with Iran and, secondarily, with Saudi Arabia – not with the UK.'[99] Indeed, it is difficult to dispute Palmer's contention that 'the Nixon Doctrine, as implemented in the Persian Gulf, was actually little more than an Iranian policy eagerly embraced by an administration caught in the morass of the Vietnam War'.[100]

Contrary to the drift of American thinking, Shaikh Isa of Bahrain still harboured hopes that the Americans would replace the British in the Gulf after 1971.[101] 'I am firmly certain', recorded the Political Agent in Bahrain, A. D. Parsons, 'that Shaikh Isa has in mind the possibility of trying to suck the Americans in to help him out after we have gone, i.e. of trying to make the tail wag the dog'. Apparently in pursuit of this aim, the Bahrain government was seeking to attract large amounts of US capital to the island. The egregious Admiral King continued to spread rumours about an increase in the US presence in the Gulf and called regularly on the Ruler of Bahrain in the company of Josephson. Parsons also reported that during a recent visit to the Gulf, a member of the Senate Foreign Relations Committee had maintained that the idea of increasing the US naval strength, in order to make it a credible force, was being tossed around not only by the US Navy, but also by his own Committee. Trying to tease out the implications of this inference for British policy, Parsons posed the question, 'would we wish to see the Americans drawn onto the hook from which we are engaged in extracting ourselves?' While not suggesting the signature of new agreements with the Rulers along the lines of the existing British treaties, Parsons did float the idea that relations between America and the newly emergent Gulf States might become a 'modernized version' of the traditional British ties with the Gulf States. In the military sphere, he speculated that America could 'hold the ring' as Britain had done in the past.

The FO poured cold water on Parsons', admittedly tentative, suggestions. 'We have always acted on the assumption', remarked one official, '. . . that there was no prospect of even a relatively interventionist democratic administration taking over our role in any way.'[102] Another warned that any pressure on the Americans would invite the retort that if a Western presence were necessary, why were the British withdrawing.[103] In its brief for a meeting of Commonwealth Prime Ministers, the FCO rejected the notion that 'any outside countries need or ought to take over our present role'.[104] McCarthy conceded that there were elements in the Defense Department who wished to build up COMIDEASTFOR, but he also recognized that there would be strong political resistance in America to new commitments.[105] Moreover, the ability of American oil companies operating in the Gulf to influence policy was limited by the fact that their production, despite earning over $1billion in foreign exchange, met only around two per cent of domestic US requirements. Quite apart from possible adverse Soviet reactions to an expansion in America's military deployments, the Iranians were considered not to welcome 'backdoor imperialism' by the US. 'While . . . it is difficult to predict with any certainty at so early a stage what the Nixon administration's attitude will be,' summed up McCarthy, 'it seems unlikely that they will wish to expand their presence in the Gulf to any significant extent'. As regards the British attitude, McCarthy pointed to recent remarks made by the Secretary of State in Delhi to the effect that, while he deprecated a vacuum in the Gulf, he did not believe it should be filled by outside powers. Expanding on this point, McCarthy described the British position in the Gulf since 1947 as an 'anachronism that worked'. 'For another power to try to pick up anything resembling the anachronism but without the local habit of acceptance which made it work in our case,' reasoned McCarthy, 'seems to me out of the question.' He concluded:

> we should encourage the US to maintain sympathetic interest and political help wherever appropriate . . . but . . . we should not do anything to overcome the US Government's reluctance to assume a commitment comparable to the one we are terminating. An attempt on their part to do this would probably only ensure reactions (pan-Arab or Soviet) which on balance were damaging.

Sir Stewart Crawford was in agreement with these views, adding that an expansion in COMIDEASTFOR'S role might generate local misunderstanding, particularly in the mind of the Ruler of Bahrain.[106] The difficulties of any such policy were soon evident.

Senator Symington of Missouri, who chaired an ad hoc subcommittee of Senate Foreign Relations Committee which was said to be on the warpath against any extension of US commitments overseas, was reported to have given a 'snort of indignation' when the question of US naval expansion in the Gulf was broached.[107] Indeed, there was a strong feeling in Congress against new commitments abroad. The FCO's Arabian Department added that 'The Johnson Administration did not, and the present Administration probably would not, think of a US presence in our place'.[108] In an interview with the *New York Times*, moreover, the Shah proclaimed his view that in future the Gulf powers themselves should handle their own problems without any attempt by the outside powers to fill the void created by the impending British withdrawal.[109] No doubt with his ongoing claim to Bahrain firmly in mind, the Shah declared his opposition to the retention by the US of naval facilities in Bahrain after 1971. In discussions with the British Ambassador in Tehran, the Iranian ruler elaborated on his approach, explaining that he welcomed British withdrawal since it would 'enable him and the other powers in the region to say that they did not want the forces of any outside power in the Gulf'.[110] Not surprisingly, the retention of US forces in Bahrain provoked an angry response from Iran.

Towards the end of 1970, the President made a decision in principle not to reduce the American naval presence in the Gulf 'unless further exploration should prove it politically unacceptable to friends of the US in the area'.[111] Subsequent discussions had apparently revealed no objection to the continued presence of US military forces; indeed, the government of Bahrain had welcomed it.[112] As if to underline this, the Bahrainis asked for the comparatively small sum of $400,000 for the facilities and services required by US forces. Almost from a sense of embarrassment, America's principal officer in Manama, John Newton Gatch, suggested that the sum be increased by $200,000. Even an annual payment of $600,000, he noted, 'would still be an excellent bargain'.[113] The US, however, was careful to limit its responsibilities towards Bahrain. Referring to the impending accord with Bahrain, Deputy Under Secretary of State Johnson stressed: 'Neither title nor tone should convey impression that this is a base rights agreement, with quid pro quo implications. Moreover, we have no commitment or underlying defence arrangement with Bahrain, and agreement should neither create nor imply one.'[114] What Johnson was looking for was a relatively short and straightforward text which would simply seek to continue the existing deployment of COMIDEASTFOR on mutually acceptable terms, while eschewing 'as much legalistic recitation as possible'. Accordingly, on 23 December 1971 exchanges took place with Foreign Minister Mohammed bin Mubarak and Prime Minister Khalifah constituting stationing and facilities agreements.[115]

While the State Department anticipated no difficulty with either Saudi Arabia or Kuwait over the base arrangements, it was 'apprehensive' about the attitude of the Shah.[116] This concern was soon justified. After several days of silence, *Etela'at* and the *Tehran Journal* carried long editorials expressing surprise at, and objection to, the agreements. Reading between the lines, the US Ambassador in Tehran, Douglas MacArthur II, tentatively suggested that this reaction represented a desire to

> place Iran on record against external presence in the Gulf and thus associate itself with other countries of region on this issue, and . . . to be in a position to criticize and object to any efforts by [the] Soviets to establish [a] presence in Gulf or step up their activities there.[117]

MacArthur's surmise proved accurate. Several days after the appearance of the *Etela'at* editorial, Foreign Minister Khalatbari reassured the Ambassador that it was not directed against the United States. Rather it had been necessary to put something on record that Iran opposed foreign forces replacing the British in the Gulf, not least because of Iran's 'long and strongly held position that after [the] withdrawal of [the] British, Gulf littoral states should maintain peace, security, and stability there'.[118] At the end of January 1972, however, the Shah re-ignited the controversy by telling reporters that 'we should not like to see a foreign power in the Persian Gulf. Whether that power be Britain, the United States, the Soviet Union or China our policy has not changed.'[119] Any hope that the issue would subside was frustrated by developments in US domestic politics.

In early December the Chairman of the Senate Committee on Foreign Relations, Senator J. W. Fulbright, had expressed concern about the forthcoming agreements with Bahrain on the grounds that 'there is a great deal more involved here than a simple decision to continue something which has been going on before'.[120] 'Given the far reaching implications of this proposal,' he continued, 'I find it difficult to understand why the negotiations with Bahrain were not brought to the attention of the Committee on Foreign Relations long ago.' David Abshire, the Assistant Secretary for Congressional Relations, attempted to mollify Fulbright by emphasizing that the administration had 'no intention' of assuming the former British role in the Gulf and welcomed the willingness of the Gulf littoral states, notably Iran and Saudi Arabia, to assume an increased responsibility for the region's security.[121] Abshire also assured the Senator that the agreement with Bahrain would 'not contain any explicit or implicit United States military or political commitments to Bahrain or any other government'. Fulbright and his colleagues were far from satisfied. On 6 March 1972 a resolution was passed by a 50–6 vote calling on the administration to submit as treaties to the Senate the recent agreements with Bahrain.[122]

Such wrangling between the executive and legislature ensured that the question received wide media attention. As early as January 1972, the Bahrain government felt it necessary to issue a statement regretting the manner in which international news agencies and the American press had treated the nature of Bahrain–American relations and stressing that Bahrain's sovereignty and independence were in no way compromised by recent agreements with the US government.[123] During discussions with Gatch, the Bahraini Foreign Minister admitted that continuing publicity was making the Bahrain government 'more and more uncomfortable and exposed not only with Arab neighbors but also with Bahraini people'.[124] To illustrate his point he referred to Kuwaiti Foreign Minister, Shaikh Sabah's, advice to cancel the stationing agreement. 'If you really need 600,000 dollars a year,' he said dismissively, 'Kuwait will give it to you.' Gatch was sufficiently alarmed to suggest that the government of Bahrain would give 'serious consideration to closing out US naval presence here if stationing agreement remains in [the] public eye'.[125] If the decision to retain COMIDEASTFOR had raised the US profile in the Gulf, so too did the decision to sell arms to the countries of the region.

In the early 1960s, a tacit understanding had been reached between the transatlantic allies that America would be the prime arms supplier in Saudi Arabia, while Britain would have the same position in Kuwait. By the mid-1960s, however, Kuwait began to investigate the possibility of purchasing military equipment from the US, including sophisticated aircraft. Kuwaiti enquiries were politely rebuffed. In response to requests from the Kuwaiti Defence Minister, Shaikh Sa'ad, for F-4 Phantoms, the American Ambassador in Kuwait, Howard Cottam, remarked:

> If the US sold aircraft to Kuwait, it might adversely affect our whole military relationship with the British. In the light of our global commitments this relationship transcends in importance any benefit the US would gain from an arms sale to Kuwait.[126]

The Lockheed Aircraft Corporation was specifically discouraged by the State Department from a sales drive to Kuwait on the grounds it might weaken Britain's defence commitment to the Amirate.[127] Drawing together the strands of State Department thinking on the matter, Under Secretary of State, George Ball, told the US Embassy in London that

> We do not desire [to] introduce US arms into Kuwait in any way which would (1) undermine Britain's ability [to] perform its defense commitment to Kuwait, (2) encourage British [to] relinquish that commitment, (3) give Kuwaitis renewed idea of turning to US for defense of [the] country, or (4) result in US–UK friction which could limit our efforts [to] work with [the] British for orderly political development in Lower Gulf or lead to UK hindering our commercial activities in that region.[128]

The British decision to leave the Gulf clearly challenged these assumptions.

Initially, Britain's role as Kuwait's primary supplier appeared unimpaired by the withdrawal announcement. In February 1968, Shaikh Sa'ad visited Britain, ostensibly for a medical check-up. Philip M. Kaiser, Minister at the US Embassy in London, reported that the 'British percieve [*sic*] considerable therapeutic value in military sales promotion. There is no question in our mind that UK [is] prepared to sell Sa'ad just about anything short of a do-it-yourself bomb kit'.[129] The FO remained confident that Britain could continue to satisfy Kuwait's defence requirements and expressed hope that the US government would maintain its existing policy of encouraging the Kuwaitis to look, in the first instance, to their traditional arms supplier.[130] Although the State Department was initially prepared to acquiesce in this, doubts began to be raised about maintaining the status quo. Ambassador Cottam opined that 'it may be appropriate for us to reexamine policy with [a] view to making it more flexible', justifying his remarks with reference to 'Scheduled UK withdrawal, fact that Kuwait will never be a military threat to anyone, Kuwait's need to maintain internal stability in order [to] be able [to] play increasingly decisive role in Lower Gulf combined with U.S.'[131] Despite earlier FO bullishness, the US Ambassador in London, David Bruce, related that FO officials had 'privately acknowledged Brits could not reasonably expect their automatic monopoly [in] this field to continue after [the] expiry [of] UK defense commitment to Kuwait'.[132] Pressure also came from the US military for a change in policy towards arms sales to Kuwait.

'[I]f the UK is unable or unwilling to respond to Kuwait's legitimate needs,' observed US commanders to the Joint Chiefs of Staff, 'it would be deemed prudent that the USG reconsider its policy if only to preclude Kuwait's resorting to communist suppliers'.[133] Reflecting this subtle shift in American thinking, Secretary of State Rusk informed the US Embassy in London that

> While we continued to want Kuwaitis to get as much of their military equipment from UK as possible, we would not wish them [to] feel so locked in by this policy that they turned to radically new sources of supply – possibly Communist – for their needs.[134]

Examining the possible consequences of maintaining the British arms monopoly in Kuwait and the Lower Gulf, the Joint Chiefs reached a similar conclusion. '[I]f we were unwilling even to consider requests for purchase of arms to assist in their self-defense,' the Chiefs cautioned, 'we could soon find those states turning to radical Arab or communist sources to meet requirements not filled by the British'.[135] To avoid such an eventuality, the Chiefs recommended that

> while we should continue to look to the United Kingdom as the principal arms supplier in this area, the United States should be prepared to consider favorably on a case-by-case basis limited sales of arms to Kuwait and the lower Gulf States to meet legitimate defense needs not met by the United Kingdom.[136]

At this stage, nevertheless, there was no fundamental reversal of American policy on arms sales. 'We hoped [the] British would maintain significant position in [the] Gulf after 1971 and believed traditional British arms supplier role to Kuwait could usefully be continued', Assistant Secretary of State Battle told the Kuwaiti Ambassador in Washington.[137] At first this line was followed by the new Nixon administration. Secretary of State Rogers informed the US Embassy in London that American policy regarding arms sales to Kuwait was to favour 'continuation [of] traditional British procurement pattern', adding: 'We would not want to upstage UK if it can supply Kuwait with desired weapons'.[138] Doubts about the viability of this policy soon began to resurface and intensify.

Reporting a formal request for US military equipment at the beginning of 1970, the US Ambassador in Kuwait, John Walsh, conceded that

> It is my firm belief that our deference to the British in selling equipment to the Kuwaitis is no longer tenable. The Kuwaitis are not prepared to be solely dependent upon the British market. They regard the existing understanding as an insult to their sovereignty and an impediment to their efforts to create an effective relationship with Saudi Arabia and Iran in the Gulf. Furthermore, they simply cannot accept the logic of our competitive efforts to compete commercially in their market if we are unable to sell them modest quantities of defensive military equipment on cash terms.[139]

Walsh concluded that the Kuwaitis viewed arms sales as 'their test of our willingness to treat them on a fully friendly and independent basis'. A little later, Walsh increased the pressure for a change of tack by warning that if America refused the Kuwaiti request to purchase US equipment, 'they will turn directly to [the] Russians and/or French without reference to the British'.[140] Walsh also predicted that if America went ahead with supplying the Israelis with sophisticated equipment, while denying the same to friendly Arabs, 'Virtually all the local people, including our closest friends, would interpret it as conclusive proof that we were pro-Israeli and very indifferent about them, particularly since they would be inundated with Israeli and Arab propaganda.'[141]

At first, Walsh's arguments did not find a receptive audience in Washington. Under the terms of the 1968 Foreign Military Sales Act, a presidential determination was required to demonstrate that the sale of defence items to Kuwait would strengthen the security of the United States and promote world peace. As Assistant Secretary of State Richardson pointed out, Kuwait's non-acceptance of the 1967 cease-fire and November 1967 UN Security Council Resolution, as well as its maintenance of a token military force in the UAR, made such a case difficult to establish.[142] '[I]f we were to accede to Kuwait's request', continued Richardson, 'we would be reversing policy [of] deferring to British on military sales to Kuwait at time when we wish [to] encourage UK [to] maintain as much influence as possible in [the] region'. The Defense Department was also sceptical about a fundamental policy shift. Noting that the British intended to remain the major arms supplier for the region, Deputy Assistant Secretary for Near East Affairs, Robert J. Pranger, concluded that 'We should not therefore enter into arms competition with them at the present time, and particularly not when the British Government is reviewing its own Persian Gulf policy.'[143] As the date for the British departure drew ever closer, however, the pressure for policy change became irresistible.

During talks at the State Department on the Middle East towards the end of 1970, J. J. Sisco (Assistant Secretary of State for Near East Affairs) told the British delegation that the Americans hoped that Saudi Arabia, Iran and Kuwait would take 'an increasingly important role in the Gulf', and were considering 'how they could help these countries by way of military assistance'.[144] Summing up for the President the specific issue of arms sales to Kuwait, Secretary of State Rogers stressed that

> US interest in Kuwait's security centers on oil and oil wealth. Appropriate sales of US defense articles to Kuwait will strengthen the security of the United States by assuring Kuwait's continued ability to provide uninterrupted oil shipments to our allies in Western Europe and Japan, whose economies are heavily dependent on the nearly three million barrels of oil which they draw daily from Kuwait. Enhancement of Kuwait's ability to defend itself will discourage local risk-taking by neighboring forces and help to preserve stability in the Gulf region after the UK withdrawal . . . . Finally our own balance of payments benefits considerably not only from the fact that American companies own over half of Kuwait's oil industry but also from the access we enjoy to Kuwait's lucrative commercial and financial markets.[145]

Rogers' arguments proved persuasive. On 17 January 1971, Nixon signed a presidential determination affirming that arms sales to Kuwait would 'strengthen the security of the United States and promote world peace'.[146]

The decision to allow arms sales to Kuwait presaged a transformation in relations with the US. In November 1971, Walsh remarked that 'In the course of the past two years there has been a remarkable reversal of GOK attitudes toward the United States. Starting from a position of bristling antagonism they have come full circle to a position of intimacy and basic trust'.[147] By contrast, Walsh insisted that 'No one should misunderstand the bitterness of the Kuwaitis in respect to their past contracts with the British. They are absolutely convinced that they have been consistently cheated'. As regards American defence contractors, Walsh noted that the 'throttles are down and the companies are swarming in'. The Ambassador concluded by observing that 'The Kuwaitis have been so burned, or at least have felt deeply so, by the British, French and Commies in past deals that they are absolutely set to go American.' Despite the expanded US role in the Gulf implied by these developments, Secretary of State Rogers took satisfaction from the fact that 'the transition in the Gulf has taken place in a manner permitting a continuing British role in support of the security of the region'.[148]

As these comments suggest, far from wishing the demise of the British role in the Gulf and its replacement by US influence, America made vigorous attempts to shore up the British position there through economic and diplomatic support. Fully stretched by the Vietnam conflict, and needing to demonstrate to a sceptical public that America was not alone in upholding Western interests around the globe, the British posture East of Suez came to assume new significance in the 1960s. US financial support to stave off sterling devaluation and the cuts in defence expenditure that this would foreshadow, coupled with the dismayed response of the Johnson administration to the eventual withdrawal announcement, underline the importance which America placed on Britain's world role. Although the Nixon administration adjusted to the new realities by encouraging Iran to assume responsibility for Gulf stability, and by breaking the British monopoly on arms supplies to the smaller Gulf States, the US continued to place a nostalgic importance on the British role in the region. This was symbolized by J. J. Sisco's reaction to the news, delivered by Sir William Luce during talks at the State Department in early 1971, that Britain intended to stick to the original timetable for the departure of British forces. 'I think your presentation convinced him intellectually that there was no alternative but to withdraw,' a member of the British Embassy staff told Luce, 'but emotionally he seems to put a higher value on British battalions than we do.'[149]

Conclusion

That the Persian Gulf was of vital economic importance to Britain is a truism.[1] Not only did the region possess the largest oil reserves in the world (about two-thirds of the whole), but also the cheapest as well. By 1967, it provided half the oil used by the Free World outside North America and over half of Western European, including British, requirements. Projecting ten years into the future, the Cabinet Official Defence and Oversea Policy Committee predicted that this dependency was likely to continue at a time when oil was expected to increase its share in total energy supplies.[2] While the scale and significance of Britain's economic stake in the Persian Gulf was not at issue, the means by which to protect it certainly was. Indeed, in the aftermath of the Suez debacle, the region did not escape the growing tendency to subject Britain's overseas commitments to a cost-benefit analysis. Starting with the British Ambassador in Tehran, Sir Roger Steven's penetrating analysis (see Chapter 1), questions began to be raised about the effectiveness of Britain's politico-military establishment in the Gulf in protecting its economic interests there.

Putting the annual cost of defending Middle East oil at £190m, an official of the Treasury remarked: 'This seems a disproportionately high premium, even if UK forces could provide 100 per cent insurance. But in fact they could not prevent a peaceful change which might adversely affect the bargaining power of the oil companies *vis-à-vis* the producing countries.'[3] At the beginning of 1963, another Treasury official opined: 'it is virtually inconceivable that the totality of our supplies should be threatened at one and the same time in any way that could be dealt with by the military means at our disposal in the Persian Gulf'.[4] He also presciently warned that 'If OPEC can make full use of its bargaining power it will be much more likely to affect the oil companies' position in the Middle East than Iraq's seizure of Kuwait'. Just a year later a Foreign Office official mused that 'The latest round of OPEC negotiations seem to throw considerable doubt on the reliance we can place on Kuwait following an independent oil policy.'[5] In a memorandum for the Cabinet Official Defence and Oversea Policy Committee, the FO was forced to concede that 'The presence of British forces does not of itself directly affect the oil policies of individual governments in OPEC or in their dealings with the companies in their territories'.[6] Ominously, in a joint memorandum to the same committee the Treasury, Foreign Office, and Ministry of Power conjectured that 'The Governments of producing countries might, by pursuing concerted efforts through OPEC, gradually erode the present concessionary arrangements to the disadvantage of the companies.'[7] Withdrawal presented its own dangers, however.

Writing in the aftermath of the 1961 'Kuwait incident', Political Resident Sir William Luce asserted that 'there is at present no policy within Her Majesty's Government's grasp which would enable us to withdraw from the Gulf at some point in the future in an orderly manner, leaving behind us political stability and security for our interests'.[8] Examining the possible consequences of Britain's departure from the Gulf, the Cabinet Official Defence and Oversea Policy Committee warned that 'The Gulf would become a power vacuum and our withdrawal would release all the rivalries in the area.'[9] 'The Shah's claim to Bahrein is quiescent now but it would undoubtedly be revived if we were to go', the Committee accurately predicted. The FO had also warned that 'In the absence of British forces in the Gulf, or any other equally effective peace-keeping machinery . . . the chances of serious breakdown in stability are great'.[10] Referring to British oil companies operating in the region, moreover, Sir Harold Beeley (Ambassador, Cairo) had counselled that 'the weakening of our position in the Gulf would probably increase the risk of nationalization'.[11]

Despite the election in 1964 of a Labour government vowing to 'modernize' British relations with the Gulf Shaikhdoms, initially the commitment to the Persian Gulf remained. Referring to Labour's approach to East of Suez as a whole, the former MoD mandarin, Sir Frank Cooper, recalled: 'It did not want, curiously enough I think, to tread on too many eggshells. It believed you could bring about change without doing damage to someone or something somewhere.'[12] With such thinking in mind, the decision at the end of 1965 not to maintain British forces in Aden or the South Arabian Federation after those territories became independent was accompanied by a determination to reinforce the Gulf in order to protect British interests there. With the loss of military facilities in Aden, however, the prospects for an indefinite British stay in the Gulf were undermined. As early as 1961, a Treasury official had insisted that 'If we no longer held Aden, the cost of a seaborne defence policy would be very large, and a reappraisal would be necessary.'[13] The likelihood of such a review ultimately pointing to a British withdrawal from the Gulf was increased by one of Harold Wilson's first acts, the restriction of defence spending to £2000 at 1964 prices until the end of the decade. As Defence Secretary Healey recalled: 'no government should cut a military capability without cutting the political commitment which made that capability necessary'.[14] With such sentiments in mind, the Wilson governments of the 1960s engaged in an almost perpetual reappraisal of Britain's overseas commitments. The key moment, as Saki Dockrill has persuasively argued, was the July 1967 decision to withdraw from East of Suez by the mid-1970s, itself the culmination of an ongoing review of Britain's world role. Indeed, devaluation at the end of the year merely accelerated a withdrawal decision which had already been taken in principle. As Cabinet minister and former Foreign Secretary, Patrick Gordon Walker, recalled: 'Economic emergency compelled the Cabinet to face a radical alteration of defence policy: it made articulate a decision that had, as it were, subconsciously been reached'.[15]

Far from engaging in programmed decision-making, whereby British governments clung blindly and instinctively to an imperial past, the documentary record suggests that policy-makers were more rational and analytical, than earlier accounts of British decolonization have given credit for. For the most part, they were fully aware that the decisions they were forced to take defied easy or superficial prescriptions harking back to a bygone, imperial era. Even the Conservative government of Edward Heath, despite its stated preference for reversing the previous administration's decision regarding withdrawal from East of Suez, approached the question pragmatically. At the end of 1970, Foreign Secretary Douglas-Home told his colleagues on the Cabinet Defence and Oversea Policy Committee that 'The larger States with a stake in the area were now actively pressing us to go, while we could no longer find any justification on military grounds for giving continued military support to the separate Trucial States'.[16] The Secretary of State for Defence, Lord Carrington, agreed that 'it was true that a continuing British presence would act chiefly as an irritant'.[17] The Cabinet Secretary, Burke Trend, had already informed the Prime Minister that 'To continue to station committed forces in the Gulf would prolong the period when . . . we should be in a position of responsibility without control. With Rhodesia and the Caribbean in mind this is an uninviting prospect'.[18] Similar pragmatism underpinned the approach of British governments, both Conservative and Labour, to the question of closer association among the Gulf States.

With the wrecks of numerous failed federal experiments to guide them, the British were extremely wary of any attempt to impose unity on the Gulf States. 'Our best course', Foreign Secretary Gordon Walker told Wilson, 'will be to press on with building up common services for the Trucial States and not to come out openly for the time being with a formal plan for federation, which would be liable to arouse antagonisms and increase the difficulty of welding the area together.'[19] Specifically drawing lessons from the disastrous South Arabian Federation, the Head of the FO's Aden Department, D. J. McCarthy, asserted: 'A structure over-dependent on British participation and support is no good. A structure, even if sounder, which appears to be bound to follow the political and administrative pattern which British practice normally involves is little better.'[20] Shortly before the formal withdrawal announcement was made, moreover, the

FO warned that 'by trying to force the Rulers into an uncongenial mould we should probably cause more instability than we should save'.[21] In his final despatch before stepping down as Political Resident, Sir Stewart Crawford pointed out that

> Britain is not in the Gulf as an imperial Power; the Protected States are not dependencies and as they have for long had their own systems of government, however imperfect, there is no question of our having, as in Aden and other colonies, to create them.[22]

While Britain was a consistent supporter of bringing the small Gulf States together, the emergence of the United Arab Emirates from the old Trucial States essentially derived from the initiative of Shaikhs Zaid of Abu Dhabi and Rashid of Dubai. The perils of direct involvement in the internal affairs of the Gulf States were highlighted during the October 1969 Supreme Council when formal British intervention in favour of harmonization precipitated the collapse of the meeting. Despite supporting the concept of unity for the Lower Gulf, America adopted the stance of an onlooker, albeit an interested one.

In contrast with those interpretations which identify a seamless transfer of power from Britain to America following the Suez episode, successive US administrations neither desired, nor saw the necessity for, such a geo-political innovation. This is not to suggest that the Americans were uncritical of Britain's handling of relations with the Gulf States. 'The British have no monopoly on goofing things up, by any means,' expostulated the US Vice-Consul in Dhahran, 'but they manage to achieve more than their fair share in the Persian Gulf.'[23] Such vituperation notwithstanding, there were clear strategic, economic, and domestic political advantages in the maintenance of the British presence in the Gulf, not least against the background of America's ever-deepening commitment to South-East Asia. During Wilson's first trip to Washington in December 1964, Secretary Rusk emphasized that the US 'would look with the greatest concern at a diminution of the UK's [worldwide] role'.[24] In its brief to the Prime Minister in advance of his visit to Washington in mid-1966, the FO ruminated that 'The Americans, from the security point of view, would welcome our presence in the Gulf for as long as possible.'[25]

Even though the Nixon presidency witnessed an erosion of Britain's traditional predominance in supplying arms to the Gulf States, Assistant Secretary of State Sisco still felt able to emphasize that the State Department 'did not want to take over in any way from the British'.[26] Secretary of State Rogers specifically stated that, if the British chose not to remain in the Gulf, America had 'no intention' of taking their place.[27] So far as the Nixon administration saw anyone assuming the British role of policing the Gulf, it was the Iranians, a development which the British themselves had anticipated. Not until the Iranian revolution, and subsequent fall of the Shah in early 1979, was this policy abandoned in favour of a more pro-active and prominent American role.

At the beginning of 1980, in what became known as the Carter doctrine, President Jimmy Carter announced that

> An attempt by an outside force to gain control of the Persian Gulf region will be regarded as an assault on the vital interests of the United States of America, and such an assault will be repelled by any means necessary, including military force.[28]

This commitment was given military credibility by the formation of a Rapid Deployment Force. The unveiling of the Carter doctrine, argues Douglas Little, signalled that 'at long last, the United States was reluctantly willing to assume the lonely burden of protecting Western interests in the Persian Gulf that Great Britain had shouldered through the early 1970s'.[29] It was to be Carter's Republican successors, however, who were to give his doctrine practical application.

In March 1987, President Ronald Reagan agreed to re-flag Kuwaiti oil tankers, thus providing them with US military protection in the context of the escalating Iran–Iraq war. This decision has been seen as the point at which the Americans had become the 'guardians of the Gulf'.[30] The leading role that the Americans played in evicting Iraq from Kuwait in 1991, and in toppling Saddam Hussein twelve years later in the face of considerable international opposition, underlined this point. Although Britain participated in both actions, it was by now very much the junior partner. Indeed, the British experience after withdrawal in 1971 had indicated the difficulties of maintaining informal influence after formal withdrawal.

In mid-1967, the Cabinet Official Defence and Oversea Policy Committee had prophetically noted that 'Our present political position in the Gulf is now interlocked with our military presence. Neither could survive for long without the other.'[31] John Darwin has also observed that informal empire 'was not a technique which worked very well where the competition for influence was intense and where richer and stronger patrons were waiting in the wings'.[32] This was increasingly the case in the Gulf. Equally, the extent to which a continued British presence could have insulated the Gulf Shaikhdoms from the influence of other oil-producing nations is doubtful.[33]

In February 1971, the six Gulf producers, including Kuwait, Qatar, and Abu Dhabi, concluded the Tehran Agreement with twenty-three oil companies to increase the 'posted-price', an artificial figure which had been used by the companies to calculate the host governments' share of oil profits. Four months later, OPEC agreed that individual governments should demand an increasing stake in the oil companies operating in their countries, negotiations to bring this principle to fruition starting the following year. Against the backdrop of renewed Arab-Israeli conflict, the Organization of Arab Petroleum Exporting Countries, which included

Bahrain, resolved in October 1973 to cut oil production in order to increase pressure for an Israeli withdrawal from the occupied territories. Concerned about the production cutbacks, and frustrated by slow progress in negotiations with the oil companies, OPEC unilaterally hiked oil prices a few days later. The early 1970s had, therefore, witnessed not only far-reaching alterations in the relationship between oil companies and hosts countries, but also the systematic use of oil as a tool of diplomacy. Whether a continued British presence in the Gulf could have prevented the participation of its former charges in these developments is debatable. After all, Kuwait's participation in the oil boycott by some Arab producers of Britain and the United States in the aftermath of the 1967 Six Day War had already indicated the limits of British influence. Perhaps more by luck than design, therefore, the British had withdrawn before their growing frailty, in the face of seemingly inexorable developments, was exposed.

Notes

Preface and acknowledgements

1 Harold Macmillan, *Riding the storm, 1956–9*, London: Macmillan, 1971, p. 523.

Introduction

1 Chris Wrigley, 'Now you see it, now you don't: Harold Wilson and Labour's foreign policy', in R. Coopey, S. Fielding, and N. Tiratsoo (eds), *The Wilson governments, 1964–70*, London: Pinter, 1993, p. 133.
2 Letter from Sir William Luce to Lord Home, No. 98, 22 November 1961, T 317/41.
3 Minute by J. G. S. Beith, 23 January 1962, FO 371/156670/B 1019/2.
4 Political Agents' conference, 20–23 January 1965: Summary record of discussions: Part I: General political discussion, FO 371/179749/B 1051/5/G.
5 'Defence expenditure study No. 6: Long-term policy in the Persian Gulf', report by the Defence Review Working Party, 7 June 1967, OPDO (67) 8, CAB 148/80.
6 Ibid.
7 'Oil aspects of Middle East defence policy', memorandum by the Treasury, Foreign Office, and Ministry of Power, 7 September 1964, DO (O) (S) (64) 17, CAB 148/9.
8 Ibid.
9 See Rosemarie Said Zahlan, *The making of the modern Gulf States: Kuwait, Bahrain, Qatar, the United Arab Emirates and Oman*, Reading: Ithaca Press, 1998, pp. 14–17; 'Relations between Her Majesty's Government and the Rulers of the Persian Gulf States', Foreign Office note, undated, FO 371/185177/B 1051/22.
10 Peter Lienhardt, *Shaikhdoms of Eastern Arabia*, Basingstoke: Palgrave, 2001, p. 9.
11 Simon C. Smith, *Kuwait, 1950–65: Britain, the al-Sabah, and Oil*, Oxford: Oxford University Press, 1999, p. 15.
12 Rosemarie Said Zahlan, 'Hegemony, dependence, and development in the Gulf', in Tim Niblock (ed.), *Social and economic development in the Arab Gulf*, London: Croom Helm, 1980, p. 67.
13 See Robert J. Blyth, 'Britain versus India in the Persian Gulf: The struggle for political control, c. 1928–48', *Journal of Imperial and Commonwealth History*, 28, 1 (2000): 90–111.
14 Letter from the Foreign Office to Bernard Burrows, No. 125, 24 July 1953, FO 371/104270/EA 1053/8.
15 Letter from Sir George Middleton to Selwyn Lloyd, No. 19, 25 February 1959, FO 371/140110/BA 1053/3.

16 Miriam Joyce, *Ruling Shaikhs and Her Majesty's Government 1960–9*, London and Portland, Oregon: Frank Cass, 2003, p. 44.
17 Letter from A. S. Halford to Lloyd, No. 42, 13 August 1959, FO 371/140084/BA 1017/44.
18 Glen Balfour-Paul, *The end of empire in the Middle East: Britain's relinquishment of power in her last three Arab dependencies*, Cambridge: Cambridge University Press, 1991, p. 116.
19 Phillip Darby, *British defence policy East of Suez, 1947–68*, London: Oxford University Press, 1973, p. 330.
20 Phillip Darby, 'East of Suez reassessed', in John Baylis (ed.), *British defence policy in a changing world*, London: Croom Helm, 1977, p. 56.
21 Ibid.
22 John Darwin, *Britain and decolonisation: The retreat from empire in the post-war world*, Basingstoke: Macmillan, 1988, p. 294.
23 Wm. Roger Louis, 'The British withdrawal from the Gulf, 1967–71', *Journal of Imperial and Commonwealth History*, 31, 1 (2003): 84.
24 F. Gregory Gause, 'British and American policies in the Persian Gulf, 1968–73', *Review of International Studies*, 11, 4 (1985): 250.
25 Karl Pieragostini, *Britain, Aden and South Arabia*, Basingstoke: Macmillan, 1991, p. 185.
26 Ibid., p. 33.
27 Anthony Parsons, *They say the lion: Britain's legacy to the Arabs: A personal memoir*, London: Jonathan Cape, 1986, p. 121.
28 John Darwin, 'Britain's withdrawal from East of Suez', in Carl Bridge (ed.), *Munich to Vietnam: Australia's relations with Britain and the United States since the 1930s*, Carlton, Victoria: Melbourne University Press, 1991, p. 145.

1 Responsibility without power: British policy towards the Gulf, 1950–67

1 Letter from Sir George Middleton to Selwyn Lloyd, No. 19, 25 February 1959, FO 371/140110/BA 1053/3.
2 For accounts of the nationalization crisis, see Mostafa Elm, *Oil, power and principle: Iran's nationalization and its aftermath*, Syracuse: Syracuse University Press, 1994; Mary Ann Heiss, *Empire and nationhood: The United States, Great Britain, and Iranian Oil, 1950–4*, New York: Columbia University Press, 1997.
3 Minute by Sir William Strang, 10 September 1951, FO 371/91341/EA 15316/2.
4 The following is based on report on a visit to the States of the Persian Gulf under British protection, with some observations on Iraq and Saudi Arabia and with conclusions and recommendations by Sir Roger Makins, 20 March 1952, FO 371/98343/EA 1051/53.
5 Letter from Sir Rupert Hay to G. W. Furlonge, No. 126/37/50, 14 June 1950, FO 371/82006/EA 1015/13.
6 'Current political developments in Qatar', memorandum by M. R. Rutherford, 31 October 1950, enclosed in telegram from Parker T. Hart to Department of State, No. 46, 31 October 1950, RG 59, Central Decimal Files 1950–4, 786F.00/10–3150.
7 Minute by L. A. C. Fry, 25 September 1950, FO 371/82157/EA 1891/1/G.
8 'Group Captain Plant', minute by C. M. Rose, 3 October 1950, FO 371/82157/EA 1891/2/G.
9 Letter from Hay to Furlonge, No. P14/9/50, 18 December 1950, FO 371/82157/EA 1891/5/G.

10 For an account of the circumstances surrounding the appointment of the adviser, see Simon C. Smith, *Kuwait, 1950–65: Britain, the al-Sabah, and Oil*, Oxford: Oxford University Press, 1999, pp. 16–25.
11 Minute by R. F. G. Sarell, 25 September 1951, PRO, FO 371/91283/EA 10510/3.
12 Minute by D. R. Serpell, 3 March 1952, T 236/4287.
13 Ibid.
14 Jill Crystal, *Oil and Politics in the Gulf: Rulers and merchants in Kuwait and Qatar*, Cambridge: Cambridge University Press, 1990, p. 69.
15 Telegram from Pelly to the Foreign Office, No. 85, 29 March 1953, FO 371/104272/EA 1055/2G.
16 Letter from Jakins to Hay, No. 54/42/50, 28 November 1950, FO 371/82010/EA 1018/48.
17 Letter from Pelly to Hay, No. 95/9/53, 8 April 1954, FO 371/104326/EA 1103/36.
18 Ibid.
19 Copy of a note by Loombe given to Pelly, 10 February 1953, PRO, FO 371/104325/EA 1103/4.
20 Minute by Richmond, 10 June 1953, PRO, FO 371/104272/EA 1055/10.
21 'Sir Roger Makins report on the Persian Gulf', minute by D. A. Greenhill, 2 December 1952, FO 371/98343/1051/58.
22 For an account of the origins of the Higher Executive Committee, see Rosemarie Said Zahlan, *The making of the modern Gulf: Kuwait, Bahrain, Qatar, the United Arab Emirates and Oman*, Reading: Ithaca Press, 1998, pp. 66–8.
23 Telegram from Bahrain to the Foreign Office, No. 166, 3 March 1956, PREM 11/1471.
24 Evelyn Shuckburgh, *Descent to Suez: Diaries 1951–6*, London: Weidenfeld and Nicolson, 1986, p. 344.
25 Minute from Eden to Minister of Defence, No. M 42/56, 10 March 1956, PREM 11/1471.
26 Minute from Eden to the Foreign Secretary, No. M 43/56, 16 March 1956, PREM 11/1471.
27 Telegram from Bahrain (Burrows) to the Foreign Office, No. 226, 15 March 1956, PREM 11/1471.
28 Minister of State at the Foreign Office.
29 Shuckburgh, *Descent to Suez*, p. 346.
30 Ibid., p. 348.
31 'Bahrain', minute by D. M. H. Riches, 17 March 1956, FO 371/120544/EA 1016/30.
32 'Bahrain', minute by C. T. E. Ewart-Biggs, 19 March 1956, FO 371/120545/EA 1016/39.
33 Telegram from Bahrain (Burrows) to the Foreign Office, No. 267, 24 March 1956, FO 371/120545/EA 1016/36.
34 Annexes to memorandum by Secretary of State for Foreign Affairs, 14 April 1956, C.P. (56) 98, CAB 129/80.
35 Memorandum by Secretary of State for Foreign Affairs, 14 April 1956, C.P. (56) 98, CAB 129/80.
36 The following is based on conclusions of a meeting of the Cabinet, 17 April 1956, CM (56) 29th conclusions, CAB 128/30 Part 1.
37 Minute from Eden to the Foreign Secretary, No. M105/56, 10 May 1956, PREM 11/1472.
38 'Bahrain', minute by Selwyn Lloyd to the Prime Minister, No. 426, 9 May 1956, PREM 11/1472.
39 In conversations with Burrow, Belgrave had indicated that he intended to remain in Bahrain for a further two years. (Telegram from Bahrain (Burrows) to the Foreign Office, No. 419, 7 May 1956, PREM 11/1472.)

40 Conclusions of a meeting of the Cabinet, 11 July 1956, CM (56) 48th conclusions, CAB 128/30 Part 2.
41 Telegram from Bahrain (Gault) to the Foreign Office, No. 608, 9 July 1956, FO 371/120547/EA 1016/103.
42 Telegram from Bahrain (Gault) to the Foreign Office, No. 614, 10 July 1956, FO 371/120547/EA 1016/105.
43 'Bahrain', minute by Riches, 24 July 1956, FO 371/120548/EA 1016/121.
44 'Relations with the rest of the Arab world', minute by C. M. Rose, 8 February 1952, FO 371/98364/EA 1071/1.
45 Letter from Burrows to Lloyd, No. 143, 24 December 1955, FO 371/120561/EA 10316/1.
46 Letter from the Secretary of State to Burrows, 19 January 1956, FO 371/120561/EA 10316/3.
47 Telegram from Bahrain (Burrows) to the Foreign Office, No. 733, 16 August 1956, FO 371/120555/EA 10111/5.
48 Telegram from Burrows to the Foreign Office, No. 961, 31 October 1956, FO 1016/478.
49 Letter from Carden to Burrows, No. 1092/110/56G, 13 November 1956, FO 1016/522.
50 Telegram from Bahrain (Burrows) to the Foreign Office, No. 984, 3 November 1956, FO 371/120557/EA 10113/10.
51 See Miriam Joyce, 'The Bahraini three on St. Helena, 1956–61', *Middle East Journal*, 4 (2000): 613–23.
52 Letter from Burrow to Riches, No. 1011/1/40/57G, 4 April 1957, FO 371/126896/EA 1016/54. See also letter from Riches to Burrows, 23 March 1957, FO 371/126896/EA 1016/46.
53 Letter from Riches to Burrows, 23 March 1957, FO 371/126896/EA 1016/46.
54 Letter from Burrows to Lloyd, No. 127, 23 November 1956, FO 371/120558/EA 10113/50.
55 Trucial States Diary No. 11 for the period 1–30 November: Confidential Annex: Reactions to the Anglo-French intervention in Egypt, FO 371/120553/EA 1019/11. On 4 November 1956, the Soviet Union had occupied the Hungarian capital to re-assert Moscow's influence there. (See John C. Campbell, 'The Soviet Union, the United States, and the twin crises of Hungary and Suez', in Wm. Roger Louis and Roger Owen (eds), *Suez 1956: The crisis and its consequences*, Oxford: Clarendon Press, 1989, pp. 233–53.)
56 Letter from Burrows to Lloyd, No. 127, 23 November 1956, FO 371/120558/EA 10113/50.
57 Telegram from Burrows to the Foreign Office, No. 971, 2 November 1956, FO 371/120567/EA 1052/7.
58 Letter from Bell to Burrows, 9 November 1956, FO 371/120557/EA 10113/35.
59 Foreign Service Despatch from William D. Brewer to the Department of State, No. 119, 27 November 1956, RG 59, Central Decimal Files 1955–9, 786D.00/11–2756.
60 Letter from Sir Michael Wright to Lloyd, No. 5, 4 January 1957, FO 371/126923/EA 1071/1.
61 Letter from Sir Roger Stevens to Lloyd, No. 140, 8 December 1956, FO 371/120571/EA 1055/17.
62 Letter from Burrows to Lloyd, No. 12, 24 January 1957, FO 371/126915/EA 1051/2.
63 'Persian Gulf', memorandum by the Secretary of State for Foreign Affairs, 7 June 1957, C. (57) 138, CAB 129/87.
64 Ibid.

65 Memorandum of 30 September 1958 by the Kuwait Government, C (58) 228, CAB 129/95.
66 Letter from D. J. McCarthy to Sir George Middleton, No. 16427/59, 6 October 1959, FO 371/140246/BA 1647/20.
67 Telegram from Richmond to the Foreign Office, No. 6, 4 January 1961, FO 371/156834/BK 1051/2.
68 Substantive text of a letter of assurance to the Ruler of Kuwait on 23 October 1958, C (58) 228, CAB 129/95.
69 Cabinet conclusions, 11 November 1958, CC 80 (58), CAB 128/32 Part 2.
70 'Second Transfer of Jurisdiction in Kuwait', minute by A. R. Walmsley, 22 April 1960, FO 371/149111/BA 1643/41.
71 *Exchange of notes regarding relations between the United Kingdom of Great Britain and Northern Ireland and the State of Kuwait, 19 June 1961*, Cmnd. 1409.
72 Letter from Richmond to Walmsley, No. 1117/60, 26 April 1960, T 236/6314; letter from Cranston to Beaumont, No. 1117/60, 17 May 1960, FO 371/148997/ BA 1114/62; letter from Cranston to Mackay, No. 11116/61, 26 March 1961, T 236/6315.
73 'Kuwait Currency', note by C. E. Loombe, 4 December 1959, FO 371/ 140157/BA 1117/70.
74 Letter from Richmond to Beaumont, No. 1119/61, 12 April 1961, FO 371/ 156860/BK1111/17.
75 *Exchange of notes regarding relations between the United Kingdom of Great Britain and Northern Ireland and the State of Kuwait, 19 June 1961*, Cmnd. 1409.
76 'Jurisdiction in Kuwait', minute by Beaumont, 23 October 1959, FO 371/ 140247/BA 1647/27.
77 Letter from A. S. Halford to Selwyn Lloyd, No. 42 (101122/59), 13 August 1959, FO 371/140084/BA 1017/44.
78 'International Status of Kuwait', memorandum by the Secretary of State for Foreign Affairs, 26 January 1959, CAB 134/2230.
79 Letter from the Secretary of State for Foreign Affairs to Sir William Luce, No. 77, 25 May 1961, FO 371/156673/B 1052/23.
80 'Jurisdiction in Kuwait', minute by Beaumont, 23 October 1959, FO 371/140247/BA 1647/27.
81 Letter from W. P. Cranston to A. Mackay, No. 11116/61, 16 July 1961, FO 371/156860/BK 1111/28. In July 1961, King Hussein of Jordan specifically told Kuwait that it could not expect help from other Arab countries unless it showed willingness to help them. (Telegram from John Henniker-Major to the Foreign Office, No. 591, 25 July 1961, FO 371/156852/BK 1083/141.) In 1962, the Kuwait Fund for Arab Economic Development was established with capital of a billion Kuwaiti dinars. (Ahmed A. Ahmed, 'Kuwait public commercial investments in Arab countries', *Middle Eastern Studies*, 31, 2 (1995): 294.)
82 British Petroleum had a two-thirds share in Abu Dhabi Marine Areas Limited, the remaining one third was held by Compagnie Française des Petroles.
83 A subsidiary of the Iraq Petroleum Company in which BP and Shell each held a 23.75 per cent share.
84 Letter from Sir George Middleton to R. A. Beaumont, No. 1535/1, 11 February 1960, FO 371/149084/B 1534/7.
85 Letter from J. P. E. C. Henniker-Major to R. S. Crawford, No. 10226/61, 29 December 1961, FO 371/162792/B 1052/2.
86 'Policy in the Persian Gulf', minute by G. F. Hiller, 5 March 1962, FO 371/162793/B 1054/3.

87 'British policy in the Persian Gulf', minute by K. H. Jones, 28 February 1962, FO 371/162793/B 1054/3.
88 The following is based on a letter from Luce to Sir Roger Stevens, No. 1040/63, 17 January 1963, FO 371/168632/B 1052/5G.
89 'Sir W. Luce's letter on M.E. policy', minute by R. S. Crawford, 4 February 1963, FO 371/168632/B 1052/5/G.
90 Letter from Roderick Parkes to Stevens, No. 1053/63, 1 February 1963, FO 371/168632/B 1052/9/G.
91 Letter from Richmond to Stevens, No. 1059/63G, 3 February 1963, FO 371/168632/B 1052/9/G.
92 'Middle East Oil and Defence', minute from R. L. Sharp to Hubback, 24 January 1963, T 317/41.
93 'Middle East Oil and Defence', note by J. E. Lucas, 13 March 1963, T 317/42.
94 'Middle East Oil and Defence', minute from Sharp to Hubback, 24 January 1963, T 317/41.
95 'Cost of Middle East Defence', minute by Lucas, 21 January 1963, T 317/41.
96 'Oil and Defence Costs in the Persian Gulf Area', minute by Sharp, 1 February 1963, T 317/42.
97 'Middle East Oil and Defence', note by Lucas, 13 March 1963, T 317/42.
98 'Standing Defence Economic Brief', attached to P. J. Kicatt's minute to Marshall, 3 April 1964, T 317/508.
99 Letter from Luce to Crawford, No. 1040G, 17 June 1964, FO 371/174488/B 1052/13/G.
100 Minute by J. A. Snellgrove, 2 July 1964, FO 371/174488/B 1052/13G.
101 Minute by D. J. McCarthy, 14 July 1964, FO 371/174488/B 1052/13G.
102 'British interests and commitments in the area served by the Aden Base', memorandum by the Foreign Office, 16 July 1964, DO (O) (S) (64) 9, CAB 148/8.
103 'Middle East oil and defence', minute from Sharp to Morton, 1 October 1964, T 317/663.
104 Letter from Geoffrey Harrison to Luce, 10 November 1964, FO 371/174489/B 1052/29.
105 Minute by Patrick Gordon Walker, 27 November 1964, FO 371/174702/BT 1016/35/G.
106 The following is based on letter from Luce to Gordon Walker, No. 38, 11 November 1964, FO 371/179749/B 1051/1/G.
107 Record of a meeting in the Secretary of State's office, 3 December 1964, FO 371/179749/B 1051/1/G.
108 Record of a meeting between Phillips Talbot and R. S. Crawford at the State Department, 23 March 1965, FO 371/179749/B 1051/11.
109 Telegram from the Foreign Office to certain of Her Majesty's Representatives, No. 10, 18 February 1965, FO 371/179749/B 1051/7.
110 Letter from Michael Stewart to Luce, No. 21, 1 April 1965, FO 371/179749/B 1051/9.
111 Ibid.
112 'The Middle East', memorandum by the Secretary of State for Foreign Affairs, 24 March 1965, C. (65) 49, CAB 129/120 Part 2.
113 Telegram from the Foreign Office to certain of Her Majesty's representatives, No. 135, 2 April 1965, FO 371/179789/BB 1015/30.
114 Telegram from Luce to the Foreign Office, No. 186, 13 March 1965, FO 371/179788/BB 1015/4.
115 'Disturbances in Bahrain', minute by T. F. Brenchley, 13 March 1965, FO 371/179788/BB 1015/10.
116 Ibid.

117 'The use of tear gas in Bahrain', Arabian Department minute, 25 March 1965, FO 371/179788/BB 1015/21.
118 Letter from Balfour-Paul to Luce, No. 5 1965, FO 371/179916/BT 1103/86.
119 Ibid.
120 Letter from Crawford to P. S. Milner-Barry (Treasury), 26 April 1965, FO 371/179916/BT 1103/22.
121 'Trucial States', memorandum by the Secretary of State for Foreign Affairs, 24 May 1965, O.P.D. (65) 85, CAB 148/21.
122 Defence and Oversea Policy Committee minutes, 26 May 1965, O.P.D. (65), 27th meeting, CAB 148/18.
123 'Trucial States: aid consortium for Middle East', report by the Minister of Overseas Development, 15 May 1965, O.P.D. (65), 99, CAB 148/21.
124 Defence and Oversea Policy Committee minutes, 26 May 1965, O.P.D. (65), 27th meeting, CAB 148/18.
125 Telegram from Slater to the Foreign Office, No. 54, 7 June 1965, FO 371/179917/BT 1103/140.
126 Telegram from Slater to the Foreign Office, No. 55, 16 June 1965, FO 371/179918/BT 1103/174; telegram from Luce to the Foreign Office, No. 523, 18 June 1965, FO 371/179918/BT 1103/191.
127 Telegram from Tripp to the Foreign Office, No. 513, 15 June 1965, FO 371/179918/BT 1103/172.
128 Telegram from Luce to the Foreign Office, No. 1120, 9 June 1965, FO 371/179918/BT 1103/147.
129 Defence and Oversea Policy Committee minutes, 16 June 1965, O.P.D. (65), 29th meeting, CAB 148/18.
130 Telegram from Luce to the Foreign Office, No. 528, 21 June 1965, FO 371/179918/BT 1103/195.
131 Telegram from Luce to the Foreign Office, No. 559, 28 June 1965, FO 371/179919/BT 1103/211.
132 Telegram from Man to the Foreign Office, No. 356, 25 July 1965, FO 371/179920/BT 1103/261.
133 Minute by Christopher Gandy, 18 July 1965, FO 960/5.
134 'Trucial States Development Fund', minute by Brenchley, 18 October 1965, FO 371/179921/BT 1103/318.
135 Ritchie Ovendale, *Britain, the United States, and transfer of power in the Middle East, 1945–62*, London and New York: Leicester University Press, 1996, p. 225.
136 'Middle East policy', Defence Review Study, 15 October 1965, O.P.D. (O) (65) 67, CAB 148/45.
137 Ibid.
138 Minute by S. Falle, 17 November 1965, FO 371/185177/B 1051/3.
139 Marginal note to Falle's minute, 17 November 1965, FO 371/185177/B 1051/3.
140 Minute by E. M. Rose, 19 November 1965, FO 371/185177/B 1051/3.
141 Letter from Luce to Brenchley, No. 1040, 27 December 1965, FO 371/185177/B 1051/4.
142 Letter from M. C. G. Man to Brenchley, No. 1072/29/12, 29 December 1965, FO 371/185177/B 1051/4.
143 'Persian Gulf currency', minute by J. E. Lucas, 2 May 1966, T 317/841.
144 Telegram from the Foreign Office to Bahrain, No. 453, 3 May 1966, T 317/841.
145 Telegram from the Foreign Office to Dubai, No. 216, 19 May 1966, T 317/841.
146 Robin Neillands, *A fighting retreat: the British empire, 1947–97*, London: Coronet Books, 1996, p. 354.
147 Letter from Sir Charles Johnston to Reginald Maudling, No. 726, 20 May 1962, FO 371/162785/B 1051/21. The former Commonwealth Secretary, George Thomson, recollected that 'we were trying to force together a society which

was not capable of being melded into one'. (Peter Catterall (ed.), Witness seminar: 'The East of Suez decision', *Contemporary Record*, 7, 3 (1993): 641.)

148 Karl Pieragostini, *Britain, Aden and South Arabia*, Basingstoke: Macmillan, 1991, p. 39.

149 Minutes of a meeting of the Defence and Oversea Policy committee, 5 August 1965, OPD (65) 36th meeting, CAB 148/18.

150 'Middle East policy', Defence Review Study, 15 October 1965, OPD (O) (65) 67, CAB 148/45.

151 Minutes of a meeting of the Defence and Oversea Policy Committee, 24 November 1965, OPD (65) 52nd meeting, CAB 148/18.

152 'Middle East policy', Defence Review Study, 15 October 1965, OPD (O) (65) 67, CAB 148/45.

153 'The Persian Gulf', minute by Michael Stewart to the Prime Minister, PM/66/5, 25 January 1966, PREM 13/2209; letter from Crawford to Brown, No. 31, 28 December 1966, PREM 13/2209.

154 'Middle East policy', Defence Review Study, 15 October 1965, OPD (O) (65) 67, CAB 148/45.

155 The following is based on 'Defence expenditure No. 6: long-term policy in the Persian Gulf', report by the Defence Review Working Party, 7 June 1967 OPDO (67) 8, CAB 148/80.

2 Defence reviews, devaluation, and Britain's departure from The Gulf

1 John Darwin, 'Britain's withdrawal from East of Suez', in Carl Bridge (ed.), *Munich to Vietnam: Australia's relations with Britain and the United States since the 1930s*, Carlton, Victoria: Melbourne University Press, 1991, p. 150.

2 Chris Wrigley, 'Now you see it, now you don't: Harold Wilson and Labour's foreign policy', in R. Coopey, S. Fielding and N. Tiratsoo (eds), *The Wilson Governments, 1964–1970*, London: Pinter, 1993, p. 130.

3 The following is based on 'Defence withdrawals', memorandum by Richard Crossman, 4 July 1967, C (67) 116, CAB 129/131 Part 2.

4 The following is based on Cabinet conclusions, 6 July 1967, CC (67) 45, CAB 128/42 Part 2.

5 'The Persian Gulf', minute by M. S. Weir, 22 September 1967, FCO 8/41.

6 Telegram from W. P. Cranston (Counsellor, British Embassy, Jedda) to the Foreign Office, No. 693, 8 October 1967, FCO 8/41.

7 Letter from Sir Stewart Crawford to Sir Richard Beaumont, 28 October 1967, FCO 8/41.

8 *Supplementary statement on defence 1967*, London: HMSO, July 1967, Cmnd. 3357.

9 Report of the Defence Review Working Party, 25 July 1967, OPDO (67) 11, CAB 148/81.

10 Saki Dockrill, *Britain's retreat from East of Suez: The choice between Europe and the world*, Basingstoke: Palgrave, 2002, p. 212.

11 Ibid., p. 206.

12 Ibid., p. 194.

13 Ibid., pp. 133–4.

14 Ibid., p. 141.

15 Ibid., p. 204.

16 Jeffrey Pickering, 'Politics and "Black Tuesday": Shifting power in the Cabinet and the decision to withdraw from East of Suez, November 1967–January 1968', *Twentieth Century British History*, 13, 2 (2002): 147.

17 Ibid., p. 152.

18 Ibid., p. 154.
19 Ibid.
20 Ibid., p. 156.
21 Ibid., p. 162.
22 Telegram from the American Embassy to the Secretary of State, No. 5847, 24 January 1968, RG 59, Subject-Numeric Files 1967–9, Box 1640, DEF 1 UK.
23 Jeffrey Pickering, *Britain's withdrawal from East of Suez: The politics of retrenchment*, Basingstoke: Macmillan, 1998, p. 186.
24 Matthew Jones, 'A decision delayed: Britain's withdrawal from South East Asia reconsidered, 1961–8', *English Historical Review*, 117, 472 (2002): 571.
25 Ibid., p. 584.
26 Ibid., p. 585.
27 'Public expenditure: post-devaluation measures: defence cuts', memorandum by the Secretary of State for Foreign Affairs and the Secretary of State Commonwealth Affairs, 3 January 1968, C (68) 7 (revise), CAB 129/135 (emphasis in original).
28 Telegram from the Embassy in the United Kingdom to the Department of State, 9 January 1968, cited in *Foreign Relations of the United States, 1964–8: Volume XII: Western Europe*, Washington: United States Government Printing Office, 2001, p. 599.
29 Denis Healey, *The time of my life*, London: Michael Johnson, 1989, p. 280.
30 Cabinet conclusions, 15 January 1968, CC 7 (68), CAB 128/43 Part 1.
31 'Withdrawal from the Gulf', minute by P. Nicholls, 12 January 1968, T 225/3144.
32 'Withdrawal from the Gulf', minute from S. H. Wright to Figgures, 23 January 1968, T 317/1069.
33 Minute by I. P. Bancroft, 12 January 1968, T 225/3144.
34 Minutes of the Defence Review Working Party, 13 October 1969, OPDO (DR) (69) 2nd meeting, CAB 148/97.
35 'Persian Gulf', minute by P. S. Mewes to Nicholls, 10 October 1969, T 225/3404.
36 Letter from Parsons to Weir, No. 2/4, 3 December 1968, FCO 8/915.
37 Cited in 'British withdrawal from the Persian Gulf: local views', memorandum by the Arabian Department, 11 June 1969, FCO 8/979.
38 Ibid.
39 Ibid.
40 Minute by Goronwy Roberts, 26 June 1969, FCO 8/979.
41 The following is based on letter from Weir to A. A. Acland, No. 3/15, 23 June 1970, FCO 8/1315.
42 Telegram from Alec Douglas-Home to the Bahrain Residency, No. 293, 26 June 1970, PREM 15/538.
43 Telegram from Crawford to the Foreign and Commonwealth Office, No. 318, 1 July 1971, PREM 15/538.
44 Telegram from Sam Falle to the Foreign and Commonwealth Office, No. 243, 27 June 1970, FCO 8/1315.
45 Telegram from F. A. Warner to the Foreign and Commonwealth Office, No. 1440, 26 June 1970, FCO 8/1315.
46 'Policy in the Gulf: consultations with the Shah', minute by Acland, 29 June 1970, FCO 8/1315.
47 Telegram from Falle to the Foreign and Commonwealth Office, No. 240, 25 June 1970, FCO 8/1315.
48 Letter from D. L. Stewart to P. T. Pyman, 1 July 1970, FCO 8/1316.
49 Telegram from Freeman (Washington) to the Foreign and Commonwealth Office, No. 1968, 29 June 1970, FCO 8/1315.
50 Telegram from Morris to the Foreign and Commonwealth Office, No. 387, 30 June 1970, FCO 8/1315.

51 'The Persian Gulf: Questions to be considered if the British military withdrawal from the Gulf and the termination of the special treaty relationship is to be cancelled or delayed', paper attached to Acland's minute 22 June 1970, FCO 8/1315.
52 'Consultations with the Shah', minute by Alec Douglas-Home to the Prime Minister, PM/70/75, 13 July 1970, FCO 8/1316.
53 Letter from Falle to Acland, 15 July 1970, FCO 8/1317. See also telegram from Falle to the Foreign and Commonwealth Office, No. 265, 28 July 1970, FCO 8/1318.
54 Telegram from Falle to the Foreign and Commonwealth Office, No. 270, 30 July 1970, FCO 8/1318.
55 Ibid.
56 Telegram from Weir to the Foreign and Commonwealth Office, No. 384, 2 August 1970, FCO 8/1318.
57 Letter from Crawford to Douglas-Home, 28 July 1970, FCO 8/1318.
58 Ibid.
59 'Military options for the Gulf after 1971', note by Luce, 17 August 1970, FCO 8/1319.
60 Ibid.
61 'British policy in the Persian Gulf', note by Luce, 2 October 1970, PREM 15/538.
62 The following is based on 'Policy in the Persian Gulf', Sir William Luce's recommendations, 4 December 1970, DOP (70) 44, CAB 148/102.
63 Minutes of a meeting of the Defence and Oversea Policy Committee, 11 December 1970, DOP (70) 12th meeting, CAB 148/101.
64 Minutes of the Cabinet Defence and Oversea Policy Committee, 24 February 1971, DOP (71) 6th meeting, CAB 148/115.
65 Cabinet conclusions, 25 February 1971, CM (71) 11th conclusions, CAB 128/49 Part 1.
66 *Parliamentary Debates (Commons), 1970–1*, Volume 812, col. 1228, 1 March 1971.
67 Ibid., col. 1229.
68 Ibid., col. 1230.
69 Minute by P. S. Milner-Barry, 9 March 1961, T 317/662.
70 'Kuwait: Future relations with the United Kingdom', minute by A. Mackay, 10 April 1961, T 317/114.
71 'Kuwait: Future relations with the United Kingdom', memorandum by the Lord Privy Seal, 5 April 1961 C (61) 49, CAB 129/104.
72 Letter from the Secretary of State to Luce, No. 77, 25 May 1961, FO 371/156673/BA 105223.
73 Cabinet conclusions, 13 April 1961, CC 20 (61), CAB 128/35 Part 1.
74 'Anglo-Kuwaiti relations', minute by R. A. Beaumont, 17 April 1961, FO 371/156835/BK 1051/21/G.
75 Telegram from the Foreign Office to Bahrain, No. 501, 28 April 1961, FO 371/156835/BK 1051/22.
76 Letter from Luce to Crawford, No. 1040/64, 3 July 1964, FO 371/174489/B 1052/26/G.
77 The following is based on 'Kuwait', memorandum by the Foreign Office and Ministry of Defence, 25 September 1961, GEN 745/4, CAB 130/178.
78 Letter from Luce to Home, No. 98, 22 November 1961, FO 371/156670/B 1019/2.
79 Letter from Richmond to Luce, No. 1059/61G, 10 December 1961, FO 371/156670/B 1019/3.
80 'Defence in the Persian Gulf', minute from A. Mackay to P. S. Milner-Barry, 9 May 1962, T 317/41.

81 Minute by Milner-Barry, 12 October 1962, T 317/41.
82 'Middle East oil and defence', minute from R. L. Sharp to Morton, 1 October 1964, T 317/663.
83 Letter from Christopher Gandy to Crawford, No. 1033/64, 30 June 1964, FO 371/174488/B 1052/15/G.
84 'A heresy', minute by D. P. Gracie, 13 July 1964, FO 371/174610/BK 1193/2.
85 Letter from G. N. Jackson to Stewart, No. 32, 30 May 1965, FO 371/179839/BK 1051/12.
86 Miriam Joyce, *Ruling Shaikhs and Her Majesty's Government 1960–9*, London: Frank Cass, 2003, p.66.
87 Robert L. Jarman, *Sabah al-Salim al-Sabah, Amir of Kuwait, 1965–77: A political biography*, London: The London Centre of Arab Studies, 2002, p. 168.
88 Letter from Jackson to Stewart, No. 32, 30 May 1965, FO 371/179839/BK 1051/12.
89 'United Kingdom commitments in the Persian Gulf', Defence Review Study, 27 October 1965, OPO (O) (65) 66, CAB 148/45.
90 'Some general considerations of foreign policy with particular reflections on the Middle East', memorandum by the Secretary of State for Foreign Affairs, 22 November 1965, OPD (65) 174, CAB 148/23.
91 The following is based on letter from D. J. McCarthy to M. S. Weir, No. 1193/65, 24 November 1965, FO 371/179842/BK 1091/11/G.
92 The following is based on letter from Luce to Brenchley, No. 1040G, 8 November 1965, FO 960/13.
93 Letter from Jackson to Brenchley, 23 November 1965, FO 960/13.
94 Minute from George Thomson to the Secretary of State for Defence, FS/GMT/65/155, 1 December 1965, PREM 13/2181.
95 Karl Hack, *Defence and decolonisation in Southeast Asia: Britain, Malaya and Singapore, 1941–68*, Richmond: Curzon, 2001, p. 285.
96 'Kuwait', minute by T. F. Brenchley, 23 May 1966, FO 371/185420/BK 1194/3.
97 Minute from Denis Healey to the Foreign Secretary, MO/3/7/3, 30 September 1966, DEFE 11/513.
98 'Defence of Kuwait', minute by Brenchley, 6 October 1966, FO 371/185420/BK 1194/8/G.
99 Ibid.
100 'Defence of Kuwait', minute by George Brown to the Secretary of State for Defence, No. PS/66/100, 7 November 1966, DEFE 11/513.
101 'Defence of Kuwait', minute by Healey to the Foreign Secretary, MO/3/7/3, Pt. 6, 5 December 1966, FO 371/185420/BK 1194/17/G.
102 'Military assistance to Kuwait', minute from Healey to the Prime Minister, MO 3/7/3, 2 January 1967, FCO 8/659. A copy of this minute can be found in PREM 13/2181.
103 Telegram from the Foreign Office to Kuwait, No. 717, 9 December 1966, FO 371/185420/BK 1194/17/G.
104 Telegram from Kuwait to the Foreign Office, No. 580, 13 December 1966, FO 371/185420/BK 1194/17/G.
105 *Parliamentary Debates (Commons), 1966–7*, Volume 737, col. 1281, 6 December 1966.
106 The following is based on letter from G. N. Jackson to T. F. Brenchley, No. 11931/66G, 3 January 1967, FCO 8/657.
107 The following is based on letter from A. Campbell to Brenchley, No. DS 1/4/5, 4 May 1967, FCO 8/623.
108 The following is based on 'Defence expenditure study no. 5: The Kuwait commitment in the period to 1970–71', report by the Defence Review Working Party, 23 May 1967, OPDO (67) 7, CAB 148/80.

109 The Committee did admit that diversification was 'already present in the minds of the present Kuwaiti regime'.
110 Letter from G. G. Arthur to George Brown, No. 17, 1 July 1967, FCO 8/614.
111 Ibid.
112 Letter from J. A. N. Graham to M. S. Weir, No. 10711, 25 June 1967, FCO 8/620.
113 Letter from Crawford to Brown, No. 19, 23 June 1967, FCO 8/44.
114 'Kuwait', minute by D. J. Maitland, 16 June 1967, FCO 8/614.
115 'Kuwait', minute by M. S. Weir, 28 June 1967, FCO 8/677.
116 Minute by Brenchley, 28 June 1967, FCO 8/677.
117 'Kuwait', minute by Weir, 21 July 1967, FCO 8/677.
118 Minute by Brenchley, 21 July 1967, FCO 8/677.
119 'Kuwait', minute by Brenchley, 25 July 1967, FCO 8/677.
120 Ibid.
121 Minute by P. H. Gore-Booth, 25 July 1967, FCO 8/677.
122 Letter from G. G. Arthur to Brenchley, No. 1041/67G, 9 July 1967, FCO 8/677.
123 Letter from Crawford to Brenchley, No. 11948/2G/12/67, 22 July 1967, FCO 8/677.
124 Letter from D. M. Day (Assistant Private Secretary to the Secretary of State for Foreign Affairs) to R. M. Hastie-Smith (Assistant Private Secretary to the Secretary of State for Defence), 14 August 1967, DEFE 11/548.
125 Letter from D. E. Munson (Assistant Private Secretary to Secretary of State for Defence) to Day, No. MO. 3/7/3, 23 August 1967, DEFE 11/548.
126 'Persian Gulf commitments', memorandum by the Secretary of State for Foreign Affairs, 27 March 1968, OPD (68) 25, CAB 148/36.
127 Letter from Arthur to Weir, No. 2/33, 29 February 1968, FCO 8/657.
128 Telegram from Arthur to the Foreign Office, No. 202, 28 April 1968, FCO 8/657.
129 *Exchange of notes between the Government of the United Kingdom of Great Britain and Northern Ireland and the Government of the State of Kuwait terminating the Agreement of 19 June 1961, regarding relations between the United Kingdom of Great Britain and Northern Ireland and the State of Kuwait, 13 May 1968*, Cmnd. 3720.
130 Letter from Arthur to Stewart, 13 May 1968, FCO 8/657.
131 Ibid.
132 'British withdrawal from the Persian Gulf: local views', memorandum by the Arabian Department, 11 June 1969, FCO 8/979.
133 'British withdrawal from the Persian Gulf: Local views', memorandum by the Arabian Department, 11 June 1969, FCO 8/979.
134 Letter from S. Falle to Stewart, No. 1/12, 12 March 1969, FCO 8/1027.
135 Letter from Falle to Stewart, No. 2/13, 15 May 1969, FCO 8/1027.
136 Ibid.
137 Letter from A. C. Goodison to D. J. McCarthy, No. 1/2, 17 September 1969, FCO 8/1028/1.
138 Letter from Falle to Stewart, No. 26/5, 1 December 1969, FCO 8/1028/1.

3 The failure of the federal idea in the Gulf, 1950–68

1 Letter from C. J. Treadwell to Alec Douglas-Home, 11 May 1972, FCO 8/1923.
2 Letter from M. Vassighy (Charge d'Affaires, Iranian Embassy) to B. A. B. Burrows, No. 1369, 24 August 1949, FO 371/74966/E10405.
3 Letter from H. G. Jakins to Sir Rupert Hay, No. 124/26/50, 8 November 1950, FO 371/82008/EA 1017/2.
4 Letter from Jakins to Hay, No. 124/27/50, 9 November 1950, FO 371/82008/EA 1017/2.

5 Letter from Hay to Jakins, No. 523/3/50, 18 November 1950, FO 371/82008/EA 1017/3.
6 The following is based on letter from Hay to the Secretary of State for Foreign Affairs, No. 13, 29 January 1951, FO 371/91326/EA 1511/1.
7 Minute by C. M. Rose, 13 March 1951, FO 371/91326/EA 1511/1.
8 Letter from the Secretary of State to Hay, No. 48, 2 April 1951, FO 371/91326/EA 1511/1.
9 Minute by Rose, 13 March 1951, FO 371/91326/EA 1511/1.
10 Minute by Rose, 30 May 1951, FO 371/91326/1511/5.
11 Frauke Heard-Bey, *From Trucial States to United Arab Emirates*, new edition, Harlow: Longman, 1996, p. 342.
12 Letter from Hay to Anthony Eden, No. 48, 9 May 1952, FO 371/98331/EA 10110/1.
13 Letter from D. A. Greenhill to Hay, 16 March 1953, FO 371/104261/EA 1015/2.
14 Letter from Hay to Sir Winston Churchill, No. 46, 14 May 1953, FO 371/104261/EA 1015/3.
15 Letter from Hay to Churchill, No. 56, 25 June 1953, FO 371/104270/EA 1053/7.
16 Letter from B. A. B. Burrows to Eden, No. 106, 5 December 1953, FO 371/104261/EA 1015/4.
17 Minute by M. S. Buckmaster, 13 January 1953, FO 371/104261/EA 1015/4.
18 Letter from C. M. Pirie-Gordon to Burrows, No. 4, 1 December 1953, FO 371/104261/EA 1015/4.
19 The following is based on letter from Pirie-Gordon to Burrows, No. 5, 5 July 1954, FO 371/109814/EA 1011/1.
20 The following is based on letter from Pirie-Gordon to Burrows, No. 1, 2 January 1955, FO 371/114592/EA 10111/2.
21 Letter from Tripp to C. A. Gault, No. 15, 27 August 1955, FO 371/114592/EA 10111/1.
22 Letter from Roger Stevens to Harold Caccia, No. 1828/4/56, 3 April 1956, FO 371/120552/EA 1018/1.
23 Letter from Caccia to Stevens, 19 April 1956, FO 371/120552/EA 1018/1.
24 Letter from Sir Michael Wright to Selwyn Lloyd, No. 5, 4 January 1957, FO 371/126923/EA 1071/1.
25 The Baghdad Pact was a defensive alliance of pro-Western 'Northern Tier' countries which Britain joined in April 1955. For an account of the formation of the Baghdad Pact, see Brian Holden Reid, 'The "Northern Tier" and the Baghdad Pact', in John W. Young (ed.), *The foreign policy of Churchill's peacetime administration, 1951–5*, Leicester: Leicester University Press, 1988.
26 Letter from Sir Bernard Burrows to Selwyn Lloyd, No. 12, 24 January 1957, FO 371/126915/EA 1051/2.
27 The following is based on Simon C. Smith, 'Rulers and Residents: British relations with the Aden Protectorate, 1937–59', *Middle Eastern Studies*, 31, 3 (1995): 517–18. See also, Spencer Mawby, 'Britain's last imperial frontier: The Aden Protectorates, 1952–9', *Journal of Imperial and Commonwealth History*, 29, 2 (2001): 75–100.
28 Letter from Burrows to Lloyd, No. 12, 24 January 1957, FO 371/126915/EA 1051/2.
29 'The future of the Persian Gulf States', paper by Burrows attached to his letter to H. Beeley, No. 1041 G, 27 May 1957, FO 371/126916/EA 1051/16.
30 'United Kingdom Position in the Persian Gulf', minute by J. B. Denson, 9 March 1957, FO 371/126915/EA 1051/11.
31 'Anglo-American talks: Persian Gulf', brief by Sir Humphrey Trevelyan attached to his minute of 28 August 1957, FO 371/126924/EA 1072/1.

32 Further political marriages were contracted with Ajman, Umm al Qawain, and Sharjah.
33 Letter from D. F. Hawley to Sir George Middleton, No. 14, 6 December 1959, FO 371/148946/BA 1071/1.
34 Minute by W. J. Adams, 20 May 1959, FO 371/140103/BA 1041/1.
35 The following is based on letter from Hawley to Middleton, No. 6, 11 May 1959, FO 371/140103/BA 1041/1.
36 Minute by R. A. Beaumont, 25 May 1959, FO 371/140103/BA 1041/1.
37 Letter from Hawley to Middleton, No. 6, 11 May 1959, FO 371/140103/BA 1041/1.
38 Ibid.
39 Minute by W. J. Adams, 20 May 1959, FO 371/140103/BA 1041/1.
40 Letter from R. G. Giddens to M.C.G. Man, No. 5, 10 June 1959, FO 371/140103/BA 1041/2.
41 Telegram from J. C. Moberly to the Foreign Office, No. 38, 2 May 1960, FO 371/148946/BA 1071/2; telegram from Sir M. Crosthwaite to the Foreign Office, No. 438, 12 May 1960, FO 371/148946/BA 1071/3.
42 Letter from the Chancery, British Embassy (Beirut) to the Political Agency (Doha), No. 1026/19/60, 14 May 1960, FO 371/148946/BA 1071/4.
43 The following is based on despatch from American Consul, Dhahran, to the Department of State, No. 201, 1 February 1961, RG 59, Central Decimal Files 1960–63, 786G.00/2–161. See also, Miriam Joyce, *Ruling Shaikhs and Her Majesty's Government 1960–9*, London: Frank Cass, 2003, p.10.
44 Airgram from American Consul, Dhahran, to the Secretary of State, No. A-58, 6 June 1962, RG 59, Central Decimal Files, 786G.00/6–662.
45 Letter from W. H. Luce to Lord Home, No. 98, 22 November 1961, T 317/41.
46 'Discussion with the State Department on British policy', draft Foreign Office brief, undated, FO 371/162812/B 1195/1.
47 Ibid.
48 'Oil and interdependence in the Middle East', State Department paper, enclosed in D. J. Speares' letter for Walmsley, No. 1030/11/62G, 4 December 1962, FO 371/162783/B 103145/2.
49 Minute by C. C. Wilcock, 3 January 1963, FO 371/162783/B 103145/12.
50 'US paper on the Persian Gulf', minute by D. G. Crawford, 22 January 1963, FO 371/162783/B 103145/12.
51 Ibid.
52 Letter from D. F. Hawley to Sir George Middleton, No. 14, 6 December 1959, FO 371/148946/BA 1071/1.
53 Letter from G. N. Jackson to T. F. Brenchley, No. 10717/63, 19 November 1963, FO 371/168624/B 1016/5.
54 Letter from Jackson to Brenchley, No. 10717/63, 27 November 1963, FO 371/168624/B 1016/6.
55 Ibid.
56 Minute by D. G. Crawford, 5 December 1963, FO 371/168624/B 1016/6.
57 Minute by D. P. Gracie (Second Secretary, Foreign Office), 3 December 1963, FO 371/168624/B 1016/6.
58 The following is based on 'Relations between Kuwait and the Southern Gulf States', minute by Gracie, 1 October 1963, FO 371/168624/B 1016/4.
59 'Kuwait and the Southern Gulf States', minute by J. A. Snellgrove, 3 October 1963, FO 371/168624/B 1016/4.
60 Minute by Crawford, 11 December 1963, FO 371/168624/B 1016/6.
61 'Kuwait and the Southern Gulf States', minute by Snellgrove, 3 October 1963, FO 371/168624/B 1016/4.

62 Telegram from American Consul, Dhahran, (Horner) to Secretary of State, No. 133, 7 November 1963, RG 59, Subject-Numeric Files, 1963, Box 4070, POL 15 Trucial St.
63 The following is based on letter from Luce to Sir Geoffrey Harrison, No. 1040/64, 4 February 1964, FO 371/174481/B 1016/1.
64 Letter from Colin Crowe to Sir Geoffrey Harrison, No. 10510 G, 27 February 1964, FO 371/174481/B 1016/4.
65 Letter from G. N. Jackson to Harrison, No. 1059/64 G, 17 March 1964, FO 371/174481/BT 1016/6.
66 Letter from H. G. Balfour-Paul to Luce, No. 1, 4 January 1965, FO 371/179902/BT 1015/3.
67 Letter from Balfour-Paul to Luce, No. 1012/65, 27 January 1965, FO 371/179902/BT 1015/5.
68 Letter from Balfour-Paul to Luce, No. 4, 3 March 1965, FO 371/179902/BT 1015/11.
69 Telegram from Luce to the Foreign Office, No. 354, 16 May 1965, PREM 13/3326.
70 Telegram from Balfour-Paul to the Foreign Office, No. 61, 27 March 1965, FO 371/179749/B 1016/2; letter from Balfour-Paul to H. Phillips, No. 1092/65, 28 March 1965, FO 371/179740/B 1016/4.
71 During a visit to London in 1964, Rashid had already expressed enthusiasm for closer co-operation between the Gulf States. (Joyce, *Ruling Shaikhs and Her Majesty's Government*, p.15.)
72 Telegram from Balfour-Paul to the Foreign Office, No. 105, 27 May 1965, FO 371/179740/B 1016/14.
73 Letter from R. H. M. Boyle to Luce, No. 1036/65, 29 May 1965, FO 371/179740/B 1016/16.
74 Ibid.
75 Telegram from Balfour-Paul to the Foreign Office, No. 105, 27 May 1965, FO 371/179740/B 1016/14.
76 Telegram from the Foreign Office to certain missions, No. 226, 24 June 1965, FO 371/179903/BT 1015/44.
77 The following is based on letter from Luce to Michael Stewart, No. 23, 19 July 1965, FO 371/179740/B 1016/25.
78 Letter from Phillips to Brenchley, No. 1017, 10 August 1965, FO 371/179740/B 1016/29.
79 Letter from Boyle to Phillips, No. 1036, 28 August 1965, FO 371/179740/B 1016/29.
80 'Persian Gulf', minute by J. E. Lucas, 16 June 1964, T 317/510.
81 Letter from Sir D. Wright to the Foreign Office, No. 1103, 27 September 1963, FO 371/179765/B 1111/87.
82 Letter from Boyle to Luce, No. 1115, 20 November 1965, FO 371/179765/B 1111/97.
83 Telegram from Luce to the Foreign Office, No. 45, 25 January 1966, FO 371/185187/B 1111/13.
84 Telegram from the Foreign Office to Bahrain, No. 37, 18 February 1966, T 317/840.
85 'Gulf currency', note by R. I. Hallows, 27 April 1966, T 317/840.
86 'Persian Gulf currency', paper attached to Lucas' letter to J. A. Snellgrove, 29 October 1963, T 317/509.
87 Telegram from Luce to the Foreign Office, No. 182, 23 March 1966, FO 371/185188/B 1111/37.
88 Telegram from Luce to the Foreign Office, No. 464, 6 July 1966, FO 371/185190/B 1111/101.

89 Letter from S. J. Nuttall to Balfour-Paul, No. 1071/66, 30 August 1966, FO 371/185192/B 1111/139.
90 Letter from A. T. Lamb to Balfour-Paul, No. 1112/66, 25 October 1966, FO 371/185192/B 1111/52.
91 Letter from F. D. W. Brown to J. A. Snellgrove, No. 11110, 3 June 1964, T 317/509.
92 Letter from J. P. Tripp to Brown, No. 1112/64, 5 May 1964, T 317/509.
93 Letter from Luce to Michael Stewart, No. 23, 19 July 1965, FO 371/179740/B 1016/25.
94 Ibid.
95 Letter from Luce to Brenchey, No. 1032, 24 December 1965, FO 371/185166/B 1016/13.
96 Letter from Boyle to Phillips, No. 1062, 15 March 1966, FO 371/185167/B 1016/22.
97 Letter from Luce to Brenchley, No. 1041, 7 February 1966, FO 371/185166/B 1016/12.
98 Letter from Luce to Boyle, No. 1041, 13 April 1966, FO 371/185167/B 1016/36.
99 Letter from Luce to Roberts, No. 1041, 2 May 1966, FO 371/185167/B 1016/38.
100 'The Rulership of Abu Dhabi', minute by Gordon Walker to the Prime Minister, PM/64/142, 22 December 1964, PREM 13/3326.
101 Letter from Luce to R. S. Crawford, No. 1946/65G, 27 May 1964, FO 371/174701/BT 1016/14G.
102 'Main points of a discussion with Shaikh Zaid at Buraimi, October 22–23', note by Luce, 27 October 1964, FO 371/174702/BT 1016/26G.
103 Letter from Luce to Crawford, No. 1946/G, 28 October 1964, FO 371/174702/BT 1016/26G.
104 Minute by Crawford, 27 November 1964, FO 371/174702/BT 1016/35/G.
105 'Minister of State's visit to the Persian Gulf, 9–16 May 1965: Trucial States', 7 May 1965, FO 371/179902/BT 1015/19.
106 Letter from Luce to Stewart, No. 24, 19 July 1965, FO 371/179905/BT 1015/79.
107 Ibid.
108 Political Agents' Conference, 7–9 December 1965: Summary record of discussions: Part II: Trucial States – political and economic development, FO 371/185177/B 1051/2.
109 Letter from Luce to Stewart, No. 24, 19 July 1965, FO 371/179905/BT 1015/79.
110 Letter from Luce to Brenchley, No. 1040, 6 November 1965, FO 371/179905/BT 1015/106.
111 Telegram from Lamb to the Foreign Office, No. 66, 19 May 1966, FO 371/185167/B 1016/40.
112 Ibid.
113 Telegram from Luce to the Foreign Office, No. 364, 4 June 1966, FO 371/185167/B 1016/44.
114 Letter from Luce to Lamb, No. 1946, 4 June 1966, FO 371/185167/B 1016/46.
115 Telegram from Ward to the Foreign Office, No. 65, 5 June 1966, FO 371/185167/B 1016/44.
116 Telegram from Luce to the Foreign Office, No. 369, 7 June 1966, FO 371/185167/B 1016/45.
117 The following is based on letter from Luce to Michael Stewart, No. 18, 19 July 1966, FO 371/185167/B 1016/51.
118 Letter from Crawford to M. N. F. Stewart, 23 December 1964, FO 371/174702/BT 1016/36/G.
119 Telegram from the Foreign and Commonwealth Office to certain missions, No. 242, 6 August 1966, FO 371/185527/BT 1016/24. See also 'Persian Gulf', minute by M. S. Weir, 18 August 1966, FO 371/185528/BT 1016/60.

120 The following is based on Miriam Joyce, 'On the road to unity: The Trucial States from a British perspective, 1960–6', *Middle Eastern Studies*, 35, 2 (1999): 57.
121 'The Rulership of Abu Dhabi', minute by Gordon-Walker to the Prime Minister, PM/64/142, 22 December 1964, PREM 11/3326.
122 Letter from Crawford to George Brown, No. 24, 14 November 1966, FO 371/185529/BT 1016/79.
123 Letter from A. T. Lamb to Crawford, No. 3, 5 November 1966, FO 371/185529/BT 1016/79.
124 Minute by P. Gent, 24 November 1966, FO 371/185529/BT 1016/79.
125 Letter from Balfour-Paul (Deputy Political Resident) to Weir, No. 1015/3, 29 December 1966, FCO 8/825.
126 Letter from S. J. Nuttall to Balfour-Paul, No. 1072/67, 16 September 1967, FCO 8/825.
127 Letter from Balfour-Paul to Nuttall, No. 1015/3/40/67, 22 September 1967, FCO 8/825.
128 Minute by E. F. Henderson, 2 November 1966, FO 371/185167/B 1016/56.
129 Letter from Boyle to Crawford, No. 1087, 5 November 1966, FO 371/185167/B 1016/59.
130 Letter from Boyle to Crawford, No. 1038, 12 November 1966, FO 371/185167/B 1016/56.
131 Letter from Crawford to George Brown, No. 31, 28 December 1966, FO 371/185167/B 1016/62.
132 Minute by S. Falle, 17 November 1965, FO 371/185177/B 1051/3.
133 'Future of British Protected States in the Persian Gulf', minute by Brenchley, 18 November 1965, FO 371/185177/B 1051/3.
134 Letter from J. T. Fearnley to A. B. Powell, No. B3/5, 15 February 1967, FCO 8/31.
135 'Long-term policy in the Persian Gulf', minute by P. R. Spendlove, 3 May 1967, FCO 8/623.
136 Note of meeting between Secretary of State for Defence and the Kuwaiti Ambassador, 4 May 1967, FCO 8/625.
137 The following is based on 'Defence expenditure study No. 6 : Long-term policy in the Persian Gulf', report by the Defence Review Working Party, 7 June 1967, OPDO (67) 8, CAB 148/80.
138 Letter from Fearnley to Powell, No. B3/5, 15 February 1967, FCO 8/31.
139 Letter from Crawford to Brenchley, No. 1041/22/67, 1 March 1967, FCO 8/17.
140 Letter from Sir Denis Wright to the Foreign Office, No. 527, 20 April 1967, FCO 8/17.
141 Letter from Crawford to Brenchley, 16 May 1967, FCO 8/17.
142 Letter from Crawford to Brenchley, No. 1041/22/67, 1 March 1967, FCO 8/17.
143 The following is based on letter from Crawford to Brenchley, No. 1041G/16/87, 13 May 1967, FCO 8/31.
144 The following is based on telegram from Crawford to the Foreign Office, No. 671, 12 October 1967, FCO 8/31.
145 Telegram from Man to the Foreign Office, No. 749, 24 October 1967, FCO 8/31.
146 Letter from Balfour-Paul to Weir, No. 1639/40/67, 6 October 1967, FCO 8/140.
147 Briefs for the Minister of State's visit to the Persian Gulf, November 1967, FCO 8/142.
148 The Minister of State's visit to the Persian Gulf, November 1967: Brief No. 1: The Protected States, FCO 8/142.
149 The following is based on 'Visit to the Persian Gulf and Iran by the Minister of State, Mr Roberts, October 31–November 12, 1967', note by G. O. Roberts, 17 December 1967, FCO 8/31.

150 Letter from Brenchley to Crawford, 7 December 1967, FCO 8/31.
151 Letter from Crawford to Brenchley, No. 1041/56/67, 16 December 1967, FCO 8/31.
152 Letter from Crawford to Brown, No. 35, 25 November 1967, FCO 8/828.
153 Letter from Crawford to Brown, No. 37, 8 December 1967, FCO 8/828.
154 Letter from Crawford to Brown, No. 39, 22 December 1967, FCO 8/828.
155 Letter from Crawford to Brown, No. 3/3, 27 January 1968, FCO 8/31.
156 Telegram from Crawford to the Foreign Office, No. 43, 11 January 1968, FCO 8/47; telegram from Lamb to the Foreign Office, No. 4, 10 January 1968, FCO 8/145.
157 Telegram from Crawford to the Foreign Office, No. 34, 10 January 1968, FCO 8/47.
158 Ibid. See also telegram from Crawford to the Foreign Office, No. 29, 10 January 1968, FCO 8/145.
159 Telegram from D. A. Roberts to the Foreign Office, No. 25, 11 January 1968, FCO 8/47.
160 Telegram from Crawford to the Foreign Office, No. 43, 11 January 1968, FCO 8/47.
161 The following is based on letter from Parsons to Weir, No. 2/3, 13 January 1968, FCO 8/48. See also Joyce, *Ruling Shaikhs and Her Majesty's Government*, p. 111.
162 Telegram from Parsons to the Foreign Office, No. 18, 25 January 1968, FCO 8/526.
163 Telegram from Arthur to the Foreign Office, No. 12, 8 January 1968, FCO 8/145.
164 Telegram from Arthur to the Foreign Office, No. 14, 9 January 1968, FCO 8/145.
165 Letter from Arthur to Brown, 13 May 1968, FCO 8/657.
166 Ibid.
167 The following is based on record of meeting between the Minister of State for Foreign Affairs and King Feisal of Saudi Arabia, 10 January 1968, FCO 8/47.
168 'Talk with Shaikh Zaid', note by Crawford, 18 October 1967, FCO 8/848.
169 The following is based on letter from Lamb to Crawford, No. 3/1G, 11 January 1968, FCO 8/48.
170 'Talk with Shaikh Zaid', note by Crawford, 18 October 1967, FCO 8/848.
171 'The Trucial States', note for the Minister of State's meeting on 16 February by M. S. Weir, 14 February 1968, FCO 8/32.
172 Letter from Crawford to Brown, No. 3/3, 27 January 1968, FCO 8/31.
173 Telegram from Crawford to the Foreign Office, No. 94, 24 January 1968, FCO 8/48.
174 Telegram from Crawford to the Foreign Office, No. 43, 11 January 1968, FCO 8/47.
175 Telegram from Crawford to the Foreign Office, No. 94, 24 January 1968, FCO 8/48.
176 Ibid.
177 Telegram from the Foreign and Commonwealth Office to certain missions, No. 23, 23 January 1968, FCO 8/48. See also Joyce, *Ruling Shaikhs and Her Majesty's Government*, p. 113.
178 Telegram from Crawford to the Foreign Office, No. 85, 23 January 1968, FCO 8/48.
179 Telegram from the Foreign Office to Bahrain, No. 133, 23 January 1968, FCO 8/48.

180 The number of servicemen in the Gulf was around 6,500 – 3,600 soldiers, 200 sailors, and 2,500 airmen. (Letter from A. J. Beamish to J. H. G. Leahy, No. B 3/19, 26 January 1968, FCO 8/49.)
181 'Persian Gulf Defence: Offset offers', minute by Weir, 23 January 1968, FCO 8/48.
182 Minute by Denis Allen, 24 January 1968, FCO 8/48.
183 Minute by P. H. Gore-Booth, 24 January 1968, FCO 8/48.
184 Minute by Brenchley, 23 January 1968, FCO 8/48.
185 Minutes by Roberts, 25 January 1968 and George Brown (undated), FCO 8/48.
186 Telegram from the Foreign Office to Bahrain Residency, No. 157, 29 January 1968, FCO 8/48.
187 Minute by R. A. Sykes, 31 January 1968, FCO 8/49.
188 The following is based on letter from Parsons to Crawford, 17 February 1968, FCO 8/49.
189 Letter from Weir to Crawford, No. 1/5, 1 February 1968, FCO 8/828.

4 Unity and division in the Lower Gulf: The emergence of the United Arab Emirates

1 Wm. Roger Louis, 'The British withdrawal from the Gulf, 1967–71', *Journal of Imperial and Commonwealth History*, 31, 1 (2003): 98.
2 Letter from Sir Stewart Crawford to T. F. Brenchley, No. 1041G/16/87, 13 May 1967, FCO 8/31.
3 Letter from D. A. Roberts to Crawford, No. 2/10, 6 March 1968, FCO 8/9.
4 Telegram from Crawford to the Foreign Office, No. 179, 29 February 1968, FCO 8/9.
5 The following is based on letter from Roberts to Crawford, No. 2/10, 6 March 1968, FCO 8/9.
6 Telegram from A. D. Parsons to the Foreign Office, No. 47, 29 February 1968, FCO 8/9.
7 Letter from Parsons to Crawford, No. 2/4, 2 March 1968, FCO 8/9.
8 Ibid.
9 Ibid.
10 Telegram from Parsons to the Foreign Office, No. 47, 29 February 1968, FCO 8/9.
11 Telegram from Crawford to the Foreign Office, No. 179, 29 February 1968, FCO 8/9.
12 Letter from Crawford to Lamb, No. 1/14, 1 March 1968, FCO 8/9.
13 Letter from R. H. M. Boyle to Crawford, No. 2/2, 5 March 1968, FCO 8/9.
14 Ibid.
15 Telegram from Crawford to the Foreign Office, No. 179, 29 February 1968, FCO 8/9. Shaikhs Isa and Khailfah of Bahrain, however, insisted that the Saudi Ambassador in Kuwait had 'played no part in the meeting except to express general exhortations'. (Telegram from Parsons to the Foreign Office, No. 47, 29 February 1968, FCO 8/9.)
16 Letter from Lamb to Balfour-Paul, No. 2/5, 11 March 1968, FCO 8/9.
17 'Rulers' meeting', minute by Roberts, 4 March 1968, FCO 8/9.
18 Ibid.
19 Letter from D. M. Day to A. M. Palliser, 8 March 1968, FCO 8/9.
20 Telegram from Parsons to the Foreign Office, No. 66, 6 April 1968, FCO 8/10
21 Record of a conversation with Shaikh Rashid on 16 March 1968, FCO 8/10.
22 Telegram from Roberts (Dubai) to the Foreign Office, No. 12, 31 March 1968, FCO 8/10.
23 Letter from Lamb to H. G. Balfour-Paul, No. 2/3, 27 March 1968, FCO 8/10.

24 Ibid.
25 Telegram from Boyle to the Foreign Office, No. 37, 25 March 1968, FCO 8/10; letter from Boyle to Balfour-Paul, No. 2/2, 28 March 1968, FCO 8/10.
26 Letter from Boyle to Balfour-Paul, No. 2/2, 28 March 1968, FCO 8/10.
27 Letter from E. F. Henderson (First Secretary [Information Adviser], Bahrain Residency) to Balfour-Paul, No. 2/3, 20 April 1968, FCO 8/11.
28 Letter from Henderson to Crawford, No. 2/3G, 4 April 1968, FCO 8/11.
29 Letter from Henderson to Balfour-Paul, No. 2/3, 20 April 1968, FCO 8/11.
30 Telegram from Crawford to the Foreign Office, No. 272, 4 April 1968, FCO 8/10. See also letter from the Secretary of State to Crawford, B 3/5, 25 April 1968, T 317/1143.
31 Letter from E. F. Henderson to Balfour-Paul, No. 2/3, 20 April 1968, FCO 8/11. Reporting the views of his fellow mainland Rulers, Shaikh Rashid noted 'they believed that Zaid was out to dominate and that Britain was backing him'. (Telegram from the Foreign Office to Bahrain, No. 980, 31 July 1968, FCO 8/886.)
32 'Defence expenditure study No. 6: Long-term policy in the Persian Gulf', report by the Defence Review Working Party, 7 June 1967, OPDO (67) 8, CAB 148/80; 'Defence expenditure studies', report by the Defence Review Working Party, 21 June 1967, OPD (67) 46, CAB 148/32.
33 'Withdrawal from the Persian Gulf', paper by the Planning Staff, 11 January 1968, FCO 8/31.
34 Ibid.
35 'Union of Arab Emirates', note by Crawford, 27 April 1968, FCO 8/11.
36 Record of the Political Resident's meeting with the Ruler of Abu Dhabi in Al Din, 11 April 1968, FCO 8/11.
37 Letter from D. J. McCarthy to Crawford, No. B1/14, 2 May 1968, FCO 8/11.
38 Letter from Henderson to Balfour-Paul, No. 2/3, 20 April 1968, FCO 8/11.
39 Letter from Crawford to McCarthy, No. 10/13, 29 April 1968, FCO 8/885.
40 Telegram from Crawford to the Foreign Office, No. 349, 7 May 1968, FCO 8/12.
41 Letter from A. D. Parsons to Crawford, No. 2/4, 6 May 1968, FCO 8/12.
42 'Union of Arab Emirates', minute by Denis Allen, 10 May 1968, FCO 8/12.
43 Letter from Parsons to the Foreign Office, No. 83, 7 May 1968, FCO 8/12.
44 'Union of Arab Emirates', minute by McCarthy, 13 May 1968, FCO 8/12.
45 Telegram from the Secretary of State to Tehran, No. 1154, 15 May 1968, FCO 8/12.
46 Telegram from Abu Dhabi (Treadwell) to the Foreign Office, No. 110, 25 May 1968, FCO 8/13.
47 Telegram from Abu Dhabi (Treadwell) to the Foreign Office, No. 113, 26 May 1968, FCO 8/13.
48 Telegram from Crawford to the Foreign Office, No. 408, 31 May 1968, FCO 8/13.
49 Letter from Boyle to Crawford, No. 2/2, 4 June 1968, FCO 8/13.
50 The following is based on letter from Crawford to Michael Stewart, No. 1/14, 10 June 1968, FCO 8/14.
51 Telegram from the Secretary of State to Bahrain, No. 809, 7 June 1968, FCO 8/14.
52 Telegram from Jackson to the Foreign Office, No. 99, 28 March 1967, FCO 8/42.
53 Telegram from Jackson to the Foreign Office, No. 109, 6 April 1967, FCO 8/42.
54 'Kuwait and the Gulf', minute by M. C. S. Weston, 11 April 1967, FCO 8/42.
55 Letter from Crawford to Brenchley, No. 10310/34/67, 11 April 1967, FCO 8/42.
56 The following is based on letter from Crawford to Brown, No. 12, 13 May 1967, FCO 8/42.
57 Letter from G. G. Arthur to George Brown, No. 25, 3 December 1967, FCO 8/42.
58 Letter from Crawford to Brown, No. 38, 22 December 1967, FCO 8/42.
59 The Minister of State's visit to the Persian Gulf, November 1967: Brief No. 7: Kuwait, FCO 8/142.

60 Letter from D. E. S. Blatherwick to the Foreign Office, No. 13/3, 1 June 1968, FCO 8/13.
61 Letter from J. A. N. Graham to Stewart, No. 2/5, 18 May 1968, FCO 8/43.
62 Letter from Blatherwick to A. Ibbott, No. 13/3, 11 June 1968, FCO 8/43.
63 Telegram from Parsons to the Foreign Office, No. 123, 24 June 1968, FCO 8/14.
64 Telegram from the Foreign Office to Kuwait, No. 497, 8 July 1968, FCO 8/15.
65 Telegram from Crawford to the Foreign Office, No. 481, 10 July 1968, FCO 8/15.
66 Letter from Parsons to Crawford, No. 2/4, 9 July 1968, FCO 8/15.
67 Ibid.
68 The following is based on letter from Parsons to Crawford, No. 2/4, 22 July 1968, FCO 8/16.
69 Telegram from Boyle to Bahrain, No. 20, 15 October 1968, FCO 8/914.
70 The following is based on letter from Crawford to Treadwell, No. 1/14, 14 October 1968, FCO 8/914.
71 Telegram from Crawford to the Foreign and Commonwealth Office, No. 654, 1 November 1968, FCO 8/914.
72 Ibid.
73 Letter from Boyle to Crawford, No. 2/2, 22 October 1968, FCO 8/914.
74 Telegram from Boyle to the Foreign and Commonwealth Office, No. 181, 24 October 1968, FCO 8/914.
75 Telegram from Boyle to the Foreign and Commonwealth Office, No. 185, 13 November 1968, FCO 8/914.
76 Telegram from Parsons to the Foreign and Commonwealth Office, No. 126, 28 October 1968, FCO 8/914.
77 Telegram from Bullard to the Foreign and Commonwealth Office, No. 204, 27 October 1968, FCO 8/914.
78 Letter from Bullard to M. S. Weir, No. 2/10, 26 November 1968, FCO 8/915.
79 Letter from A. D. Harris to A. J. D. Stirling, No. 25/18, 12 December 1968, FCO 8/956.
80 Letter from Boyle to Crawford, No. 2/2, 23 November 1968, FCO 8/915.
81 Ibid.
82 Letter from W. Morris to McCarthy, No. 2/31, 23 December 1968, FCO 8/956.
83 Telegram from S. Falle to the Foreign and Commonwealth Office, No. 43, 25 January 1969, FCO 8/916.
84 The following is based on letter from Crawford to Stewart, 17 February 1969, FCO 8/917.
85 'The Union of Arab Emirates', minute by McCarthy, 18 March 1969, FCO 8/917.
86 Letter from C. J. Treadwell to Crawford, No. 2/5, 22 March 1969, FCO 8/917.
87 Letter from Boyle to Weir, No. 2/2, 25 March 1969, FCO 8/917.
88 Ibid.
89 Ibid.
90 Telegram from Henderson to the Foreign and Commonwealth Office, No. 29, 14 May 1969, FCO 8/918.
91 Telegram from Crawford to the Foreign and Commonwealth Office, No. 169, 17 May 1969, FCO 8/918.
92 The following is based on letter from Crawford to Stewart, No. 1/14, 9 July 1969, FCO 8/920.
93 Letter from Henderson to Weir, No. 2/2, 13 May 1969, FCO 8/918.
94 Telegram from Henderson to the Foreign and Commonwealth Office, No. 32, 17 May 1969, FCO 8/918.
95 Letter from Henderson to Weir, No. 2/2, 20 May 1969, FCO 8/918.
96 Letter from Stirling to Crawford, No. 2/4, 19 June 1969, FCO 8/919.
97 Letter from Crawford to Stewart, No. 1/14, 9 July 1969, FCO 8/920.
98 Letter from Henderson to T. J. Everard, No. 2/2, 23 June 1969, FCO 8/919.

99 Letter from Crawford to Stewart, No. 1/14, 9 July 1969, FCO 8/920.
100 Telegram from Stewart to Bahrain Residency, No. 275, 4 July 1969, FCO 8/919. See also records of meetings in the Foreign and Commonwealth Office, 11 June, 25 June, 27 June 1969, FCO 8/997.
101 Letter from McCarthy to Crawford, No. 26/5, 10 July 1969, FCO 8/1163.
102 Telegram from Stewart to Bahrain Residency, No. 275, 4 July 1969, FCO 8/919.
103 Letter from McCarthy to Crawford, No. 26/5, 10 July 1969, FCO 8/1163.
104 Telegram from Stewart to Bahrain Residency, No. 275, 4 July 1969, FCO 8/919.
105 The following is based on letter from Crawford to Stewart, No. 1/14, 15 July 1969, FCO 8/920.
106 Telegram from A. J. M. Craig to the Foreign and Commonwealth Office, No. 350, 15 July 1969, FCO 8/920.
107 The following is based on letter from Crawford to Stewart, No. 1/14, 15 July 1969, FCO 8/920.
108 Formed in 1950, the Trucial Oman Levies, later renamed Trucial Oman Scouts, was a small British-officered force of local people. (Peter Lienhardt, *Shaikhdoms of Eastern Arabia*, Basingstoke: Palgrave, 2001, p. 12.)
109 'Our conversations with Sheikh Zaid of Abu Dhabi and Sheikh Khalifah of Qatar', minute by Roberts, 7 July 1969, FCO 8/920.
110 'Union of Arab Emirates', minute by D. Slater, 21 July 1969, FCO 8/920.
111 Letter from Stewart to Crawford, No. NB1/1, 13 August 1969, FCO 8/920.
112 Letter from S. Falle to McCarthy, No. 2/23, 26 May 1969, FCO 8/918.
113 Letter from Henderson to Weir, No. 2/2, 15 September 1969, FCO 8/921.
114 Letter from McCarthy to Weir, 18 September 1969, FCO 8/922.
115 Telegram from Lord Caradon (UK Mission, New York) to the Foreign and Commonwealth Office, No. 2179, 9 October 1969, FCO 8/922. The Shah had expressed similar sentiments, remarking that 'if the decision [on withdrawal] were now reversed it would cause much political confusion in the area'. (Telegram from Sir Denis Wright to the Foreign and Commonwealth Office, No. 483, 27 May 1969, FCO 8/958.)
116 Telegram from Treadwell to the Foreign and Commonwealth Office, No. 305, 21 October 1969, FCO 8/923.
117 Letter from Treadwell to Crawford, 2 November 1969, FCO 8/925.
118 Telegram from Abu Dhabi to the Foreign and Commonwealth Office, No. 306, 22 October 1969, FCO 8/923.
119 Letter from Treadwell to Crawford, 2 November 1969, FCO 8/925.
120 Telegram from Stewart to the Bahrain Residency, No. 376, 22 October 1969, FCO 8/923.
121 Letter from Treadwell to Crawford, 2 November 1969, Annex II, FCO 8/925.
122 Telegram from Treadwell to the Foreign and Commonwealth Office, No. 318, 26 October 1969, FCO 8/923.
123 Letter from Treadwell to Crawford, 2 November 1969, FCO 8/925.
124 Ibid.
125 Telegram from Sir D. Wright to the Foreign and Commonwealth Office, No. 915, 1 November 1969, FCO 8/924.
126 Letter from Treadwell to Crawford, 2 November 1969, FCO 8/925.
127 Letter from Crawford to Stewart, 11 November 1969, FCO 8/925.
128 Letter from Treadwell to Crawford, 2 November 1969, FCO 8/925.
129 Telegram from J. L. Bullard to the Foreign and Commonwealth Office, No. 217, 29 October 1969, FCO 8/924.
130 Telegram from Henderson to the Foreign and Commonwealth Office, No. 114, 30 October 1969, FCO 8/924.
131 Telegram from Treadwell to the Foreign and Commonwealth Office, No. 329, 1 November 1969, FCO 8/924.

132 Letter from Crawford to Stewart, 11 November 1969, FCO 8/925.
133 Letter from Treadwell to Crawford, 2 November 1969, FCO 8/925.
134 Letter from Stewart to Crawford, 10 December 1969, FCO 8/925.
135 Telegram from Treadwell to Bahrain Residency, No. 369, 19 December 1969, FCO 8/925.
136 Letter from Henderson to Weir, No. 2/2, 19 November 1969, FCO 8/925.
137 Letter from Henderson to Weir, No. 2/2, 13 December 1969, FCO 8/1292.
138 Telegram from Morris to the Foreign and Commonwealth Office, No. 100, 20 February 1970, FCO 8/1292.
139 Telegram from Treadwell to the Foreign and Commonwealth Office, No. 35, 10 February 1970, FCO 8/1292.
140 Telegram from Treadwell to the Foreign and Commonwealth Office, No. 78, 22 March 1970, FCO 8/1292.
141 Telegram from Treadwell to the Foreign and Commonwealth Office, No. 102, 15 April 1970, FCO 8/1292.
142 Letter from Parsons to Crawford, 17 June 1968, FCO 8/519.
143 Letter from Crawford to Stewart, 25 June 1968, FCO 8/519.
144 'Iran's claim to Bahrain', memorandum by the Secretary of State for Foreign and Commonwealth Affairs, 24 July 1969, OPD (69) 39, CAB 148/93.
145 Telegram from Wright to the Foreign and Commonwealth Office, No. 1641, 29 October 1968, FCO 8/938/1.
146 Louis, 'British withdrawal from the Gulf', p. 98.
147 Telegram from Crawford to the Foreign and Commonwealth Office, No. 162, 29 April 1970, FCO 8/1293.
148 Letter from Stirling to Weir, No. 2/9, 4 May 1970, FCO 8/1293.
149 Telegram from Crawford to the Foreign and Commonwealth Office, No. 358, 25 July 1970, FCO 8/1317.
150 Record of conversation with the Ruler of Bahrain at Rifai Palace, 27 August 1970, FCO 8/1319.
151 Record of a conversation between the Foreign and Commonwealth Secretary and Shaikhs Khalifah and Muhammed [Mohammed] of Bahrain at the Foreign and Commonwealth Office, 31 July 1970, FCO 8/1318.
152 Frauke Heard-Bey, *From Trucial States to United Arab Emirates*, Harlow: Longman, 1996, p. 357.
153 Letter from Treadwell to Weir, No. 2/3, 27 October 1970, FCO 8/1296.
154 Telegram from Douglas-Home to Bahrain Residency, No. 503, 29 October 1970, FCO 8/1296.
155 Record of Political Agents' Conference, 12–13 November 1970, FCO 8/1297.
156 Telegram from Arthur to the Foreign and Commonwealth Office, No. 558, 5 November 1970, FCO 8/1296.
157 Telegram from Stirling to the Foreign and Commonwealth Office, No. 28, 6 December 1970, FCO 8/1297.
158 'Bahrain and the UAE', minute by A. A. Acland, 10 November 1970, FCO 8/1297.
159 Letter from Henderson to Weir, No. 2/2, 21 June 1970, FCO 8/1294.
160 Telegram from Falle to the Foreign and Commonwealth Office, No. 403, 10 November 1970, FCO 8/1297.
161 Ibid.
162 'The UAE', minute by D. E. T. Luard, 11 May 1970, FCO 8/1293.
163 Telegram from Michael Stewart to Bahrain, No. 171, 15 May 1970, FCO 8/1293.
164 The following is based on 'The Union of Arab Emirates', minute by A. A. Acland, 18 May 1970, FCO 8/1293.
165 Letter from Crawford to Douglas-Home, 25 July 1970, FCO 8/1318.
166 Record of a conversation in Jedda, 24 January 1971, FCO 8/1552.

167 Robert L. Jarman, *Sabah al-Salim al-Sabah, Amir of Kuwait, 1965–77: A political biography*, London: The London Centre of Arab Studies, 2002, pp. 249, 328.
168 Telegram from Luce to the Foreign and Commonwealth Office, No. 63, 1 February 1971, FCO 8/1552; telegram from Luce to the Foreign and Commonwealth Office, No. 65, 1 February 1971, FCO 8/1552; telegram from Luce to the Bahrain Residency, No. 15, 28 January 1971, FCO 8/1584.
169 Record of conversation in Doha on Wednesday 27 January 1971, FCO 8/1584.
170 Telegram from Luce to the Foreign and Commonwealth Office, No. 75, 11 February 1971, FCO 8/1553; report on Sir William Luce's mission to the Gulf area 22 January to 13 February 1971, attached to 'Policy in the Persian Gulf', memorandum by the Secretary of State for Foreign and Commonwealth Affairs, 18 February 1971, DOP (71) 13, CAB 148/116.
171 Record of a conversation between the Minister of State for Foreign and Commonwealth Affairs and Shaikh Mohammed bin Mubarak at the Foreign and Commonwealth Office, 18 February 1971, FCO 8/1554.
172 Telegram from Luce to the Bahrain Residency, No. 15, 28 January 1971, FCO 8/1584.
173 Telegram from Henderson to the Bahrain Residency, No. 70, 3 May 1971, FCO 8/1557.
174 Report on Sir William Luce's mission to the Gulf area 22 January to 13 February 1971, attached to 'Policy in the Persian Gulf', memorandum by the Secretary of State for Foreign and Commonwealth Affairs, 18 February 1971, DOP (71) 13, CAB 148/116. See also record of discussions on the Persian Gulf at the State Department on 13 January 1971, FCO 8/1583.
175 Record of a conversation with Shaikh Zaid at Rahimyar Khan on 2 and 3 February 1971, FCO 8/1585.
176 'Union of Arab Emirates (UAE)', note by A. A. Acland, 4 June 1971, FCO 8/1558.
177 Sir William Luce's visit to the Gulf and neighbouring states in May 1971, FCO 8/1560.
178 Telegram from Douglas-Home to certain missions, No. 53, 8 March 1971, FCO 8/1554.
179 Report on Sir William Luce's mission to the Gulf area 22 January to 13 February 1971, attached to 'Policy in the Persian Gulf', memorandum by the Secretary of State for Foreign and Commonwealth Affairs, 18 February 1971, DOP (71) 13, CAB 148/116.
180 Minutes of the Cabinet Defence and Oversea Policy Committee, 2 July 1971, DOP (71) 13th meeting, CAB 148/115.
181 Telegram from Morris to the Foreign and Commonwealth Office, No. 519, 4 July 1971, FCO 8/1560.
182 Telegram from R. A. Beaumont (British Ambassador, Cairo) to the Foreign and Commonwealth Office, No. 772, 28 June 1971, FCO 8/1560.
183 Telegram from Douglas-Home to Bahrain Residency, No. 317, 7 July 1971, FCO 8/1560.
184 Minutes of the Cabinet Defence and Oversea Policy Committee, 2 July 1971, DOP (71) 13th meeting, CAB 148/115.
185 Telegram from Treadwell to Bahrain Residency, No. 85, 28 April 1971, FCO 8/1556.
186 Letter from J. F. Walker to D. G. Allen, 13 December 1971, FCO 8/1569.
187 Record of a conversation with Shaikh Zaid at Rahimyar Khan on 2 and 3 February 1971, FCO 8/1585.
188 Telegram from Luce to the Foreign and Commonwealth Office, No. 17, 5 February 1971, FCO 8/1585. See also telegram from Luce to the Foreign and Commonwealth Office, No. 84, 8 February 1971, FCO 8/1585.

189 Telegram from Stirling to Bahrain Residency, No. 46, 19 July 1971, FCO 8/1561.
190 Telegram from Stirling to Bahrain Residency, No. 47, 21 July 1971, FCO 8/1561.
191 Telegram from P. A. Raftery (Assistant Political Agent, Bahrain) to Bahrain Residency, No. 50, 27 July 1971, FCO 8/1562.
192 Letter from Arthur to Douglas-Home, No. 1/22, 23 September 1971, FCO 8/1642.
193 Telegram from the Foreign and Commonwealth Office to the Bahrain Residency, No. 353, 31 July 1971, FCO 8/1562. Musing on the Qatari decision, the former Political Agent in Bahrain, Sir Anthony Parsons, remarked: 'The rivalry between Bahrain and Qatar is such (and always has been) that whatever Bahrain decided to do, Qatar would do the same.' (Sir Anthony Parsons, 'Gulf withdrawal: British withdrawal from the Gulf 1965–71', *Contemporary Record*, 2, 2 (1988): 43.)
194 Letter from Henderson to P. R. H. Wright, No. 2/3, 22 February 1971, FCO 8/1586.
195 Letter from Arthur to Douglas-Home, 21 October 1971, FCO 8/1724; *Exchange of notes concerning the termination of special treaty relations between the United Kingdom of Great Britain and Northern Ireland and the State of Qatar, 3 Sept 1971*, London: HMSO, 1972, Cmnd. 4849.
196 *Treaty of friendship between the United Kingdom of Great Britain and Northern Ireland and the State of Qatar, 3 September 1971*, London: HMSO, 1972, Cmnd. 4850; *Treaty of friendship between the United Kingdom of Great Britain and Northern Ireland and the State of Bahrain, 3 September 1971*, London: HMSO, 1972, Cmnd. 4828.
197 Telegram from Walker to the Foreign and Commonwealth Office, No. 233, 21 July 1971, FCO 8/1561.
198 Telegram from Arthur to the Foreign and Commonwealth Office, No. 520, 20 August 1971, FCO 8/1563.
199 Telegram from Tehran to the Foreign and Commonwealth Office, No. 674, 7 September 1971, FCO 8/1564.
200 Telegram from Douglas-Home to Bahrain Residency, No, 539, 19 October 1971, FCO 8/1565.
201 Telegram from Arthur to the Foreign and Commonwealth Office, No. 807, 9 November 1971, FCO 8/1566.
202 Telegram from the American Embassy, London (Annenberg) to Secretary of State, No. 10144, 3 November 1971, RG 59, Subject-Numeric Files 1970–73, Box 1996, POL 33 Persian Gulf.
203 Telegram from Walker to Bahrain Residency, No. 374, 26 November 1971, FCO 8/1567.
204 *Exchanges of notes concerning the termination of special treaty relations between the United Kingdom of Great Britain and Northern Ireland and the State of the Trucial States, 1 December 1971*, London: HMSO, 1972, Cmnd. 4941.
205 Telegram from Arthur to the Foreign and Commonwealth Office, No. 948, 2 December 1971, FCO 8/1568.
206 Telegram from American Embassy, London (Bruce), to Secretary of State, No. 7654, 29 March 1968, RG 59, Subject-Numeric Files 1967–9, Box 1640, DEF 1 UK.
207 Telegram from Luce to the Foreign and Commonwealth Office, No. 75, 11 February 1971, FCO 8/1553.
208 Report on Sir William Luce's mission to the Gulf area 22 January to 13 February 1971, attached to 'Policy in the Persian Gulf', memorandum by the Secretary of State for Foreign and Commonwealth Affairs, 18 February 1971, DOP (71) 13, CAB 148/116.
209 Record of a conversation between the Foreign and Commonwealth Secretary and the Shah of Iran at the Iranian Embassy in Brussels, 10 July 1970, FCO 8/1316.

210 'Gulf policy and the islands', minute from Alec Douglas-Home to the Secretary of State for Defence, FCS/71/71, 12 October 1971, T 225/3542.
211 Department of State telegram, No. 179656, 30 September 1971, RG 59, Subject-Numeric Files 1970–73, Box 1996, POL 33 Persian Gulf.
212 Telegram from Department of State (Irwin) to American Embassies, London and Tehran, No. 172104, 18 September 1971, RG 59, Subject-Numeric Files 1970–73, Box 1996, POL 33 Persian Gulf.
213 'Gulf policy and the islands', minute from Douglas-Home to the Secretary of State for Defence, FCS/71/71, 12 October 1971, T 225/3542.
214 Telegram from American Consul General, Dhahran (Dinsmore), to the Secretary of State, No. 1284, 9 September 1971, RG 59, Subject-Numeric Files 1970–73, Box 1996, POL 33 Persian Gulf.
215 Telegram from American Embassy, Tehran, to the Secretary of State, No. 6452, 15 November 1971, RG 59, Subject-Numeric Files 1970–73, Box 1996, POL 33 Persian Gulf.
216 Conclusions of a meeting of the Cabinet, 18 November 1971, CAB 128/49 Part 2, CM (71) 56th conclusions.
217 Telegram from American Embassy, Tehran, to the Secretary of State, No. 6452, 15 November 1971, RG 59, Subject-Numeric Files 1970–73, Box 1996, POL 33 Persian Gulf.
218 Minutes of the Cabinet Defence and Oversea Policy Committee, 20 October 1971, DOP (71) 20th meeting, CAB 148/115.
219 Telegram from Department of State (Irwin) to American Embassy, Tel Aviv, No. 214109, 26 November 1971, RG 59, Subject-Numeric Files 1970–73, Box 1996, POL 33 Persian Gulf.
220 Telegram from American Embassy, Tehran, to Secretary of State, No. 6747, 29 November 1971, RG 59, Subject-Numeric Files 1970–73, Box 1996, POL 33 Persian Gulf.
221 Telegram from American Embassy, Jidda, to Secretary of State, No. 4051, 29 November 1971, RG 59, Subject-Numeric Files 1970–73, Box 1996, POL 33 Persian Gulf.
222 Telegram from American Embassy, Tehran, to Secretary of State, No. 901, 11 March 1970, RG 59, Subject-Numeric Files 1970–73, Box 1774, DEF 1 Near East.
223 Conclusions of a meeting of the Cabinet, 2 December 1971, CAB 128/49 Part 2, CM (71) 61st conclusions.
224 Telegram from American Embassy, London (Annenberg) to Secretary of State, No. 10982, 1 December 1971, RG 59, Subject-Numeric Files 1970–73, Box 2640, POL 7 UAE.
225 Ibid.; 'Death of Shaikh Khalid bin Mohammed al Qasimi, Ruler of Sharjah', minute by Acland, 25 January 1972, FCO 8/1925.
226 'Persian Gulf: coup and countercoup in Sharjah', Intelligence note: Bureau of Intelligence and Research, 4 February 1972, RG 59, Subject-Numeric Files 1970–73, Box 2640, POL 7 UAE; letter from Walker to Treadwell, 1 February 1972, FCO 8/1925.
227 Letter from Julian Amery to Douglas-Home, 17 February 1972, FCO 8/1925.
228 Telegram from American Consul General (Dinsmore) to the Secretary of State, No. 368, 23 February 1972, RG 59, Subject-Numeric Files 1970–73, Box 2560, POL 23–9 Qatar.
229 Telegram from Henderson to the Foreign and Commonwealth Office, No. 61, 22 February 1972, FCO 8/1891.
230 Telegram from Treadwell to the Foreign and Commonwealth Office, No. 155, 11 March 1972, FCO 8/1893.
231 Letter from P. J. F. Manley to A. D. Harris, No. 3/8, 21 August 1972, FCO 8/1894.
232 Letter from Walker to Treadwell, No. 1/1,14 March 1972, FCO 8/1923.

233 The following is based on letter from Treadwell to Douglas-Home, 11 May 1972, FCO 8/1923.
234 M. E. Yapp, *The Near East since the First World War*, London and New York: Longman, 1991, p. 374.

5 Conflict and co-operation: Anglo-American relations in the Gulf from the nationalisation of Anglo-Iranian Oil to the Yemeni revolution

1 Christopher Thorne, *Allies of a kind: The United States, Britain and the war against Japan, 1941–5*, London: Hamilton, 1978.
2 D. Cameron Watt, 'Demythologizing the Eisenhower era', in Hedley Bull and William Roger Louis (eds), *The 'special relationship': Anglo-American relations since 1945*, Oxford: Clarendon Press, 1986, pp. 65–85.
3 In particular see Wm. Roger Louis and Ronald Robinson, 'The imperialism of decolonization', *Journal of Imperial and Commonwealth History*, 22, 3, (1994): 462–511.
4 Ritchie Ovendale, *Britain, the United States and the transfer of power in the Middle East, 1945–62*, London and New York: Leicester University Press, 1996, p. 211. See also Ritchie Ovendale, *Anglo-American relations in the twentieth century*, Basingstoke: Macmillan, 1998, p. 125.
5 Ovendale, *Transfer of power in the Middle East*, p. 211.
6 Tore T. Petersen, *The Middle East between the great powers: Anglo-American conflict and co-operation, 1952–7*, Basingstoke: Macmillan, 2000, p. 42.
7 Report on a visit to the Persian Gulf States under British protection, with some observations on Iraq and Saudi Arabia and with conclusions and recommendations by Sir Roger Makins, 20 March 1952, FO 371/98343/EA 1051/53.
8 Letter from President Truman to Prime Minister Attlee, 31 May 1951, cited in *Foreign relations of the United States (FRUS), 1952–4: Volume X: Iran, 1951–4*, Washington: United States Government Printing Office, 1989, pp. 60, 61.
9 Mark J. Gasiorowski, 'The 1953 coup d'etat in Iran', *International Journal of Middle East Studies*, 19, 3 (1987): 264.
10 Moyara de Moraes Ruehsen, 'Operation "Ajax" revisited: Iran, 1953', *Middle Eastern Studies*, 29, 3 (1993): 469.
11 Steve Marsh, 'The United States, Iran and Operation "Ajax": Inverting interpretative orthodoxy', *Middle Eastern Studies*, 39, 3 (2003): 28–9.
12 Ovendale, *Transfer of power in the Middle East*, p. 73.
13 Mary Ann Heiss, 'The United States, Great Britain, and the creation of the oil consortium, 1953–4', *International History Review*, 16, 3 (1994): 534.
14 Steve Marsh, 'HMG, AIOC and the Anglo-Iranian Oil crisis: in defence of Anglo-Iranian', *Diplomacy and Statecraft*, 12, 4 (2001): 165.
15 Steve Marsh, 'The special relationship and the Anglo-Iranian oil crisis, 1950–4', *Review of International Studies*, 24, 4 (1998): 543–4.
16 Gasiorowski, 'The 1953 coup d'etat in Iran', pp. 275–6.
17 J. H. Bamberg, *The history of the British Petroleum Company: Volume 2: The Anglo-Iranian years, 1928–54*, Cambridge: Cambridge University Press, 1994, p. 511.
18 Keith Kyle, *Suez*, New York: St. Martin's Press, 1991, p. 100.
19 Petersen, *The Middle East between the great powers*, pp. 41–2.
20 Tore Tingvold Petersen, 'Anglo-American rivalry in the Middle East: The struggle for the Buraimi oasis, 1952–7', *International History Review*, 14, 1 (1992): 85.
21 Cabinet conclusions, 4 October 1955, cited John Kent (ed.), *Egypt and the Defence of the Middle East*, London: The Stationery Office, 1998, p. 447.
22 Telegram from the Foreign Office to Washington, No. 5998, 15 December 1955, FO 371/114559/E 1021/4.

23 'Oman', minute by D. H. M. Riches, 14 December 1955, FO 371/114559/E 1021/5.
24 Petersen, 'Anglo-American rivalry in the Middle East', p. 72.
25 Petersen, *The Middle East between the great powers*, p. 71.
26 Nigel John Ashton, *Eisenhower, Macmillan and the problem of Nasser: Anglo-American relations and Arab nationalism, 1955–9*, Basingstoke: Macmillan, 1996, p. 67; Ashton, 'The hijacking of a pact: the formation of the Baghdad Pact and Anglo-American tensions in the Middle East, 1955–8', *Review of International Studies*, 19, 2 (1993): 132–5.
27 Petersen, *The Middle East between the great powers*, p. 75.
28 Scott Lucas, *Britain and Suez: The lion's last roar*, Manchester: Manchester University Press, 1996, p. 98.
29 Memorandum by the President, 1 November 1956, cited in *FRUS, 1955–7: Volume XVI: Suez crisis*, Washington: United States Government Printing Office, 1990, p. 924.
30 Peter L. Hahn, *The United States, Great Britain, and Egypt, 1945–56: Strategy and diplomacy in the early Cold War*, Chapel Hill and London: University of North Carolina Press, 1991, p. 230.
31 John Charmley, *Churchill's grand alliance: The Anglo-American special relationship, 1940–1957*, London: Hodder and Stoughton, 1995, pp. 353, 349.
32 W. Scott Lucas, *Divided we stand: Britain, the United States and the Suez crisis*, London: Hodder and Stoughton, 1991, p. 324.
33 Muhammad Abd el-Wahab Sayed-Ahmed, *Nasser and American foreign policy, 1952–56*, London: LAAM, 1989, p. 144.
34 Douglas Little, *American orientalism: The United States and the Middle East since 1945*, London: I. B. Tauris, 2003, p. 119.
35 Steven Z. Freiberger, *Dawn over Suez: The rise of American power in the Middle East, 1953–7*, Chicago: Ivan R. Dee, 1992, p. 206.
36 Ray Takeyh, *The origins of the Eisenhower doctrine*, Basingstoke: Macmillan, 2000, p. xiii.
37 Ibid., pp. xiii–xiv.
38 Ibid., p. 147.
39 Ibid., p. 145.
40 Ashton, *Eisenhower, Macmillan and the problem of Nasser*, p. 100.
41 Nigel Ashton, 'Macmillan and the Middle East', in Richard Aldous and Sabine Lee (eds), *Harold Macmillan and Britain's world role*, Basingstoke: Macmillan, 1996, p. 46.
42 Ibid., p. 49.
43 Hahn, *The United States, Great Britain, and Egypt*, p. 240.
44 Petersen, *The Middle East between the great powers*, p. 68.
45 Telegram from Burrows to the Foreign Office, No. 2, 16 January 1957, FO 371/126910/EA 10345/1.
46 Minute by J. C. Moberly, 24 January 1957, FO 371/126910/EA 10345/1.
47 Minute from D. H. M. Riches, 25 January 1957, FO 371/126910/EA 10345/1.
48 Letter from Riches to Bernard Burrows, 8 February 1957, FO 371/126910/EA 10345/1.
49 Bermuda Conference – March 1957: Persian Gulf States, Foreign Office brief, FO 371/126915/EA 1051/6.
50 Petersen, *The Middle East between the great powers*, p. 111.
51 Bermuda Conference – March 1957: Persian Gulf States, Foreign Office brief, FO 371/126915/EA 1051/6.
52 Ibid.
53 Letter from Burrows to Riches, No. 1631/57, 23 May 1957, FO 371/126910/EA 10345/7.

54 Bermuda Conference – March 1957: Persian Gulf States, Foreign Office brief, FO 371/126915/EA 1051/6.
55 Herbert Hoover, Jr., Under Secretary of State.
56 'United Kingdom position in the Persian Gulf', minute by John B. Denson, 9 March 1957, FO 371/126915/EA 1051/11.
57 Minute by A. R. Walmsley, 4 April 1957, FO 371/126915/EA 1051/11.
58 Letter from Sir Roger Stevens to Selwyn Lloyd, No. 140, 8 December 1956, FO 371/120571/EA 1055/71.
59 Letter from Burrows to Riches, No. 1051/13/57, 11 April 1957, FO 371/126910/EA 10345/5.
60 Minute by Denson, 17 April 1957, FO 371/126910/EA 10345/5.
61 Undated comment by D. H. M. Riches on Walmsley's minute, 4 April 1957, FO 371/126915/EA 1051/11.
62 'Persian Gulf', memorandum by the Secretary of State for Foreign Affairs, 7 June 1957, C. (57) 138, CAB 129/87.
63 Harold Macmillan, *Riding the storm, 1956–9*, London: Macmillan, 1971, p. 511.
64 E. Bruce Geelhoed and Anthony O. Edmonds, *Eisenhower, Macmillan and Allied Unity, 1957–61*, Basingstoke: Palgrave, 2003, pp. 51–3.
65 Ibid., p. 53.
66 Wm. Roger Louis, 'Britain and the crisis of 1958', in Wm. Roger Louis and Roger Owen (eds), *A revolutionary year: The Middle East in 1958*, London: I. B. Tauris, 2002, p. 68.
67 Memorandum of conversation, 17 July 1958, cited in *FRUS, 1958–60: Volume XII: Near East region; Iraq; Iran; Arabian Peninsula*, Washington: United States Government Printing Office, 1993, p. 777.
68 Irene L. Gendzier, 'Oil, politics, and US intervention', in Louis and Owen, *A revolutionary year*, p. 108.
69 Memorandum of conversation with President Eisenhower, 20 July 1958, cited in *FRUS, 1958–60: Volume XII*, p. 84.
70 Ibid.
71 Memorandum from the Assistant Secretary of State for Near Eastern, South Asian, and African Affairs (Rountree) to Secretary of State Dulles, 23 July 1958, cited in ibid., p. 94.
72 Paper prepared by the National Security Council Planning Board, 29 July 1958, cited in ibid., p. 119.
73 'The British position in the Persian Gulf-Arabia Peninsula area', Special National Intelligence Estimate, 28 October 1958, cited in ibid., p. 782.
74 Memorandum from the legal adviser (Becker) to Secretary of State Herter, 15 May 1959, cited in ibid., p. 787.
75 Richard A. Mobley, 'Deterring Iraq: The UK experience', *Intelligence and National Security*, 16, 2 (2001): 58.
76 Letter from Sir George Middleton to R. A. Beaumont, No. 1094G, 11 February 1960, FO 371/148947/BA 1072/4/G.
77 Letter from Beaumont to Middleton, 8 March 1960, FO 371/148947/BA 1072/4/G.
78 'Anglo-American planning for intervention in the Persian Gulf', minute by Beaumont, 24 May 1961, FO 371/156694/ B1198/2G.
79 Minutes of a meeting of the Defence Committee, 27 April 1961, D (61) 5th meeting, CAB 131/25.
80 Minute by F. R. Hoyer Millar, 25 May 1961, FO 371/156694/ B1198/2G.
81 Minute from P. F. de Zulueta to the Prime Minister, 1 June 1960, PREM 11/3169.
82 For accounts of the 1961 Kuwait 'incident', see Miriam Joyce, 'Preserving the Sheikhdom: London, Washington, Iraq and Kuwait, 1958–61', *Middle Eastern Studies*, 31, 2 (1995): 281–92; Joyce, *Kuwait, 1945–96: An Anglo-American perspective*, London and Portland, Oregon: Frank Cass, 1998, pp. 92–118.

83 'The possibility of assistance from the United States in defending Kuwait', minute by Walmsley, 27 June 1961, FO 371/156874/BK 1193/16/G.
84 Telegram from the Department of State to the Consulate in Kuwait, 27 June 1961, cited in *FRUS: 1961–3: Volume XVII: Near East, 1961–2*, Washington: United States Government Printing Office, 1994, p. 163.
85 Cabinet conclusions, 29 June 1961, CC 36 (61), CAB 128/35 Part 1.
86 Message from Home to Rusk, 29 June 1961, cited in *FRUS, 1961–63: Volume XVII*, p. 171.
87 Ibid., p. 172.
88 For an account of the growth of US oil interests in the region, see Fiona Venn, '"A futile paper chase": Anglo-American relations and Middle East Oil, 1918–34', *Diplomacy and Statecraft*, 1, 2, (1990): 165–84.
89 Nigel Ashton, 'Britain and the Kuwait crisis, 1961', *Diplomacy and Statecraft*, 9, 1 (1998): 170.
90 Ibid., p. 171.
91 Telegram from Rusk to American Consul (Kuwait), 30 June 1961, JFK Library, National Security File: Countries, Box 129A, Kuwait: General 6/61–7/61 (Folder A).
92 Ibid.
93 Ashton, 'Britain and the Kuwait crisis', p. 172.
94 Ibid.
95 Telegram from Baghdad (Jernegan) to the Secretary of State, No. 15, 5 July 1961, JFK Library, National Security File: Countries, Box 129A, Kuwait: General 6/61–7/61 (Folder A).
96 Ibid.
97 Telegram from Baghdad (Jernegan) to Secretary of State, No. 56, 25 July 1961, JFK Library, National Security File: Countries, Box 129A, Kuwait: General 6/61–7/61 (Folder B).
98 Airgram from American Embassy Baghdad (Jernegan) to the Secretary of State, No. A-171, 21 December 1961, JFK Library, National Security File: Countries, Box 129A, Kuwait: General 8/61–5/62.
99 Memorandum from the Assistant Secretary of State for Near Eastern and South Asian Affairs (Talbot) to the Under Secretary of State for Political Affairs (McGhee), 29 December 1961, cited in *FRUS, 1961–3: Volume XVII*, p. 376.
101 Ibid., p. 377.
101 Ibid., p. 378.
102 The following is based on telegram from Baghdad (Jernegan) to Secretary of State, No. 286, 28 December 1961, JFK Library, National Security File: Countries, Box 129A, Kuwait: General 8/61–5/62. See also *FRUS, 1961–3: Volume XVII*, pp. 374–5.
103 Telegram from Baghdad (Jernegan) to Secretary of State, No. 289, 29 December 1961, JFK Library, National Security File: Countries, Box 129A, Kuwait: General 8/61–5/62.
104 Message from McGeorge Bundy to the President, 30 December 1961, JFK Library, National Security File: Countries, Box 129A, Kuwait: General 8/61–5/62.
105 Telegram from Rusk to American Embassy, Kuwait, No. 390, 4 January 1962, JFK Library, National Security File: Countries, Box 129A, Kuwait: General 8/61–5/62.
106 Telegram from Cairo (Badeau) to Secretary of State, No. 1024, 30 December 1961, JFK Library, National Security File: Countries, Box 129A, Kuwait: General 8/61–5/62.
107 Telegram from Amman (Macomber) to Secretary of State, No, 292, 2 January 1962, JFK Library, National Security File: Countries, Box 129A, Kuwait: General 8/61–5/62.

108 Minutes of a meeting of the Cabinet Official Committee on the Middle East, 21 August 1961, OME (61) 3rd meeting, CAB 134/2345.
109 Letter from Richmond to Walmsley, No. 11115/62, 4 January 1962, FO 371/162906/BK 1114/6.
110 Minute by Walmsley, 13 February 1962, FO 371/162906/BK 1114/6.
111 Telegram from Rusk to American Embassy, Kuwait, 29 July 1963, JFK Library, National Security File: Countries, Box 129A, Kuwait: General 6/62–11/63.
112 Letter from Sir William Luce to the Earl of Home, No. 98, 22 November 1961, FO 371/156670/B 1019/2.
113 'Anglo-American discussions on Kuwait', minute by R. S. Crawford, 8 January 1962; Minute by P. A Wilkinson, 9 January 1962, FO 371/162812/B 1195/1.
114 'Discussions with the State Department on British policy', draft Foreign Office brief (undated), FO 371/162812/B 1195/1.
115 Letter from J. C. W. Bushell to Walmsley, No. 104/01/62, 26 January 1962, FO 371/162812/B 1195/2.
116 Minute by H. B. Walker, 9 January 1961 [1962], FO 371/156670/B 1019/2.
117 Letter from David Ormsby-Gore to Sir Roger Stevens, 2 January 1962, FO 371/162812/B 1195/1.
118 Letter from D. A. Greenhill to A. R. Walmsley, No. 10815/62, 23 January 1962, FO 371/162783/B 103145/2.
119 Ibid.
120 Letter from Walmsley to D. J. Speares, 2 August 1962, FO 371/162783/B 103145/9.
121 For an account of Anglo-American relations over Yemen, see Simon C. Smith, 'Revolution and reaction: South Arabia in the aftermath of the Yemeni revolution', *Journal of Imperial and Commonwealth History*, 28, 3 (2000): 193–208.
122 Alistair Horne, *Macmillan, 1957–86*, London: Macmillan, 1989, p. 420.
123 Douglas Little, 'The new frontier on the Nile: JFK, Nasser, and Arab nationalism', *Journal of American History*, 75, 2 (1988): 514.
124 Telegram from the Foreign Office to Washington, No. 8290, 16 November 1962, enclosing texts of messages received by Macmillan from Kennedy, PREM 11/3878.
125 Telegram from the Foreign Office to Washington, No. 8199, 14 November 1962, enclosing message from the Prime Minister to the President, PREM 11/3878.
126 Memorandum for the President from R. W. Komer, 14 February 1963, JFK Library, President's Office File: Countries: Box 128A, Yemen Security.
127 Telegram from Sir Charles Johnston to the Secretary of State for Colonies, No. 155, 8 February 1963, PREM 11/4357.
128 Michael Kandiah and Gillian Staerck, '"Reliable allies": Anglo-American relations', in Wolfram Kaiser and Gillian Staerck (eds), *British foreign policy, 1955–64*, Basingstoke: Macmillan, 2000, p. 144.
129 Telegram from the Foreign Office to Washington, No. 801, 15 February 1963, enclosing a message from the Prime Minister to the President, PREM 11/4357.
130 Fawaz A. Gerges, *The superpowers and the Middle East: Regional and international politics, 1953–67*, Boulder: Westview Press, 1994, pp. 147–8; Gerges, 'The Kennedy administration and the Egyptian-Saudi conflict in Yemen: Co-opting Arab nationalism', *Middle East Journal*, 49, 2 (1995): 296–7. See also Little, 'JFK, Nasser, and Arab nationalism', pp. 501–27.
131 Nigel J. Ashton, *Kennedy, Macmillan and the Cold War: The irony of interdependence*, Basingstoke: Palgrave, 2002, p. 16.
132 Ibid., p. 223.
133 Ibid., p. 226.

134 W. Taylor Fain, 'John F. Kennedy and Harold Macmillan: Managing the "special relationship" in the Persian Gulf region, 1961–3', *Middle Eastern Studies*, 38, 4 (2002): 111. See also W. Taylor Fain, '"Unfortunate Arabia": The United States, Great Britain and Yemen, 1955–63', *Diplomacy and Statecraft*, 12, 2 (2001): 146.
135 Kandiah and Staerck, '"Reliable allies"', p. 152.
136 'Oil and interdependence in the Middle East', State Department paper, enclosed in Speares' letter to Walmsley, No. 1030/11/62G, 4 December 1962, FO 371/162783/B 103145/9.
137 Ibid.
138 'State Department Planning Paper', minute by D. G. Crawford, 1 March 1963, FO 371/162783/B 103145/9.
139 Letter from Luce to Sir Roger Stevens, No. 1040/63, 17 January 1963, FO 371/168632/B 1052/5/G.
140 'Sir William Luce's letter on British policy in the Middle East', minute by G. F. Hiller, 30 January 1963, FO 371/168632/B 1052/5/G.
141 'Sir W. Luce's letter on M.E. policy', minute by R. S. Crawford, 4 February 1963, FO 371/168632/B 1052/5/G.
142 Letter from Stevens to Luce, 8 February 1963, FO 371/168632/B 1052/5/G.
143 Letter from J. E. Killick to Stevens, No. 10523/3/63G, 13 February 1963, FO 371/168632/B 1052/10/G.
144 Record of a meeting between Sir Roger Stevens and Mr. Phillips Talbot of the State Department, 6 February 1963, FO 371/168627/B 103145/1.
145 'British interests and commitments in the area served by the Aden base', memorandum by the Foreign Office, D.O. (O) (S) (64) 9, 16 July 1964, CAB 148/8.
146 Letter from P. R. H. Wright (First Secretary, British Embassy, Washington) to J. A. Snellgrove, No. 10417G, 3 December 1964, FO 371/174485/B103145/10.
147 Matthew Elliot, 'Defeat and revival: Britain in the Middle East', in Kaiser and Staerck (eds), *British foreign policy*, 2000, p. 251.
148 Telegram from American Consul, Dhahran (Horner), to Secretary of State, No. 133, 7 November 1963, RG 59, Subject-Numeric Files 1963, Box 4070, POL 15 Trucial St. See also Miriam Joyce, *Ruling Shaikhs and Her Majesty's Government, 1960–9*, London: Frank Cass, 2003, p. 14.

6 The 'special relationship' and the withdrawal from East of Suez

1 David Reynolds, 'A "special relationship"? America, Britain and the international order since the Second World War', *International Affairs*, 62, 1 (1986): 2.
2 David Reynolds, 'Rethinking Anglo-American relations', *International Affairs*, 65, 1 (1989): 98.
3 Geoffrey Warner, 'The Anglo-American special relationship', *Diplomatic History*, 13, 4 (1989): 480.
4 Ian Clark, *Nuclear diplomacy and the special relationship: Britain's deterrent and America, 1957–62*, Oxford: Clarendon Press, 1994, p. 14.
5 Matthew Elliot, 'Defeat and revival: Britain in the Middle East', in Wolfram Kaiser and Gillian Staerck (eds), *British foreign policy, 1955–64*, Basingstoke: Macmillan, 2000, p. 245.
6 Alex Danchev, *On specialness: Essays on Anglo-American relations*, Basingstoke: Macmillan, 1998, pp. 11–12.
7 Alan P. Dobson, *Anglo-American relations in the twentieth century*, London: Routledge, 1995, p. 97.
8 John Dumbrell, *A special relationship: Anglo-American relations in the Cold War and after*, Basingstoke: Macmillan Press, 2001, p. 13.
9 Nigel J. Ashton, *Kennedy, Macmillan and the Cold War: The irony of interdependence*, Basingstoke: Palgrave, 2002, p. 6.

10 Matthew Jones, 'Anglo-American relations after Suez, the rise and decline of the working group experiment, and the French challenge to NATO, 1957–9', *Diplomacy and Statecraft*, 14, 1 (2003): 73.
11 W. Scott Lucas, 'Neustadt revisited: a new look at Suez and the Anglo-American "alliance"', in Anthony Gorst, Lewis Johnman and W. Scott Lucas (eds), *Post-war Britain, 1945–64: Themes and perspectives*, London: Pinter, 1989, p. 198.
12 Letter from P. R. H. Wright to J. A. Snellgrove, No. 19093, 25 September 1964, FO 371/174485/B103145/8.
13 Letter from Snellgrove to F. D. W. Brown, 15 October 1964, FO 371/174485/B 103145/8; 'Talks between Sir G. Harrison and Mr. Phillips Talbot', Arabian Department paper, 4 December 1964, FO 371/1745515/B1903/6.
14 Letter from Brown to Snellgrove, No. 1902, 3 November 1964, FO 371/174485/B 103145/9.
15 Letter from Wright to M. S. Weir, No. 19093, 7 January 1965, FO 371/179783/ B1903/1.
16 Letter from Weir to R. J. R. Owen, 2 February 1965, FO 371/179783/B1903/1.
17 Letter from Sir William Luce to T. F. Brenchley, No. 1902, 17 April 1965, FO 371/179783/B1903/3.
18 Letter from H. G. Balfour-Paul to Luce, No. 1901/65, 1 May 1965, FO 371/179783/B101903/4.
19 Letter from Brenchley to Luce, 29 April 1965, FO 371/179783/B1903/3.
20 Letter from Sir Michael Stewart to Sir Roger Allen, 2 September 1966, FO 371/185172/B103145/6.
21 Letter from Stewart to Allen, 29 September 1966, FO 371/185172/B103145/8G.
22 Telegram from Dean to the Foreign Office, No. 2571, 21 September 1966, FO 371/185172/B103145/7G.
23 Jeremy Fielding, 'Coping with decline: U.S. policy towards the British defense reviews of 1966', *Diplomatic History*, 23, 4 (1999): 637–8.
24 Alan Dobson, 'The years of transition: Anglo-American relations 1961–7', *Review of International Studies*, 16, 3, (1990): 251.
25 Fielding, 'Coping with decline', p. 641.
26 Dumbrell, *A special relationship*, p. 151.
27 Memorandum from McGeorge Bundy to the President, 10 September 1965, cited in *Foreign Relations of the United States, 1964–8: Volume XII: Western Europe*, Washington: United States Government Printing Office, 2001, p. 506.
28 Telegram from George Ball, 9 September 1965, cited in *FRUS, 1964–8: Volume XII*, p. 508.
29 Ibid., pp. 508–9.
30 Ibid., p. 509.
31 Fielding, 'Coping with decline', p. 646.
32 'Visit of Prime Minister Wilson, December 15–19, 1965', memorandum by the Executive Secretary, Department of State (undated), cited in *FRUS, 1964–8: Volume XII*, p. 510.
33 Fielding, 'Coping with decline', p. 647.
34 'UK Defence Review: UK position in Aden and the Persian Gulf', position paper by the State Department, 27 January 1966, RG 59, Lot Files: Conference Files, 1964–66, Lot 67 D305, Box 398, UK Defence Review – January 1966: Vol. I: Briefing Book.
35 Memorandum of conversation, 27 January 1966, cited in *FRUS, 1964–8: Volume XII*, p. 526.
36 Letter from Stewart to Allen, 29 September 1966, FO 371/185172/B103145/8G.
37 Fielding, 'Coping with decline', p. 653.
38 Memorandum from Secretary of State Rusk to Foreign Secretary Brown, 21 April 1967, cited in *FRUS, 1964–8: Volume XII*, p. 568.

39 Airgram from American Consul-General, Dhahran, to the Secretary of State, No. A-80, 21 December 1966, RG 59, Subject-Numeric Files, 1964–66, Box 1909, POL Bahrain IS.
40 National Intelligence Estimate, 18 May 1967, cited in *FRUS, 1964–8: Volume XXI: Near East Region; Arabian Peninsula*, Washington: United States Printing Office, 2000, p. 207.
41 Information memorandum from the Assistant Secretary of State for Near Eastern Affairs and South Asian Affairs (Battle) to Secretary of State Rusk, 20 November 1967, cited in ibid., p. 245.
42 Dumbrell, *A special relationship*, p. 63.
43 Ashton, *Kennedy, Macmillan and the Cold War*, p. 222. For an account of Wilsonian meddling in Vietnam, see Rolf Steininger, '"The Americans are in a hopeless position": Great Britain and the war in Vietnam, 1964–5', *Diplomacy and Statecraft*, 8, 3 (1997): 237–285.
44 Sylvia A. Ellis, 'Lyndon Johnson, Harold Wilson and the Vietnam War: A *not* so special relationship?', in Jonathan Howell (ed.), *Twentieth-century Anglo-American relations*, Basingstoke: Palgrave, 2002, p. 193.
45 Kevin Boyle, 'The price of peace: Vietnam, the pound, and the crisis of the American empire', *Diplomatic History*, 27, 1 (2003): 46.
46 Message from President Johnson to Prime Minister Wilson, 11 January 1968, cited in *FRUS, 1964–8: Volume XII*, p. 609.
47 Message from President Johnson to Prime Minister Wilson, 15 January 1968, cited in ibid., p. 610.
48 The following is based on Cabinet conclusions, 12 January 1968, CC 6 (68), CAB 128/43 Part 1. In the American version of the discussions, Rusk is more restrained, saying merely 'be Britain'. (Memorandum of conversation, 11 January 1968, cited in *FRUS, 1964–8: Volume XII*, p. 604).
49 Memorandum of conversation, 11 January 1968, cited in *FRUS, 1964–8: Volume XII*, p. 608. See also Wm. Roger Louis, 'The dissolution of the British empire in the era of Vietnam', *American Historical Review*, 107, 1 (2002): 3.
50 Barbara Castle, *The Castle diaries, 1964–70*, London: Weidenfeld and Nicolson, 1984, p. 354.
51 Ibid.
52 Tony Benn, *Office without power: Diaries, 1968–72*, London: Hutchinson, 1988, p. 13.
53 John Dumbrell, 'The Johnson administration and the British Labour Government: Vietnam, the pound and East of Suez', *Journal of American Studies*, 30, 2 (1996): 219.
54 Matthew Jones, 'A decision delayed: Britain's withdrawal from South East Asia reconsidered, 1961–8', *English Historical Review*, 117, 472 (2002): 591. See also, Matthew Jones, *Conflict and confrontation in South East Asia, 1961–5: Britain, the United States and the creation of Malaysia*, Cambridge: Cambridge University Press, 2002, pp. 292–3.
55 Saki Dockrill, *Britain's retreat from East of Suez: The choice between Europe and the world*, Basingstoke: Palgrave, 2002, p. 222. See also ibid., pp. 204–5.
56 'United States participation in the Persian Gulf Fund', paper attached to a memorandum by Raymond A. Hare to the Acting Secretary, 22 November 1965, RG 59, Lot Files: Middle/Near East, Entry 5267, Lot 67D 619 Box 2, Economic Affairs (Gen.) 1965: Qatar and Trucial States.
57 Boyle, 'The price of peace', p. 44.
58 Dumbrell, 'The Johnson administration and the British Labour government', p. 230.
59 Jones, 'A decision delayed', p. 589.
60 Dobson, 'Anglo-American relations 1961–7', pp. 257–8.

61 Dumbrell, 'The Johnson administration and the British Labour government', p. 225.
62 The following is based on Cabinet conclusions, 12 January 1968, CC 6 (68), CAB 128/43 Part 1.
63 Cabinet conclusions, 15 January 1968, CC 7 (68), CAB 128/43 Part 1.
64 Telegram from Prime Minister Wilson to President Johnson, 15 January 1968, cited in *FRUS, 1964–8: Volume XII*, pp. 612–13.
65 Message from President Johnson to Prime Minister Wilson, 15 January 1968, cited in ibid., pp. 610–11.
66 Telegram from Prime Minister Wilson to President Johnson, 15 January 1968, cited in ibid., p. 613.
67 Briefing memorandum from the Assistant Secretary of State for Near Eastern and South Asian Affairs (Battle) to Secretary of State Rusk, 9 January 1968, cited in *FRUS, 1964–8: Volume XXI*, p. 257.
68 Letter from A. B. Urwick to A. J. D. Stirling, No. U 10/1/2, 18 January 1968, FCO 8/36. See also 'Visit of British Prime Minister Wilson, February 1968: Persian Gulf', background paper prepared in the Department State, 2 February 1968, cited in *FRUS, 1964–8: Volume XXI*, p. 275.
69 Memorandum from Harold H. Saunders to the President's Special Assistant (Rostow) and Edward Fried of the National Security Council Staff, 2 February 1968, cited in *FRUS, 1964–8: Volume XXI*, p. 276.
70 Letter from Urwick to Weir, No. 10/37, 29 January 1968, FCO 8/36.
71 Anglo-American talks on the Middle East in the State Department, 13 September 1968, FCO 8/37.
72 Telegram from Rusk to American Embassies in London, Jidda, Tehran, Aden, Kuwait, and American Consul General, Dhahran, No. 113711, 12 February 1968, RG 59, Subject-Numeric Files 1967–69, Box 1640, DEF 1 UK.
73 Letter from Urwick to Stirling, U 10/1/2, 18 January 1968, FCO 8/36.
74 Letter from Urwick to Weir, No. 10/37, 29 January 1968, FCO 8/36; letter from Urwick to Weir, No. 10/37, 15 February 1968, FCO 8/36.
75 Letter from A. D. Parsons to Balfour-Paul, 14 March 1968, FCO 8/36.
76 Miriam Joyce, *Ruling Shaikhs and Her Majesty's Government 1960–9*, London: Frank Cass, 2003, pp. 114–15.
77 Memorandum of conversation, 25 January 1968, cited in *FRUS, 1964–8: Volume XXI*, pp. 264–5.
78 Telegram from the State Department (Rusk) to the Embassy in Southern Yemen, 3 February 1968, cited in ibid., pp. 277–8.
79 Interdepartmental regional group for Near East and South Asia: Record of meeting, 1 February 1968, cited in ibid., p. 273. See also interdepartmental regional group for Near East and South Asia: Record of meeting, 10 July 1968, cited in ibid., p. 300.
80 Interdepartmental regional group for Near East and South Asia: Record of meeting, 4 June 1968, cited in ibid., p. 412.
81 'US arms sales in the Persian Gulf', memorandum from the Deputy Assistant Secretary of Defense for International Security Affairs (Schwartz) to the Assistant Secretary of Defense for International Security Affairs (Warnke), cited in ibid., p. 292; memorandum from Deputy Secretary of Defense (Nitze) to the Chairman of the Joint Chiefs of Staff (Wheeler), 2 August 1968, cited in ibid., p. 304.
82 Telegram from Rusk to American Embassies in Jidda, Kuwait, London, and Tehran, No. 286621, 13 December 1968, RG 59, Subject-Numeric Files 1967–69, Box 2284, POL 7 KUW.
83 Letter from D. J. McCarthy to Urwick, 4 October 1968, FCO 8/37.
84 Letter from W. Morris to McCarthy, 24 December 1968, FCO 8/1005.
85 Ibid.
86 Ibid.

87 The following is based on letter from Sir Patrick Dean to Sir Paul Gore-Booth, 8 January 1969, FCO 8/934/1. See also Joyce, *Ruling Shaikhs and Her Majesty's Government*, p. 141.
88 Minute by McCarthy, 14 January 1969, FCO 8/934/1.
89 Letter from Gore-Booth to Dean, 27 January 1969, FCO 8/934/1.
90 Letter from Urwick to A. A. Acland, No. B/3/11, 27 January 1969, FCO 8/934/1.
91 Telegram from Arthur to the Foreign Office, No. 85, 24 February 1968, FCO 8/957. The Amir evidently took Arthur's words to heart and during his visit to the United States between 10 and 16 December 1968, he made it plain that he was not thinking in terms of an alliance between Kuwait and the United States. (Letter from Urwick to McCarthy, No. 3/63, 20 December 1968, FCO 8/1035.)
92 Anglo-American talks on the Middle East, New York and Washington, 7–11 March 1969: the Persian Gulf and Arabia: Steering brief, FCO 8/934/1.
93 Anglo-American talks on the Middle East held at Washington on 10 and 11 March 1969: Persian Gulf, FCO 8/934/1.
94 Letter from Weir to McCarthy, No. 3/3, 14 May 1969, FCO 8/934/1.
95 The following is based on letter from E. E. Tomkins to McCarthy, No. 10/18/13, 20 May 1969, FCO 8/934/1.
96 Michael A. Palmer, *Guardians of the Gulf: A history of America's expanding role in the Persian Gulf, 1833–1992*, New York: The Free Press, 1992, p. 86.
97 Telegram from American Embassy, Tehran (MacArthur), to the Secretary of State of State, No. 36, 5 January 1970, RG 59, Subject-Numeric Files 1970–73, Box 1774, DEF 1 Near East.
98 National Security Decision Memorandum 92, 7 November 1970, RG 273, NSDM 92, Box 1.
99 'The Tories and the Persian Gulf', memorandum from Joseph W. Neubert to the Secretary, 24 June 1970, RG 59, Subject-Numeric Files 1970–73, Box 1994, POL 33 Persian Gulf.
100 Palmer, *Guardians of the Gulf*, p. 88.
101 The following is based on letter from Parsons to Weir, No. 3/31, 26 November 1968, FCO 8/935.
102 'An American presence in the Gulf', minute by C. D. Powell, 16 December 1968, FCO 8/1005.
103 Minute by C. H. D. Everett, 20 December 1968, FCO 8/1005.
104 'Persian Gulf', brief by the Foreign and Commonwealth Office for meeting of Commonwealth Prime Ministers, 1969, 17 December 1968, FCO 8/958.
105 The following is based on letter from McCarthy to Weir, No. BB 3/304/1, 5 February 1969, FCO 8/935.
106 Telegram from Sir Stewart Crawford to the Foreign and Commonwealth Office, No. 38, 14 February 1969, FCO 8/935.
107 Letter from Urwick to Acland, No. 10/18/13, 12 February 1969, FCO 8/935.
108 'Bilateral talks with the U.S. Secretary of State on 26 May: the Gulf', brief No. 2 by the Arabian Department, FCO 8/958.
109 Telegram from Washington to the Foreign and Commonwealth Office, No. 894, 25 March 1969, FCO 8/935.
110 Telegram from Sir Denis Wright to the Foreign and Commonwealth Office, No. 483, 27 May 1969, FCO 8/958.
111 National Security Council Decision memorandum 92, 7 November 1970, RG 273, Box 1, NSDM 92.
112 Action memorandum from Joseph Sisco to the Acting Secretary, circular 175, 10 June 1971, RG 59, Subject-Numeric files 1970–73, Box 1690, DEF 15-4 BAHRAIN IS-US.

113 Telegram from Manama (Gatch) to Secretary of State, No. 96, 26 November 1971, RG 59, Subject-Numeric Files 1970–73, Box 1690, DEF 15 BAHRAIN-US.

114 Telegram from Department of State (Johnson) to American Consul General, Dhahran, COMIDEASTFOR, and American Embassy, London, No. 90123, 5 May 1971, RG 59, Subject-Numeric Files 1970–73, Box 1690, DEF 15–4 BAHRAIN IS-US.

115 Telegram from Gatch to Secretary of State, No. 160, 23 December 1971, RG 59, Subject-Numeric Files 1970–73, Box 1690, DEF 15–4 BAHRAIN-US.

116 Letter from Weir to Acland, No. 3/17, 1 December 1970, FCO 8/1304.

117 Telegram from American Embassy, Tehran, (MacArthur) to the Secretary of State, No. 279, 15 January 1972, RG 59, Subject-Numeric Files 1970–73, Box 1690, DEF 15–4 BAHRAIN-US.

118 Telegram from American Embassy, Tehran, (MacArthur) to the Secretary of State, No. 322, 17 January 1972, RG 59, Subject-Numeric Files 1970–73, Box 1690, DEF 15–4 BAHRAIN-US.

119 Palmer, *Guardians of the Gulf*, p. 90.

120 Letter from J. W. Fulbright to William P. Rogers, 14 December 1971, RG 59, Subject-Numeric Files 1970–73, Box 1690, DEF 15–4 BAHRAIN-US.

121 Letter from David M. Abshire to Fulbright, 17 December 1971, RG 59, Subject-Numeric Files 1970–73, Box 1690, DEF 15–4 BAHRAIN-US.

122 Letter from Senator Clifford P. Case to Rogers, 6 March 1972, RG 59, Subject-Numeric Files 1970–73, Box 1690, DEF 15–4 BAHRAIN-US.

123 Telegram from American Embassy, Manama, (Gatch) to American Embassy, Tehran, No. 60, 23 January 1972, RG 59, Subject-Numeric Files 1970–73, Box 2113, POL BAHRAIN IS-A [POL BAHRAIN-US].

124 Telegram from American Embassy, Manama, (Gatch) to Secretary of State, No. 229, 3 April 1972, RG 59, Subject-Numeric Files 1970–73, Box 1690, DEF 15–4 BAHRAIN-US.

125 Ibid.

126 Airgram from American Embassy, Kuwait (Cottam), to Department of State, No. A-300, 19 May 1966, RG 59, Subject-Numeric Files 1964–66, Box 1654, DEF 12–5 KUW-US.

127 Memorandum of conversation: subject: Lockheed Aircraft interests in sales of F-104 to Kuwait and Jordan, 11 February 1966, RG 59, Subject-Numeric Files 1964–66, Box 1654, DEF 12–5 KUW-US.

128 Telegram from Department of State (Ball) to the American Embassy, London, No. 7326, 7 June 1966, RG 59, Subject-Numeric Files 1964–66, Box 1654, DEF 12–5 KUW-US. See also *FRUS, 1964–8: Volume XXI*, p. 398.

129 Telegram from American Embassy, London (Kaiser), to the Secretary of State, No. 6321, 8 February 1968, RG 59, Subject-Numeric Files 1967–69, Box 1569, DEF 12–5 KUW.

130 Telegram from Department of State (Rusk) to American Embassy, Kuwait, No. 119386, 22 February 1968, RG 59, Subject-Numeric Files 1967–69, Box 1569, DEF 12–5 KUW.

131 Telegram from American Embassy, Kuwait (Cottam), to Secretary of State, No. 1017, 1 May 1968, RG 59, Subject-Numeric Files 1967–69, Box 1569, DEF 12–5 KUW.

132 Telegram from American Embassy, London (Bruce), to Secretary of State, No. 8610, 2 May 1968, RG 59, Subject-Numeric Files 1967–69, Box 1569, DEF 12–5 KUW.

133 Telegram from CINCSTRIKE/USCINCMEAFSA (Commander in Chief, Strike Command/United States Commander in Chief, Middle East/South Asia and Africa South of the Sahara) to the Joint Chiefs of Staff, No. 71701Z, 6 May 1968, RG 59, Subject-Numeric Files 1967–69, Box 1569, DEF 12–5 KUW.

134 Telegram from Department of State (Rusk) to American Embassy, London, No. 179095, 7 June 1968, RG 59, Subject-Numeric Files 1967–69, Box 1569, DEF 12–5 KUW.
135 Memorandum from the Joint Chiefs of Staff to Secretary of Defense McNamara, 19 June 1968, cited in *FRUS, 1964–8, Volume XXI*, p. 298.
136 Ibid., pp. 298–9.
137 Telegram from Department of State (Battle) to American Embassy, London, No. 190642, 25 June 1968, RG 59, Subject-Numeric Files 1967–69, Box 1569, DEF 12–5 KUW.
138 Telegram from Department of State (Rogers) to American Embassy, London, No. 99984, 18 June 1969, RG 59, Subject-Numeric Files 1967–69, Box 1569, DEF 12–5 KUW.
139 Telegram from American Embassy, Kuwait (Walsh), to Secretary of State, No. 57, 21 January 1970, Nixon Presidential Materials, National Security Council Files: Country Files: Middle East: Kuwait, Vol. I.
140 Telegram from Walsh to Secretary of State, No. 76, 27 January 1970, Nixon Presidential Materials, National Security Council Files: Country Files: Middle East: Kuwait, Vol. I. This telegram can also be found in RG 59, Subject-Numeric Files 1970–73, Box 1762, DEF 12–5 KUW.
141 Telegram from Walsh to Secretary of State, No. 108, 5 February 1970, Nixon Presidential Materials, National Security Council Files: Country Files: Middle East: Kuwait, Vol. I.
142 Telegram from Department of State (Richardson) to American Embassy, Kuwait, No. 26892, 21 February 1970, RG 59, Subject-Numeric Files 1970–73, Box 1762, DEF 12–5 KUW.
143 Letter from Robert J. Pranger to Rodger P. Davies (Deputy Assistant Secretary of States) 10 July 1970, RG 59, Subject-Numeric Files 1970–73, Box 1762, DEF 12–5 KUW.
144 Record of Anglo-American talks on the Middle East held at the State Department, 18 November 1970, FCO 8/1304.
145 Memorandum for the President from Rogers, 22 December 1970, RG 59, Subject-Numeric Files 1970–73, Box 1762, DEF 12–5 KUW.
146 Memorandum for the Secretary of State from Nixon, Presidential Determination No. 71–6, 17 January 1971, RG 59, Subject-Numeric Files 1970–73, Box 1762, DEF 12–5 KUW.
147 Telegram from Walsh to the Secretary of State, No. 1293, 17 November 1971, RG 59, Subject-Numeric Files 1970–73, Box 2432, POL 23 KUW.
148 'Persian Gulf': Memorandum for the President from Rogers, 16 December 1971, RG 59, Subject-Numeric Files 1970–73, Box 1774, DEF 1 Near East.
149 Letter from G. E. Millard (Minister, British Embassy, Washington) to Luce, 20 January 1971, FCO 8/1583.

Conclusion

1 The following is based on 'Defence expenditure study No. 6: Long-term policy in the Persian Gulf', report by the Defence Review Working Party, 7 June 1967, OPDO (67) 8, CAB 148/80.
2 Ibid.
3 'Western oil interests in the Middle East', note by G. S. Downey, July 1964, T 317/663.
4 'Middle East oil and defence', minute from R. L. Sharp to Hubback, 24 January 1963, T 317/41.
5 Minute by A. T. Lamb, 1 January 1964, FO 371/174507/B 1531/1/G.
6 'British interests and commitments in the area served by the Aden base', memorandum by the Foreign Office, 16 July 1964, DO (O) (64) 9, CAB 148/8.

7 'Oil aspects of Middle East Defence Policy', memorandum by the Treasury, Foreign Office and Ministry of Power, 7 September 1964, CAB 148/9.
8 Letter from Sir William Luce to Lord Home, No. 98, 22 November 1961, T 317/41.
9 'Mediterranean and the Middle East', memorandum circulated for consideration of the Committee, 5 May 1965, OPDO (O) (65) 31, CAB 148/43.
10 'British interests and commitments in the area served by the Aden base', memorandum by the Foreign Office, 16 July 1964, DO (O) (64) 9, CAB 148/8.
11 Letter from H. Beeley to Sir Geoffrey Harrison, No. 1531/10/12/63G, 10 December 1963, FO 371/174507/B 1531/1/G.
12 Peter Catterall (ed.), Witness seminar: 'The East of Suez decision', *Contemporary Record*, 7, 3 (1993): 619–20.
13 'Kuwait', Minute by A. Mackay, 11 April 1961, T 317/114.
14 Denis Healey, *The time of my life*, London: Michael Joseph, 1989, p. 256.
15 Patrick Gordon Walker, *The Cabinet*, London: Jonathan Cape, 1970, p. 129.
16 Minutes of a meeting of the Cabinet Defence and Oversea Policy Committee, 11 December 1970, DOP (70) 12th meeting, CAB 148/101.
17 Ibid.
18 'Policy in the Persian Gulf', minute from Burke Trend to the Prime Minister, 10 December 1970, PREM 15/538.
19 'The rulership of Abu Dhabi', minute by Patrick Gordon-Walker to the Prime Minister, PM/64/152, 22 December 1964, PREM 13/3326.
20 'Lessons from South Arabia?', minute by D. J. McCarthy, 20 November 1967, FCO 8/41.
21 'Withdrawal from the Persian Gulf', paper by the Planning Staff, 11 January 1968, FCO 8/31.
22 Letter from Sir Stewart Crawford to Douglas-Home, 25 July 1970, FCO 8/1318.
23 'The other five Trucial States', paper by Thomas J. Carolan, 20 July 1966, RG 59, Lot Files: Middle/Near East, Entry 5267, Lot 68 D 303, Box 6, Persian Gulf 1966: Political Affairs: Pol-General.
24 Tore Tingvold Petersen, 'Crossing the rubicon?: Britain's withdrawal from the Middle East, 1964–8: A bibliographical review', *International History Review*, 22, 2 (2000): 331.
25 Prime Minister's visit to Washington July 1966: Arabia and the UAR, brief by the Foreign Office, 21 July 1966, FO 371/185177/B 1051/21.
26 Record of Anglo-United States talks on the Persian Gulf and Arabian Peninsula in the State Department, 26 June 1972, FCO 8/1806.
27 Minute from Anthony Royle (Parliamentary Under-Secretary of State, Foreign and Commonwealth Office) to the Secretary of State, enclosing record of a conversation with US Secretary of State Rogers, 6 July 1970, FCO 8/1316.
28 Michael A. Palmer, *Guardians of the Gulf: A History of America's expanding role in the Persian Gulf, 1883–1992*, New York: The Free Press, 1992, p. 106.
29 Douglas Little, *American orientalism: The United States and the Middle East since 1945*, London: I. B. Tauris, 2003, p. 147.
30 Palmer, *Guardians of the Gulf*, p. 149.
31 'Defence expenditure study No. 6: Long-term policy in the Persian Gulf', report by the Defence Review Working Party, 7 June 1967, OPDO (67) 8, CAB 148/80 (underlining in the original).
32 John Darwin, 'Diplomacy and decolonization', *Journal of Imperial and Commonwealth History*, 28, 3 (2000): 18.
33 For an account of shifts in the relations between the producing countries on the one hand, and the oil companies and consuming countries on the other, see Fiona Venn, *The oil crisis*, London: Longman, 2002.

Bibliography

Unpublished Official Sources

National Archives (Public Record Office), Kew, London

Cabinet Office

CAB 128	Cabinet Minutes
CAB 129	Cabinet Memoranda
CAB 130	Miscellaneous Committees: Minutes and Papers
CAB 131	Defence Committee
CAB 134	Cabinet Committees: General Series from 1945
CAB 148	Defence and Overseas Policy Committee and Sub-Committee: Minutes and Papers, 1965–70

Ministry of Defence

DEFE 11	Ministry of Defence: Chiefs of Staff Committee

Foreign Office/Foreign and Commonwealth Office

FCO 8	Arabian Department and Middle East Department, 1967–72
FO 371	Political Departments: General Correspondence
FO 960	Political Agency and Embassy, Kuwait
FO 1016	Embassy and Consular Archives: Persian Gulf Residencies and Agencies

Prime Minister's Office

PREM 11	Prime Minister's Office: Correspondence and Papers, 1951–64
PREM 13	Prime Minister's Office: Correspondence and Papers, 1964–70
PREM 15	Prime Minister's Office: Correspondence and Papers, 1970–2

Treasury

T 225	Defence Policy and Material Division
T 236	Overseas Finance Division
T 317	Overseas Development Divisions and Successors

United States National Archives, College Park, Maryland

RG 59 Department of State Records: Central Decimal, Subject-Numeric, and Lot Files

RG 273 National Security Council Decision and Study Memoranda

Nixon Presidential Materials: National Security Files

John F. Kennedy Library, Boston, Massachusetts

National Security File

President's Office File

Published Official Papers

Egypt and the defence of the Middle East, edited by John Kent, London: Her Majesty's Stationery Office, 1998.

Exchange of notes between the Government of the United Kingdom of Great Britain and Northern Ireland and the Government of the State of Kuwait terminating the agreement of 19 June 1961, regarding relations between the United Kingdom of Great Britain and Northern Ireland and the State of Kuwait, 13 May 1968, London: HMSO, 1968, Cmnd, 3720.

Exchange of notes regarding relations between the United Kingdom of Great Britain and Northern Ireland and the State of Kuwait, 19 June 1961, London: HMSO, 1961, Cmnd. 1409.

Exchange of notes concerning the termination of special treaty relations between the United Kingdom of Great Britain and Northern Ireland and the State of Qatar, 3 September 1971, London: HMSO, 1972, Cmnd. 4849.

Exchange of notes concerning the termination of special treaty relations between the United Kingdom of Great Britain and Northern Ireland and the State of the Trucial States, 1 December 1971, London: HMSO, 1972, Cmnd. 4941.

Foreign relations of the United States, 1952–4: Volume X: Iran, 1951–4, Washington: United States Government Printing Office, 1989.

Foreign relations of the United States, 1955–7: Volume XVI: Suez crisis, Washington: United States Government Printing Office, 1990.

Foreign relations of the United States, 1958–60: Volume XII: Near East region; Iraq; Iran; Arabian Peninsula, Washington: United States Government Printing Office, 1993.

Foreign relations of the United States, 1961–3: Volume XVII: Near East, 1961–2, Washington: United States Government Printing Office, 1994.

Foreign relations of the United States, 1964–8: Volume XII: Western Europe, Washington: United States Government Printing Office, 2001.

Foreign relations of the United States, 1964–8: Volume XXI: Near East region; Arabian Peninsula, Washington: United States Printing Office, 2000.

Parliamentary Debates (Commons, 1966–7, Volume 737.

Parliamentary Debates (Commons), 1970–1, Volume 812.

Supplementary statement on defence 1967, London: HMSO, July 1967, Cmnd. 3357.

Treaty of friendship between the United Kingdom and Great Britain and Northern Ireland and the State of Bahrain, 3 September 1971, London: HMSO, 1972, Cmnd. 4828.

Treaty of friendship between the United Kingdom of Great Britain and Northern Ireland and the State of Qatar, 3 September 1971, London: HMSO, 1972, Cmnd. 4850.

Books and articles

Ahmed, Ahmed A., 'Kuwait public commercial investments in Arab countries', *Middle Eastern Studies*, 31, 2 (1995): 293–306.

Ashton, Nigel J., 'The hijacking of a pact: The formation of the Baghdad Pact and Anglo-American tensions in the Middle East, 1955–8', *Review of International Studies*, 19, 2 (1993): 123–37.

Ashton, Nigel J., 'Macmillan and the Middle East', in Richard Aldous and Sabine Lee (eds), *Harold Macmillan and Britain's World Role*, Basingstoke: Macmillan, 1996.

Ashton, Nigel J., *Eisenhower, Macmillan and the Problem of Nasser: Anglo-American Relations and Arab Nationalism, 1955–9*, Basingstoke: Macmillan, 1996.

Ashton, Nigel J., 'Britain and the Kuwait crisis, 1961', *Diplomacy and Statecraft*, 9, 1 (1998): 163–81.

Ashton, Nigel J., *Kennedy, Macmillan and the Cold War: The Irony of Interdependence*, Basingstoke: Palgrave, 2002.

Balfour-Paul, Glenn, *The End of Empire in the Middle East: Britain's Relinquishment of Power in her Last Three Arab Dependencies*, Cambridge: Cambridge University Press, 1991.

Bamberg, J. H., *The History of the British Petroleum Company: Volume 2: The Anglo-Iranian Years, 1928–54*, Cambridge: Cambridge University Press, 1994.

Benn, Tony, *Office without Power: Diaries 1968–72*, London: Hutchinson, 1988, p. 13.

Blyth, Robert J., 'British versus India in the Persian Gulf: The struggle for political control, c. 1928–48', *Journal of Imperial and Commonwealth History*, 28, 1 (2000): 90–111.

Boyle, Kevin, 'The price of peace: Vietnam, the pound, and the crisis of the American empire', *Diplomatic History*, 27, 1 (2003): 37–72.

Campbell, John C., 'The Soviet Union, the United States, and the twin crises of Hungary and Suez', in Wm. Roger Louis and Roger Owen (eds), *Suez 1956: The Crisis and its Consequences*, Oxford: Clarendon Press, 1989.

Castle, Barbara, *The Castle diaries, 1964–70*, London: Weidenfeld & Nicolson, 1984, p. 354.

Catterall, Peter (ed.), 'Witness seminar: "The East of Suez decision"', *Contemporary Record*, 7, 3 (1993): 612–53.

Charmley, John, *Churchill's Grand Alliance: The Anglo-American Special Relationship, 1940–1957*, London: Hodder and Stoughton, 1995.

Clark, Ian, *Nuclear Diplomacy and the Special Relationship: Britain's Deterrent and America, 1957–62*, Oxford: Clarendon Press, 1994.

Crystal, Jill, *Oil and Politics in the Gulf: Rulers and Merchants in Kuwait and Qatar*, Cambridge: Cambridge University Press, 1990.

Danchev, Alex, *On specialness: Essays on Anglo-American Relations*, Basingstoke: Macmillan, 1998.

Darby, Phillip, *British Defence Policy East of Suez, 1947–68*, London: Oxford University Press, 1973.

Darby, Phillip, 'East of Suez reassessed', in John Baylis (ed.), *British Defence Policy in a Changing World*, London: Croom Helm, 1977.

Darwin, John, *British and Decolonisation: The Retreat from Empire in the Post-war World*, Basingstoke: Macmillan, 1988.

Darwin, John, 'Britain's withdrawal from East of Suez', in Carl Bridge (ed.), *Munich to Vietnam: Australia's Relations with Britain and the United States since the 1930s*, Carlton, Victoria: Melbourne University Press, 1991.

Darwin, John, 'Diplomacy and decolonization', *Journal of Imperial and Commonwealth History*, 28, 3 (2000): 5–24.

Dobson, Alan, 'The years of transition: Anglo-American relations 1961–7', *Review of International Studies*, 16, 3 (1990): 239–58.

Dobson, Alan, *Anglo-American Relations in the Twentieth Century*, London: Routledge, 1995.

Dockrill, Saki, *Britain's Retreat from East of Suez: The Choice between Europe and the World*, Basingstoke: Palgrave, 2002.

Dumbrell, John, 'The Johnson administration and the British Labour Government: Vietnam, the pound and east of Suez', *Journal of American Studies*, 30, 2 (1996): 211–31.

Dumbrell, John, *A Special Relationship: Anglo-American Relations in the Cold War and After*, Basingstoke: Macmillan, 2001.

Elliot, Matthew, 'Defeat and revival: Britain in the Middle East', in Wolfram Kaiser and Gillian Staerck (eds), *British Foreign Policy, 1955–64*, Basingstoke: Macmillan, 2000.

Ellis, Sylvia A., 'Lyndon Johnson, Harold Wilson and the Vietnam War: A *not* so special relationship?', in Jonathan Howell (ed.), *Twentieth-century Anglo-American Relations*, Basingstoke: Palgrave, 2002.

Elm, Mostafa, *Oil, Power and Principle: Iran's Oil Nationalization and its Aftermath*, Syracuse: Syracuse University Press, 1994.

Fain, W. Taylor, '"Unfortunate Arabia": The United States, Great Britain and Yemen, 1955–63', *Diplomacy and Stagecraft*, 12, 2 (2001): 125–52.

Fain, W. Taylor, 'John F. Kennedy and Harold Macmillan: Managing the "special relationship" in the Persian Gulf region, 1961–3', *Middle Eastern Studies*, 38, 4 (2002): 95–122.

Fielding, Jeremy, 'Coping with decline: U.S. policy towards the British defense reviews of 1966', *Diplomatic History*, 23, 4 (1999): 633–56.

Freiberger, Steven Z., *Dawn over Suez: The Rise of American Power in the Middle East, 1953–7*, Chicago: Ivan R. Dee, 1992.

Gasiorowski, Mark, 'The 1953 coup d'etat in Iran', *International Journal of Middle East Studies*, 19, 3 (1987): 261–86.

Gause, F. Gregory, 'British and American policies in the Persian Gulf, 1968–73', *Review of International Studies*, 11, 4 (1985): 247–73.

Geelhoed, E. Bruce, and Edmonds, Anthony O., *Eisenhower, Macmillan and Allied Unity, 1957–61*, Basingstoke: Palgrave, 2003.

Gendzier, Irene L., 'Oil, politics, and US intervention', in Wm. Roger Louis and Roger Owen (eds), *A Revolutionary Year: The Middle East in 1958*, London: I. B. Tauris, 2002.

Gerges, Fawaz A., *The Superpowers and the Middle East: Regional and International politics, 1953–67*, Boulder: Westview Press, 1994.

Gerges, Fawaz A., 'The Kennedy administration and the Egyptian-Saudi conflict in Yemen: Co-opting Arab nationalism', *Middle East Journal*, 49, 2 (1995): 292–311.

Hack, Karl, *Defence and Decolonisation in Southeast Asia: Britain, Malaya and Singapore, 1941–68*, Richmond: Curzon, 2001.

Hahn, Peter L., *The United States, Great Britain, and Egypt, 1945–56: Strategy and diplomacy in the early Cold War*, Chapel Hill and London: University of North Carolina Press, 1991.

Healey, Denis, *The time of my life*, London: Michael Johnson, 1989.

Herad-Bey, Frauke, *From Trucial States to United Arab Emirates*, new edition, Harlow: Longman, 1996.

Heiss, Mary Ann, 'The United States, Great Britain and the creation of the oil consortium, 1953–4', *International History Review*, 16, 3 (1994): 511–35.

Heiss, Mary Ann, *Empire and nationhood: The United States, Great Britain, and Iranian Oil, 1950–4*, New York: Colombia University Press, 1997.

Horne, Alistair, *Macmillan, 1957–86*, London: Macmillan, 1989.

Jarman, Robert L., *Sabah al-Salim al-Sabah, Amir of Kuwait, 1965–77: A Political Biography*, London: The London Centre of Arab Studies, 2002.

Jones, Matthew, *Conflict and Confrontation in South East Asia, 1961–5: Britain, the United States and the Creation of Malaysia*, Cambridge: Cambridge University Press, 2002.

Jones, Matthew, 'A decision delayed: Britain's withdrawal from South East Asia reconsidered, 1961–8', *English Historical Review*, 117, 472, (2002): 569–95.

Jones, Matthew, 'Anglo-American relations after Suez, the rise and decline of the working group experiment, and the French challenge to NATO, 1957–9', *Diplomacy and Statecraft*, 14, 1 (2003): 49–79.

Joyce, Miriam, 'Preserving the Sheikhdom: London, Washington, Iraq and Kuwait, 1958–61', *Middle East Studies*, 31, 2 (1995): 281–92.

Joyce, Miriam, *Kuwait 1945–96: An Anglo-American Perspective*, London and Portland, Oregan: Frank Cass, 1998.

Joyce, Miriam, 'On the road to unity: The Trucial States from a British perspective, 1960–6', *Middle Eastern Studies*, 35, 2 (1999): 45–60.

Joyce, Miriam, 'The Bahraini three on St. Helena, 1956–61', *Middle East Journal*, 4 (2000): 613–23.

Joyce, Miriam, *Ruling Shaikhs and Her Majesty's Government 1960–9*, London and Portland, Oregan: Frank Cass, 2003.

Kandiah, Michael, and Staerck, Gillian, '"Reliable allies": Anglo-American relations', in Wolfram Kaiser and Gillian Staerck (eds), *British Foreign Policy, 1955–64*, Basingstoke: Macmillan, 2000.

Kyle, Keith, *Suez*, New York: St. Martin's Press, 1991.

Lienhardt, Peter, *Shaikhdoms of Eastern Arabia*, Basingstoke: Palgrave, 2001.

Little, Douglas, 'The new frontier on the Nile: JFK, Nasser, and Arab nationalism', *Journal of American History*, 74, 2 (1998): 514.

Little, Douglas, *American Orientalism: The United States and the Middle East since 1945*, London: I. B. Tauris, 2003.

Louis, Wm. Roger, 'Britain and the crisis of 1958', in Wm. Roger Louis and Roger Owen (eds), *A Revolutionary Year: The Middle East in 1958*, London: I. B. Tauris, 2002.

Louis, Wm. Roger, 'The dissolution of the British empire in the era of Vietnam', *American Historical Review*, 107, 1 (2002): 1–25.

Louis, Wm. Roger, 'The British withdrawal from the Gulf, 1967–71', *Journal of Imperial and Commonwealth History*, 31, 1 (2003): 83–108.

Louis, Wm. Roger and Robinson, Ronald, 'The imperialism of decolonization', *Journal of Imperial and Commonwealth History*, 22, 3 (1994): 462–511.

Lucas, W. Scott, 'Neustadt revisited: a new look at Suez and the Anglo-American "alliance"', in Anthony Gorst and W. Scott Lucas (eds), *Post-war Britain, 1945–64: Themes and Perspectives*, London: Pinter, 1989.

Lucas, W. Scott, *Divided We Stand: Britain, the United States and the Suez Crisis*, London: Hodder and Stoughton, 1991.

Lucas, W. Scott, *Britain and Suez: The Lion's Last Roar*, Manchester: Manchester University Press, 1996.

Macmillan, Harold, *Riding the Storm, 1956–9*, London: Macmillan, 1971.

Marsh, Steve, 'The special relationship and the Anglo-Iranian Oil crisis, 1950–4', *Review of International Studies*, 24, 4 (1998): 529–44.

Marsh, Steve, 'HMG, AIOC and the Anglo-Iranian oil crisis: In defence of Anglo-Iranian', *Diplomacy and Statecraft*, 12, 4 (2001): 143–74.

Marsh, Steve, 'The United States, Iran and Operation "Ajax": Inverting interpretative orthodoxy', *Middle Eastern Studies*, 39, 3 (2003): 1–38.

Mawby, Spencer, 'Britain's last imperial frontier: The Aden Protectorates, 1952–9', *Journal of Imperial and Commonwealth History*, 29, 2 (2001): 75–100.

Mobley, Richard A., 'Deterring Iraq: The UK experience', *Intelligence and National Security*, 16, 2 (2001): 55–82.

Neillands, Robin, *A Fighting Retreat: The British Empire, 1947–97*, London: Coronet Books, 1996.

Ovendale, Ritchie, *Anglo-American Relations in the Twentieth Century*, Basingstoke: Macmillan, 1998.

Ovendale, Ritchie, *Britain, the United States and the Transfer of Power in the Middle East, 1945–62*, London and New York: Leicester University Press, 1996.

Palmer, Michael A., *Guardians of the Gulf: A History of America's Expanding Role in the Persian Gulf, 1833–1992*, New York: The Free Press, 1992.

Parsons, Anthony, *They Say the Lion: Britain's Legacy to the Arabs: A Personal Memoir*, London: Jonathan Cape, 1986.

Parsons, Sir Anthony, 'Gulf withdrawal: British withdrawal from the Gulf 1965–71', *Contemporary Record*, 2, 2 (1988): 41–3.

Petersen, Tore T., 'Anglo-American rivalry in the Middle East: The struggle for the Buraimi oasis, 1952–7', *International History Review*, 14, 1 (1992): 71–91.

Petersen, Tore T., *The Middle East between the Great Powers: Anglo-American Conflict and Co-operation, 1952–7*, Basingstoke: Macmillan, 2000.

Petersen, Tore T., 'Crossing the rubicon?: Britain's withdrawal from the Middle East, 1964–8: A bibliographical review', *International History Review*, 22, 2 (2000): 318–39.

Pickering, Jeffrey, *Britain's Withdrawal from East of Suez: The Politics of Retrenchment*, Basingstoke: Macmillan, 1998.

Pickering, Jeffrey, 'Politics and "Black Tuesday": Shifting power in the Cabinet and the decision to withdraw from East of Suez, November 1967–January 1968', *Twentieth Century British History*, 13, 2 (2002): 144–70.

Pieragostini, Karl, *Britain, Aden and South Arabia*, Basingstoke: Macmillan, 1991.

Reid, Brian Holden, 'The "Northern Tier" and the Baghdad Pact', in John W. Young (ed.), *The Foreign Policy of Churchill's Peacetime Administration, 1951–5*, Leicester: Leicester University Press, 1988.

Reynolds, David, 'A "special relationship"? America, Britain and the international order since the Second World War', *International Affairs*, 62, 1 (1986): 1–20.

Reynolds, David, 'Rethinking Anglo-American relations', *International Affairs*, 65, 1 (1989): 89–111.

Ruehsen, Moyara de Moraes, 'Operation "Ajax" revisited: Iran, 1953', *Middle Eastern Studies*, 29, 3 (1993): 467–86.

Sayed-Ahmed, Muhammad Abd el-Wahab, *Nasser and American Foreign Policy, 1952–56*, London: LAAM, 1989.

Shuckburgh, Evelyn, *Descent to Suez: Diaries 1951–6*, London: Weidenfeld and Nicolson, 1986.

Smith, Simon C., 'Rulers and Residents: British relations with the Aden Protectorate, 1937–59', *Middle Eastern Studies*, 31, 3 (1995): 509–23.

Smith, Simon C., *Kuwait, 1950–65: Britain, the al-Sabah, and Oil*, Oxford: Oxford University Press, 1999.

Smith, Simon C., 'Revolution and reaction: South Arabia in the aftermath of the Yemeni revolution', *Journal of Imperial and Commonwealth History*, 28, 3 (2000): 193–208.

Steininger, Rolf, '"The Americans are in a hopeless position": Great Britain and the war in Vietnam, 1964–5', *Diplomacy and Statecraft*, 8, 3 (1997): 237–85.

Takeyh, Ray, *The Origins of the Eisenhower Doctrine*, Basingstoke: Macmillan, 2000.

Thorne, Christopher, *Allies of a Kind: The United States, Britain and the War against Japan, 1941–5*, London: Hamilton, 1978.

Venn, Fiona, '"A futile paper chase": Anglo-American relations and Middle East oil, 1918–34', *Diplomacy and Statecraft*, 1, 2 (1990): 165–84.

Venn, Fiona, *The Oil Crisis*, London: Longman, 2002.

Walker, Patrick Gordon, *The Cabinet*, London: Jonathan Cape, 1970.

Warner, Geoffrey, 'The Anglo-American special relationship', *Diplomatic History*, 13, 4 (1989): 479–99.

Watt, D. Cameron, 'Demythologizing the Eisenhower era', in Hedlely Bull and William Roger Louis (eds), *The 'special relationship': Anglo-American relations since 1945*, Oxford: Clarendon Press, 1986.

Wrigley, Chris, 'Now you see it, now you don't: Harold Wilson and Labour's foreign policy', in R. Coopey, S. Fielding, and N. Tiratsoo (eds), *The Wilson Governments, 1964–70*, London: Pinter, 1993.

Yapp, M. E., *The Near East since the First World War*, London and New York: Longman, 1991.

Zahlan, Rosemarie Said, 'Hegemony, dependence, and development in the Gulf', in Tim Niblock (ed.), *Social and Economic Development in the Arab Gulf*, London: Croom Helm, 1980.

Zahlan, Rosemarie Said, *The Making of the Modern Gulf States: Kuwait, Bahrain, Qatar, the United Arab Emirate and Oman*, Reading: Ithaca Press, 1998.

Index